LITERARY/CULTURAL THEORY

EDWARD SAID

Literary/Cultural Theory provides concise and lucid introductions to a range of key concepts and theorists in contemporary literary and cultural theory. Original and contemporary in presentation, and eschewing jargon, each book in the series presents students of humanities and social sciences with exhaustive overviews of theories and theorists, while also introducing them to the mechanics of reading literary/cultural texts using critical tools. Each book also carries glossaries of key terms and ideas, and pointers for further reading and research. Written by scholar-teachers who have taught critical theory for years, and vetted by some of the foremost experts in the field, the series Literary/Cultural Theory is indispensable to students and teachers.

Also in the series

Psychoanalytic Theory and Criticism
Feminisms
Jacques Lacan
Dalit Literature and Criticism
Ecocriticism
Postcolonialism Now
Marxist Literary and Cultural Theory
Postsecular Theory
Nations and Nationalisms
Periyar
Popular Culture
Queer Studies
Frantz Fanon
Mikhail Bakhtin
Deconstruction and Poststructuralism
Subaltern Studies

LITERARY/CULTURAL THEORY

EDWARD SAID

A CRITICAL INTRODUCTION

JAYDEEP CHAKRABARTY
Assam University, Silchar

Orient BlackSwan

EDWARD SAID: A CRITICAL INTRODUCTION

ORIENT BLACKSWAN PRIVATE LIMITED

Registered Office
3-6-752 Himayatnagar, Hyderabad 500 029, Telangana, India
Email: centraloffice@orientblackswan.com

Other Offices
Bengaluru, Chennai, Guwahati, Hyderabad, Kolkata, Mumbai, New Delhi, Noida, Patna, Visakhapatnam

First published 2023

ISBN 978 93 5442 593 6

Typeset in Aldine 401 BT 10.5/13 *by*
Akhil Offset Printers
Hyderabad 500 020

037532

Printed at
Yash Printographics,
Noida 201 301

Published by
Orient Blackswan Private Limited
3-6-752, Himayatnagar,
Hyderabad 500 029, Telangana, India
Email: info@orientblackswan.com

Contents

Preface

Contrary to common perception, Edward Said was neither an anti-Semite nor an apologist for the cultural supremacy of the Orient. While a partial or superficial reading of his works may lead one to these unidirectional conclusions, a detailed and sincere engagement with Said makes it possible for us to see him as a humanist par excellence. Interestingly, while humanism has always been his forte, the Saidian perception of humanism does not preclude its continuous critique; in fact, a continuous oppositional scrutiny of all that is human is an essential part of Said's humanism. A sustained faith in the human agency that is capable of interrogating authorities and tradition was at work behind all he said and did. This faith, which worked hand in hand with his unparalleled erudition, has broadened the horizons of human experience and our understanding of it.

It is hardly possible to over-emphasise Edward Said's crucial contributions towards a better understanding of words and the world. His reading of modern systems of thought and knowledge as colonial or Eurocentric helps us see through the garb of objectivity that covers them. Further, his works on cultural imperialism, the role of intellectuals in society and the politics of dispossession emerge, in the final analysis, as a humanist's plea for dignity which has lasting relevance for both the personal and the political. Widely regarded as the founder of postcolonial studies, his reasoning and arguments have reshaped an entire range of disciplines which constitute the area of humanities and social sciences. His works influenced fields as diverse as history, anthropology, geography and cultural studies, and the list does not end here.

In recognition of Said's enormous contributions and influence, a number of general introductions to his works (not to talk about the endless outpouring of critical engagement with his individual works or ideas) have been made available till now. However, extant introductions to Said and his works can be seen as not quite complete for three reasons: first, they approach Said mostly within the rubric of academic investments (especially that of postcolonial criticism or studies) without emphasis on his political interventions; and second, they tend to leave out his crucial works before *Orientalism* altogether, while addressing the other works mostly from the vantage point of *Orientalism;* and third, the biographical details in these works are often not adequate enough to help contextualise Said and his works effectively. Hence, there is a need for a comprehensive introduction to Edward Said and his oeuvre which seeks to address these lacunae; which is what this book has attempted to accomplish. This book proposes to make the works of Said accessible and available to a wide range of readers, without bracketing them under the prescription of postcolonial theory. While it is true that postcolonial theory and Said's works have reinforced each other to a great extent, it is more rewarding not to see them as one and the same phenomenon. Additionally, it also provides a moderately detailed intellectual genealogy of Said which is of significance for beginners in the field.

It is a perilous task to represent others; it is more so when the person in question has been one of the best critics of literary, cultural and political representations. Given the erudition and eclectic orientation of his works, I certainly do not have the authority or audacity to claim that my 'representation' of Said is a perfect one, or the final one. As a matter of fact, no representation can ever be a replacement for the original; the former actually supplements (or, at times, complements) the latter. In other words, no introduction to Said's works can be a replacement for the works themselves. My purpose is to lead the reader forward to Said's own works, and I modestly hope that this attempt will make Said's thoughts and ideas more accessible for them. The guiding principle behind this book has been famously foregrounded by Helen Gardner: the need for the critic to function as a torch bearer to illuminate the original work, to show the way to it. Therefore, instead of presenting my own views, except when absolutely necessary, I have chosen to stay close to Said's formations throughout the journey. Similarly, I have tried to ensure that this book concerns itself more with Said's works than what has been written about them, barring those situations when the distinction is not a productive one. I have also tried to follow the chronology of Said's publications while dividing this book into chapters. What follows is a brief outline of each of the chapters in the book and what texts, ideas and contexts they focus on.

Chapter 1 situates Said against the background of his own contextual specificities – historical, political and intellectual. Said's autobiography

Out of Place: A Memoir has made his life and thinking more accessible and has been used as the primary text for this chapter. If this book were to proceed in a strictly chronological order *Out of Place* would, of course, be one of the last texts to be discussed. However, for a better understanding of the contexts that produced all his works and his subject position, *Out of Place* seems to be the right text with which to begin.

Chapter 2 is based on Said's first two books, *Joseph Conrad and the Fiction of Autobiography* and *Beginnings: Intention and Method*. This chapter focuses on ideas like the relation between an author and his work, the construction and deconstruction of the concept of 'authority' and the centrality of the novel as a form in European culture – all of which become recurrent motifs in Said's later works. Additionally, *Beginnings* was one of the first books in English which introduced French critical theory to the Anglo-American world, helping the transition of literary criticism to literary theory. Said himself has said that he was seeking to establish a voice of his own by using other's voices in *Beginnings.*

Chapter 3 looks at *Orientalism* which is essentially against essentialism. Paradoxical though the statement appears it is perhaps the best one-line summary of the book. In *Orientalism,* Edward Said tries to show how (and at times, why) Western scholarship and culture have misrepresented the Orient by showing it as inferior to the West. He goes on to show how this project of misrepresenting the East was, more often than not, related to the direct colonisation and subjugation of the Oriental world.

The primary text for Chapter 4 is *The World, the Text, and the Critic* which seeks to reverse the deconstructionist dictum of 'there is nothing outside the text' by locating the text firmly in the world. This is a seminal work which offers a lot of possibilities of further research in the area but has been overshadowed by the fame and influence of *Orientalism.* Said feels that both the traditional study of literature as well as post-1960s critical theory have avoided, neglected or suppressed the social and political conditions in which literary texts are written, read and interpreted. Both 'secular criticism' and its cognate ideation of 'worldliness' seek to re-situate texts in the world that produced them.

Chapter 5 introduces *Culture and Imperialism*, another key text, which is a blend of Said's critique of colonialism and his theories of reading fiction. I seek to show how the book is also an attempt at answering, on Said's part, some of the allegations and criticisms raised against *Orientalism*. Additionally, *Culture and Imperialism* tries to take note of resistances to European cultural and political hegemonies that took place across the globe. Said's assertion here that the Orientalist's task of misrepresenting the Orientals is currently continued by Western, especially American media, is a continuation and reinforcement of the same argument he presented in his previous works.

Chapter 6 looks into the arguments offered in Said's seminal texts on Palestinian politics and representations of Islam. *The Question of Palestine*, *Covering Islam* and *The Politics of Dispossession* foreground the significance of the Palestinian struggle for space and identity in his life. One should remember that the chief ontological concern of Said's *Orientalism* is also the Palestinian struggle for a dignified existence, though this specific concern is often forgotten or underplayed by those who prefer to project the work as a critique of the politics of representation in general. It is important to point out that this chapter is focused on presenting the Saidian viewpoint on the Palestinian question and not the Israel–Palestine debate per se. Though Said has worked from the greater paradigm of human rights, one must also remember that he represents the Palestinian side of the Israel–Palestine conflict. For other viewpoints on the conflict, one has to go beyond his work.

In the concluding chapter, I have primarily dealt with the ideas and arguments presented in Said's last works: *Freud and the Non-European* and the posthumously published *Humanism and Democratic Criticism* and *On Late Style*. Taking a sharply oppositional stance to the proclamations and preoccupations of posthumanism, Said reiterates his humanist pleas in this book which can be seen as his final message to posterity. Equally significant is his call for a return to philology in this work, which seeks to repair the damage caused by the synchronic study of languages. The most outstanding trope, in my opinion, is that of 'democratic criticism' which has remained largely unexplored.

The book has adopted a communicative and functional approach in terms of language and style, keeping in mind – among other things – Said's recurrent emphasis on using language that is free from jargon, abstraction and obfuscation. I hope it meets the expectations of those for whom it is written, and beyond.

Jaydeep Chakrabarty

Acknowledgements

The book has benefitted from the critical insights and encouragement of academicians, scholars and friends who have added to my readings of Edward Said. I must begin by expressing my debt of gratitude to Professor Bijay Kumar Danta whose erudition, expertise and never failing interest in Said have been crucial in shaping my understanding of Said. I am also greatly thankful to Professor Nandana Dutta whose significant inputs, suggestions and guidance have been of immense help in giving this book its present shape. I must place on record my sincere thanks to Professors Prafulla C. Kar, R. Radhakrishnan, Himadri Lahiri and Bibhash Choudhury whose lectures, seminars and works on Said and allied areas over the years have been of great help.

It has been my privilege to have Dr Avishek Ray as a close friend whose interest in the work has been as useful as his constant encouragement to complete the work meaningfully and his vetting several of my ideas on Said.

I am deeply grateful to Sreenath S. from Orient BlackSwan for the offer to write this book for them, and for his unstinted support ever since. I am equally thankful to Namrata Kartik for her meticulous editing of the manuscript as well as the warm encouragement that helped me continue with the project with comfort and ease.

I am thankful to all my wonderful colleagues at Assam University, Silchar, as well as my students and research scholars. A special note of thanks to my scholar Longjam Gaurav Kumar Singha whose abiding interest in academic ventures of various kinds is a major source of inspiration for me.

I am equally thankful to my parents as well as all the dearest members of my family, my friends and my admirers who continue to have greater faith in my abilities than I do.

Finally, a very special note of thanks to my wife Mousumi Chatterjee and our son Jayartha Chakrabarty for everything they did for me as well as the book. I dedicate this book to them.

Chapter One

Edward W. Said

THE MAKING OF THE INTELLECTUAL

In his Edward W. Said Memorial Lecture delivered at Columbia University, Noam Chomsky categorically stated that '[i]n literary criticism and historical writing there are two times: before *Orientalism* and after *Orientalism*' (n.p.). Chomsky's statement is an honest recognition of how Edward Said's contributions and interventions have transformed the way humanity sees itself by challenging some of its very foundational assumptions. In the same lecture, Chomsky also foregrounded Said's passionate dedication to humanism, placing it alongside Said's paramount significance for intellectuals and the world at large by observing that his death 'is an irreparable loss for the poor and the suffering of the world, and for depth and clarity of thought and understanding' (n.p.). Anyone who is familiar with the words and works of Edward Said could not agree more. Said's sustained unmasking of authorities – textual and actual – will go a long way in providing humanity with the succour necessary to liberate itself from the strictures of oppressive power structures.

Said's central concern was the oppressive politics of colonialism and its widespread, debilitating effects, but his assessment of the problems of colonialism and its aftermath has a wider applicability that may be profitably used in understanding the functioning of power, knowledge and subjugation in other domains as well. Said's increasing relevance for the word and the world has perhaps been best captured by Patrick Williams in his assessment that '[it] is difficult to find his [Said's] equal today in terms of his embodiment of committed and courageous taking of positions and defending of causes combined with generosity of spirit' (32). While Said's academic interventions, reasoning and arguments have reshaped almost the entire range of disciplines which constitute the twin fields of humanities and social sciences, his relentless efforts for the uplift of Palestinians – ranging from writing to actual political engagements – have been instrumental in changing academic, political and popular perspectives on the issue. His dedication to academics and politics has led many to consider him a bi-focal intellectual, dividing his time between academics and politics, between literary criticism and the ethically-engaged activism of a public intellectual. So far as Said himself is concerned, however, he has always maintained that academic scholarship and commitment to greater public causes are inseparable from one another. This simultaneous commitment to academics and action places him in a tradition of socially committed critics beginning with Ben Jonson in the English literary tradition (if not earlier), and Socrates in the Western philosophical tradition.

While books dealing with a thinker's intellectual and academic life often attempt to keep away from their personal life, such an approach will be epistemologically as well as ethically flawed in the case of a thinker like Said. His life and works are seamlessly woven together, almost always, by a one-to-one correspondence, so much so that without some insight into the major signposts of his life, his works will remain only half intelligible.

In fact, Said himself has highlighted the significance of his personal life and its effects on his works on several occasions. The most important of all these is the identification of 'the personal dimension' (*Orientalism* 25) as one of three key aspects of his contemporary reality that have produced *Orientalism* and other works. The theoretical support behind such an approach, as Said himself acknowledges, has been drawn from Antonio Gramsci (*Orientalism* 25) whose influence on Said can hardly be overstated. We will see during the course of the book how a major part of Said's critical energy was reserved for continuous, in fact recurrent, negotiations between Gramsci and Michel Foucault.

Said also believes that the influence of the 'personal dimension' is not unique to him but common to all scholars, their claims to objectivity notwithstanding: 'No one has ever devised a method for detaching the scholar from the circumstances of life, from the fact of his involvement (conscious or unconscious) with a class, a set of beliefs, a social position, or from the mere activity of being a member of a society. These continue to bear on what he does professionally' (*Orientalism* 10). This was written in 1978, and till date, I believe, such a method is conspicuous by its absence. There seems to be some humble beginnings towards this goal of objective knowledge with advances in digital technology, but that too has a very long way to go. In any case, an engagement with Said's biological and intellectual genealogies is crucial for a meaningful introduction to his works. The subsequent sections of this chapter are dedicated to these genealogies.

In Lieu of a Biography

Edward Wadie Said[1] was born in Jerusalem on 1 November 1935 to an Arab Palestinian family which had a background of being open to Euro-American cultural traditions and were primarily based in Cairo, Egypt. Hilda Musa – his mother – was Lebanese and raised in Nazareth with an American school background, while his father – Wadie Said – was a Palestinian with US citizenship as he had served in the American army. There was a strong American connection in Said's mother's family as well. Hilda's father, a Baptist minister in Nazareth, was educated for a time in Texas. These multiple sociocultural antecedents contributed significantly towards Said's intellectual as well as emotional development.

Said, while reflecting on his past, often saw himself as 'a Palestinian going to school in Egypt, with an English first name, an American passport, and no certain identity, at all. To make matters worse, Arabic, my native language, and English, my school language, were inextricably mixed' (*Reflections on Exile* 556–57). He always found it difficult to choose one identity over the other: 'Ever since I can remember, I have felt that I belonged to both worlds, without being completely of either one or the other' (*Culture and Imperialism* xxx). This has been the fate of each and every colonial subject, though perhaps not all of them feel the rift as consciously as Said does. Derek Walcott's 'A Far Cry from Africa' gives poetic voice to the same indeterminacy and crisis that Said expresses in prose:

> I who am poisoned with the blood of both,
> Where shall I turn, divided to the vein?
> I who have cursed
> The drunken officer of British rule, how choose
> Between this Africa and the English tongue I love? (200)

The house Said was born in was located in what was then British-mandated Palestine. While he has claimed it to be his 'family house' on more than one occasion, the claim has been subsequently disputed by Justus Weiner (among others) who has tried to prove that the house belonged to Said's paternal aunt ('"My Beautiful Old House" and other Fabrications by Edward Said'). Such research, however, shows a lack of awareness about the concept of family as well as property ownership in traditional Arab societies. In reality, building a case against Said's authenticity and intellectual integrity would also amount to discrediting the movement for Palestinian rights to a great extent. As Weiner worked for the Israeli Ministry of Justice, it seems that such concerns could inform his discrediting of Said's claims to his family home.

While Said and his parents resided in Cairo for a major part of his childhood, it does not imply that his Palestinian identity is a lie or a fabrication. The family stayed in Cairo simply because his father had set up a very successful stationery business there, after having served in the American army. Weiner's claims have been exposed as having mala fide intentions by Alexander Cockburn and Christopher Hitchens. While Hitchens went to the extent of commenting that Weiner's writing is full of 'stupid blunders', Cockburn (in an article jointly written with Jeffrey St. Clair) wrote that Weiner's research on Said's early life was 'like looking at history through the wrong end of a telescope' (St. Clair and Cockburn, n.p.).

The Said family used to visit their ancestral house in Jerusalem at regular intervals and Said was born in Jerusalem during one such visit. This had something to do with a family tragedy. Hilda and Wadie had lost a son during childbirth at the Cairo Hospital which followed the Western system of medicine. Though Wadie was generally 'Eurocentric', after this tragedy he decided that the next child should be born under the care of the traditional Palestinian system. Hence, they had moved to their ancestral house in Jerusalem before Said's birth. Though it is purely coincidental, the rejection of the Western system in favour of the native Palestinian system during the process of his birth interestingly prefigures some of the agendas and choices of the future Edward Said.

Said's parents were two distinctly divergent personalities who seemed to conform to typical patriarchal expectations of how a man and a woman should be and both had a strong influence on his life either latently or blatantly. Wadie, Said's father, was a typical patriarch who controlled as many lives as he could for as long as he could. Consequently he was, for Said, 'a devastating combination of power and authority, rationalistic discipline, and repressed emotions', all of which had some 'inhibiting and debilitating effects' on Said's life (*Out of Place* 12). However, Wadie was not without any redeeming feature at all. Going by Said's own admission, his father – in addition to providing Said with a good lifestyle and education – arranged piano lessons for him from the early age of six, took him on regular visits to the opera, had a well-furnished library, and over and above everything, instilled a strong sense of discipline and hard work in Said. In the final analysis, however, Said's relation with his father is perhaps best seen as a typically Oedipal one, marked by distrust, disapproval and eventual disobedience. Predictably enough, his relationship with his mother was the very reverse of it: 'certainly my closest and most intimate companion for the first twenty five years of my life' (12). The radically opposed and divergent natures of his parents have been aptly phrased by Said in his assertion that his father and mother were 'two Palestinians with dramatically different backgrounds and temperaments living in colonial Cairo as members of a Christian minority within a large pond of minorities' (19).

The differences with his father translated to bitterness with the passage of time, and at one point we find Said writing to his father saying that he was done with being lectured on how to be a good son, brother and so on, and 'the time has come to start lecturing my sisters about how they should treat me in a way more properly befitting an older brother' (Brennan 24.) I have chosen to emphasise the strained relationship between father and son not only because Said himself chooses to do so in his memoir. Even a cursory glance at this sketchy summary of a turbulent father–son relationship, as well as a strained sibling relationship, will tell one that Said's overarching feeling of being 'out of place' or 'between worlds' was not just the result of being a Palestinian in America. This aspect, however, will remain veiled for those who try to understand Said's exilic existence only on the basis of his academic and scholarly writings like 'Reflections on Exile'. In fact, Said's musings on the twin tropes of 'filiation' and 'affiliation' in *The World, the Text, and the Critic* become more meaningful when read against his family background. The sibling rivalry continued well into his last years and his sisters denounced, or rather disowned, Said's representation of his father in his memoir.

In addition to – or perhaps owing to – these pronounced filial ruptures from early childhood, Said's performance at school was very uneven with touches of brilliance in fits and starts. He continuously shifted from one institution to another during his school days, mostly due to his inability to adjust. After a brief stint at St. George's School in Jerusalem (in the widely used Ashcroft and Ahluwalia authored *Edward Said*, the school has been erroneously located in Cairo), Said shifted back to Cairo where he attended Gezira Preparatory School (GPS) from 1941 till May 1942 and then from 1943 till 1946. Said's independent ways of thinking and behaviour manifested early and he was not at all comfortable during this period of study at GPS. Within a very short period he was marked out as a delinquent. The school, in fact, became for him the first monument of colonial authority which manifested itself primarily in 'the sheer Englishness of its teachers and many of its students' (*Out of Place* 42). A more direct and more humiliating colonial encounter during this period followed when he was told by the secretary of the Gezira Club that, as an Arab boy he could not even walk across the outlying fields of the club.

The indignation caused by this inhuman incident continued throughout Said's life. What was worse than the humiliation itself is that neither he nor his father – who was an influential person in many ways – could raise any protest against this acute racial othering. Even fifty years after the incident Said wrote in his memoir, 'that realisation shames me still' (45). Perhaps this was the most important incident which turned Said against colonialism and inhuman authoritarianisms of all kinds once and for all. As a person reading and writing on Said from India, a striking parallel that comes to my mind is the well known incident of M.K. Gandhi being thrown off a first class railway compartment in South Africa only because he was not a white person.

From 1946 to 1949, Said studied at the Cairo School for American Children (CSAC). While he found the American system of education at CSAC a little more liberating than the strict British authoritarianism at GPS, Said soon started developing a strong dislike for CSAC's own kind of discipline. In fact, during his early years in GPS as well as CSAC, Said was often well known for mostly the wrong reasons, though his nonconformity with institutional expectations or discipline seems to be the result of his instinctual anti-authoritarian stance more than anything else. In 1949, Said was admitted to Victoria College (VC) in Cairo where he completed his high school studies, against the backdrop of the onset of the Palestine–Israel crisis. It was, like GPS, a school based on the British system of education, originally intended to be a Middle Eastern replica of Eton College. However, unlike GPS, there were no British students in VC though most of the teachers were British. Though the ambience was less elegant than the previous institutions he had attended, the colonial obsession with Englishness was visible here as well. The very first rule of *The School Handbook* declared that 'English is the language of the school. Anyone caught speaking other languages will be severely punished'. Consequently, Arabic became 'a criminalised discourse' (*Out of Place* 184). The same colonial spirit of imposition was also visible in other aspects of the curriculum as well. The students learned about the British monarchy, English life and literature, 'habits and idioms' that could never be used anywhere else other than England, and so on. 'Being and speaking Arabic were delinquent activities at VC, and accordingly we were never given proper instruction in our own language, history, culture, and geography' (186).

Indeed, the imposition of the priorities and concerns of the British administration on systems of education in colonised countries was one of the characteristic features of British colonialism, and its effect on students was mainly that of alienation from their own cultures and tradition. There was also a good deal of fear psychosis at play and a feeling of inferiority, of being 'pitted against a wounded colonial power that was dangerous and capable of inflicting harm on us' (*Out of Place* 186). The situation, interestingly, is very similar to the one described by Ngũgĩ wa Thiong'o in *Decolonising the Mind*. Thiong'o, in fact, phrases the predicament with proverbial precision when he says that once he got admitted into school, 'The language of my education was no longer the language of my culture' (11). Unfortunately, many such trends of colonial education have continued into post-colonial times as well, often to be replaced by an unthinking imitation of neocolonial (especially American) education systems. Sometimes, there is also an attempt at an equally unthinking revival of a pristine, pre-colonial curriculum which never existed in the first place. More engaged and dialogic negotiations with the protocols of colonial and neocolonial systems of education are necessary at the moment, and insights from thinkers like Said and Thiong'o can give us significant inputs to that end.

Coming back to Said's student life at VC, by the end of the very first month he was identified as a 'troublemaker' here as well. There were incidents leading to physical punishments along the lines of his life in earlier institutions, though on one occasion he was praised for doing exceedingly well in physics. However, Said's image of being a 'troublemaker' overshadowed everything else. His schooling at VC also ended after a horrid experience with their English teacher Mr Lowe; one whom Said identified as a 'blustering, weak, and incompetent teacher' (*Out of Place* 206). On that fateful day, the students of the class rejected Mr Lowe's proposal to study Shakespeare and demanded Walter Scott's work instead. The teacher somehow identified Said as the naysayer and quite literally pounced on him. In a moment Said found Lowe's 'great obese body pulling me down so that he lay on top of me' (208). After this, his parents thought it would be better if Said's education was conducted via a different pedagogy and not through the British system. Their decision was also based on a similar opinion shared by the acting headmaster Mr Griffiths. It was decided that Said should be sent to the United States for further studies, and accordingly he was admitted in Mount Hermon, a boarding school in Massachusetts. He fared better in academics and the piano at this institution – a trend which continued. His achievements in academic and co-curricular activities notwithstanding, Said found life at Mount Hermon alienating in certain ways. He was particularly hurt by the fact that responsible assignments and appointments were always denied him in spite of his possessing all the requisite qualifications (229–30). Said's nonconformist attitude was strengthened further by such deprivations at Mount Hermon: 'I began a lifelong struggle and attempt to demystify the capriciousness and hypocrisy of a power whose authority depended absolutely on its ideological self-image as a moral agent, acting in good faith and with unimpeachable intentions' (230). It was a 'lifelong struggle' indeed and what Said sought to interrogate in all his works was basically this 'ideological self-image' of colonialism and imperialism.

The worst deprivation at Mount Hermon, however, came when Said was not made the salutatorian (the student who gives the opening speech at graduation ceremonies, customarily reserved for students who hold the second rank in the graduating class) in spite of securing the second position in his class in the final examination. It dawned on him that the only reason he was denied the honour was his non-white identity. From that moment onwards, Said became acutely aware of his identity as 'marginal, non-American, alienated, marked' (248).

In 1953, Said moved to Princeton University for his undergraduate studies. It was an all-male institute back then and, in Said's assessment, 'a provincial, small-minded college' which gradually transformed itself into a 'genuine university' later on (276). While Said disliked quite a few practices and rituals of Princeton life, he was full of appreciation for the courses he took there. He chose to do a major not in literature, but in humanities which put equal emphasis on music, philosophy, French and English. It was indeed a wide range of subjects whose influence on the Saidian oeuvre is perhaps most visible in Said's refusal to be bound by the borders of English studies or literary studies (despite being a Professor of English and Comparative Literature at Columbia). Of all who taught him at Princeton, Said names two professors who left 'a lasting impression' on him: R. P. Blackmur, Professor of English (though he had neither a doctorate nor even a high school diploma) and Arthur Szathmary, Professor of Philosophy, who was the symbol of intellectual life itself for a large section of students (276–77). Said generously acknowledged the formative role that the humanities courses at Princeton played in his career: 'My humanities courses were unreflectingly historical in organization, taught by men of the utmost competence and philological rigor. . . and . . . formed the foundation of everything I have done as a scholar and teacher' (277).

On graduating with a BA from Princeton in 1957, Said joined Harvard University as a graduate student in literature the following year. The formalist and historical study of literature that Harvard offered him could not, however, satisfy his intellectual curiosities. Consequently, his intellectual discoveries were made outside of what was acceptable to the establishment. While Said became increasingly distanced from his Middle Eastern moorings during his days at Harvard (1958–63), he busied himself in studying Vico, Lukács, Sartre, Heidegger and Merleau-Ponty. The insights derived from these figures helped Said shape his doctoral dissertation on Joseph Conrad written under the guidance of Monroe Engel and Harry Levin (290).

In 1963, Said joined Columbia University as an instructor in the English Department (Brennan 92). For the rest of his life and career, Said continued as a faculty member of this institution holding various prestigious posts and positions. In 1969, he was promoted to full professor at Columbia. The year 1976 was an important year for Said in terms of a wider recognition of his scholarship which followed the publication of *Beginnings* in America (1975). He was awarded the prestigious Lionel Trilling Award for *Beginnings* by Columbia University. In quick succession, he became the Parr Professor of English and Comparative Literature the following year. He was subsequently made a University Professor at Columbia, the highest academic position there. Throughout his career, he taught, researched and lectured extensively at several other prestigious institutions like Harvard, Yale and Stanford in various capacities. Said was also elected the President of the Modern Language Association in 1998. Parallel to his academic career, Said's stakes and role in the struggle for Palestinian self- determination had been on the rise since the 1967 Arab–Israel war. He was member of the PNC (Palestinian National Council) for fourteen long years (the detailed trajectory of Said's involvement in the Palestinian struggle has been charted later in this book).

It must be mentioned that discontents and detractors notwithstanding, Columbia University was overtly supportive of Edward Said and his projects, both academic and political. One such noteworthy instance of support may be cited here for further explorations. Towards the end of Said's life and career there was mounting pressure on the authorities of Columbia University to call him out and penalise him for allegedly having thrown stones at Israeli soldiers during a visit to the disputed Israel–Palestine border. The university authorities did not budge and allowed Said the freedom to continue with the institution as he had been doing. Said also acknowledged the immunity and amenities of the space provided by Columbia in particular, and American universities in general, on numerous occasions. In the introduction to *Culture and Imperialism,* for instance, Said admits that in the writing of the book he availed himself 'of the utopian space still provided by the university, which I believe must remain a place where such vital issues are investigated, discussed, reflected on'. Universities, consequently, should not be spaces 'where social and political issues are actually either imposed or resolved' as that would amount to a total negation of 'the university's function and turn it into an adjunct to whatever political party is in power' (*Culture and Imperialism* xxix). Similarly, in *Reflections on Exile*, Said has identified American universities as the 'last remaining utopia' (xi) for academics as well as students. While he did not have much faith in established religions and would more often identify himself as secular – whether as a critic or as an individual – what he deeply believed in and stood for was the sanctity of the university as an institution meant to speak truth to power. As Aram Veseer recalls, 'The popular image of Said as an activist/ideologue locked into his own doctrine is the opposite of the Said I encountered at Columbia, a restless character who could not embrace any position or idea without simultaneously pushing it away' (23).

On occasions he thought fit and just, Said generously helped his younger colleagues as well. In her 'Thinking about Edward Said: Pages from a Memoir', Gayatri Chakravorty Spivak has a crisp but powerful account of Said's humanist commitment. In 1988 due to a protocol mistake (which is natural for a newcomer to the US), a few younger colleagues ganged up against Spivak determined to label her a 'racist', with obvious consequences. Said immediately intervened without even being requested to do so. 'Edward sent a message on his own, saying, "Gayatri works for the oppressed, stop this". I was immensely grateful that he had somehow drawn me into what was surely his life—working for the oppressed' (524). One may say that by this gesture, Said too aligns himself once again with the pedagogy of speaking for the oppressed.

Said's sharp progression up the academic ladder is closely connected to his dense and dedicated scholarship which has left, for posterity, several crucial texts whose significance has continued to rise. Of these, the ones generally considered the most significant are,

Beginnings: Intention and Method (1975)

Orientalism (1978)

The World, the Text, and the Critic (1983)

Culture and Imperialism (1993)

Humanism and Democratic Criticism (2004)

Besides these works, there is also a collection of essays titled *Reflections on Exile.* The essays are mostly extensions of the arguments that he has presented in his books and had been previously published intermittently in various journals and periodicals. He did the same thing in the numerous television shows in which he appeared with a regularity not generally seen in the academics of his generation, or even now. All these paved the way for his wider recognition as a public intellectual – perhaps the most prominent one of his day, second only to Noam Chomsky. This was despite the fact that the general spirit of the American media was vehemently against the Palestinian cause that Said espoused.

What was an exceptional academic and scholarly career was unfortunately cut short by leukaemia which Said succumbed to on 24 September 2003. Though his health had been increasingly compromised ever since the detection of leukaemia in September 1991, Said continued with scholarly publications and performances of gigantic proportions. Eqbal Ahmad, a close friend and scholar, tells us how Said continued with his eighteen hour-a-day schedule in spite of being treated for leukaemia (Ahmad 10).

Though there are more than enough insights and inspirations in Said's life and writings for posterity, something equally compelling needs to be added here. Most commonly available biographical notes on Said – spread across different critical dictionaries, anthologies and so on – cite or recommend only the five texts cited on the previous page as his achievements (see for instance, David Macey's *The Penguin Dictionary of Critical Theory*, a widely used book among students and scholars of literature and humanities). In doing so, they somehow carry on the Orientalist misrepresentation, albeit in an indirect way, that Said was always up against. Apart from his Arab origins and untimely death, the life story narrated above – brilliant and attractive as it is – is not very different from his peers in academia: a smooth and fast upward career graph with commendable scholarly publications in the field. And yet, this is not the complete picture of Said at all – rather it is very, very far from the true Said. The mainstay of his life and works was the question of Palestine, the question of the rights of Palestinians in particular and Arabs in general, and a continuous interrogation of the misrepresentations of the Eastern world by the West.

SHORT TAKES

SAID THE MUSICAL MAESTRO

Music, interestingly, was Said's third space, closely following his more famous avatars as the Professor of English and Comparative Literature and the veteran activist fighting for the rights of Palestine. Though it is the least known aspect of Said's life for the majority of his readers and audience, Said has to his credit four books on music:

Musical Elaborations (1991)

Parallels and Paradoxes: Explorations in Music and Society (2002, co-author Daniel Barenboim)

On Late Style: Music and Literature Against the Grain (2006)

Music at the Limits (2007)

These can only be dealt with by specialists in music and are well beyond the scope of the present volume. However, two very important tropes of his critical writings are from or closely related to music: 'contrapuntal' and 'late style'. These will be discussed in the following chapters.

It may be noted here that Said, along with his Jewish friend Daniel Barenboim, had set up an orchestra named the West–Eastern Divan Orchestra in 1999. Their driving motive was to bring young musicians from both Palestine and Israel together to forge a better relationship between both the countries. Music was seen as an alternative platform where the contested and strife-ridden antagonistic past and present of the two people could merge into each other.

Let us have a look at a list of books by Said which are often glossed over by the protocols of mainstream academia (with the possible exception of Arab, Palestinian and Jewish academia):

The Question of Palestine (1979)

Covering Islam (1981)

Blaming the Victims: Spurious Scholarship and the Palestinian Question (co-edited with Christopher Hitchens) (1988)

The Politics of Dispossession (1994)

Peace and Its Discontents (1995)

Out of Place (1999)

From Oslo to Iraq and the Roadmap (2004)

These are, to borrow a phrase from Keats, the unheard melodies of Said, and hence sweeter!

All these unambiguously point towards the dispossession of the Palestinians as the single most important mooring of Said's utterances, critical and political. If you read between the lines, his magnum opus *Orientalism* and its sequel *Culture and Imperialism* are also based on his commitment to Palestinian cause. For those not familiar with the primacy of the Palestinian politics in Said's life, *Orientalism* would appear to be a critique of the politics of representation in general and colonial representation in particular. But for Said initiates, it is basically the beginning of a long series of books defending the rights of Palestinians, Arabs and the Orient, which spells out his 'intention' as well as 'method' of criticism for all time to come.

In fact, almost all his works stem from the anxiety of a man irreversibly dispossessed from his origins. This dispossession continued to plague him throughout his stay in the Western world as there was a constant, unrelenting demonisation of Arabs and the Islamic world by Anglo-American and Jewish cultural politics. Said, therefore, was a man forever in search of a lost identity. In more ways than one, his writings became a vicarious fulfilment for the identity and the land he had lost. Said was well aware of it himself and would often quote this famous line from Adorno: 'For a man who no longer has a homeland, writing becomes a place to live' (qtd. in 'Intellectual Exile: Expatriates and Marginals' 377)

As is often asserted by Said and corroborated by his friends and critics, the 1967 Arab–Israel war was literally the turning point of his life and career. The brutality of the war combined with the pathetic defeat of the Arab world was the final blow to the dream of an uncomplicated academic life for Said. However, if one cares to read his memoir, interviews and articles about his intellectual and political development minutely, it would be obvious that the 1967 war was not the only catalyst in his transformation; rather it was the most decisive one.

He has, for instance, spoken about his becoming aware of the acute sufferings of the Palestinians through the philanthropic moves of his Aunt Nabiha as early as 1948 (*Out of Place* 119). Even in his apparently apolitical doctoral dissertation (later published as a monograph) on Conrad, there are visible discomforts with Conrad's imperialist attitudes, though Said does not build on these. I will deal with the intricacies, contentions and nuances of the Palestinian question later, but this foregrounding is absolutely necessary for a better vision of Said. It is sufficient to remember at this point that Edward W. Said saw his existence in America as 'a uniquely punishing destiny' over and above everything (*Orientalism* 27).

THE INTELLECTUAL BACKGROUND

While Said had been making a case for the need of speaking truth to power all through his career, the 1993 Reith Lectures titled *Representations of the Intellectual* make his agenda and choices clear in this regard. This section seeks to introduce some of the major intellectuals whose influence on Said can hardly be overemphasised. Given that Said was extremely well read in multiple epistemological and cultural traditions from both the East and the West (English, French and Arabic, for instance), it is difficult to trace the influences exhaustively in an introductory work like this. Only the most prominent ones, therefore, have been chosen. Further, the influence of his teachers and mentors are always at work in his formations and formulations. Since the purpose of this chapter is to provide a summative critical background to Said, the specifics of his engagement with these thinkers will be dealt with in the following chapters as and when relevant. For example, here we would highlight Said's overall assessment of Foucault (and obviously Foucault's overall influence on Said), but the relevance of Foucault for *Orientalism* will be specifically dealt with in Chapter 3. Similarly, Said's critique of Foucauldian formulations on power has been engaged with elsewhere in the book. It must be remembered, however, that Said never allows his intellectual affiliations to override or overwrite his own intellectual, cultural or racial priorities – whichever way one takes it. In other words, other theories and theorists are acceptable to him only as far as they corroborate (or at least do not contradict) his convictions. For ease of reference, a list of the prominent intellectual influences on Said is given here:

Karl Marx (his discontent with Marxism's shortcomings are well known)

Michel Foucault

Antonio Gramsci
Raymond Williams
Noam Chomsky
Erich Auerbach
Giambattista Vico
Joseph Conrad
Theodor Adorno

It needs to be noted here that sometimes Frantz Fanon is added to this list, but this is a little erroneous. The trajectory of Said's core critique of colonialism is independent of Fanon; there is no engagement with Fanon at all in *Orientalism,* for instance. It was only after this absence of Fanon was pointed out as a flaw by critics that Said attempted to placate them with summative discussions on Fanon and other such 'omissions', in his *Culture and Imperialism.* There is also a group of thinkers who extended Said's arguments and supported and reinforced his line of work, but with whom there is no detailed critical engagement in Said's critical and political writings. To this group belong Gayatri Chakravorty Spivak, Homi Bhabha, Eqbal Ahmed (to whom *Culture and Imperialism* is dedicated) and Salman Rushdie. In addition, there have been quite a few students and scholars who studied with Said and carry on his legacy of exposing the politics of culture, among other things. Most noteworthy among them are Gauri Viswanathan, Sara Suleri, Moustafa Bayoumi, Andrew Rubin and Timothy Brennan.

An engaged reading of *Beginnings*; *The World, the Text, and the Critic*; and above all *Orientalism*, is bound to reveal that his sustained critiques of Western epistemology notwithstanding, Said has often enriched himself with the insights offered by leading intellectuals of the West. Again, so far as the dominant note of Said's writings has been an oppositional one (as we will subsequently see), the influence of Marx – the arch oppositional thinker of the Western world – can hardly be overstated. In fact, Marx – and to some extent, Freud – have influenced following generations of thinkers to a much greater degree than any other intellectual. While communism as a political system or Freudian coordinates of psychological treatment may have lost their charm, the relevance of Marx and Freud as scholars and thinkers continue. This is not to say, however, that the following generations only replicated what Marx (and Freud) did; in most cases there were strong disagreements too. But these strong disagreements are also significant indicators of their overriding presence. Two outstanding instances are Foucault's disagreement with Freud on the issue of repression of sexuality in Victorian England and Said's critique of Marx for the latter's views on the colonisation of Asia by Europe.

It is somewhat easier, however, to assess the influence of Foucault on Said. The ease comes from Said's own candid, and even categorical, assertions of Foucault's influence as well as their differences. His *Orientalism,* for instance, is in many ways a textbook example of the application of the Foucauldian idea of discourse, the clamour against the book's so-called methodological inconsistency notwithstanding. In fact, among Said's contemporary poststructuralist theorists, Foucault's critical strategies appear to have been more useful for Said's purposes than any other. Critics have indeed often pointed to Said's methodological inconsistencies in using Foucault, whether alone or in combination with Gramsci. Those who feel that Said did not use Foucault's methodology consistently would be surprised if they care to check that Foucault himself has never used any methodology consistently, nor has he advocated using only one.

The main idea behind Foucault's (and Said's) interventions is to look for the fissures and ruptures in histories of culture as well as cultures of history; and making explicit the operations of power that are otherwise implicit. It is interesting to note that in 'Thinking about Edward Said', Gayatri Chakravorty Spivak also recounts her supervisor Paul de Man introducing Said to her as a scholar working on Foucault (521). Though Said finally went well beyond the boundaries of a mere Foucault scholar, there is no doubt that Foucault's intricate formulations on the questions of power and knowledge as well as ethics and epistemology were very instructive for Said. Indeed, the way anyone sees the relationship between power and knowledge has undoubtedly undergone a radical change after the interventions of Foucault. Further, Said's epistemological debt to Foucault mandates that any sincere discussion of Said's intellectual affiliations and antecedents cannot ignore dealing with Foucault, however cursorily. One, of course, has to also identify the point at which he finds Foucault ethically disempowering which in turn leads him to the Gramscian model of counter-hegemony. In *Beginnings* as well as *The World, the Text, and the Critic*, Said engages in a detailed study of the critical methodologies of poststructuralist critics like Derrida, Foucault and others and indicates his preference for Foucault's more politically pronounced interventions than Derrida's textual strategies. In his attempt to highlight the contrasts between these two high priests of poststructuralism, Said tells us that 'Derrida's criticism moves us into the text, Foucault's in and out' (*The World, the Text, and the Critic* 183). After a certain point however, Said moves away from both Foucault and Derrida. I will look into the issue of Said's critical engagement with Foucault and Derrida in greater detail later. What may be highlighted here is that for Said, the counterpoints to Foucault and Derrida are provided by arguably more politically committed thinkers and intellectuals like Antonio Gramsci, Raymond Williams, Georg Lukács and Noam Chomsky.

Gramsci, Williams and Lukács belong to what has been rather loosely called 'Western Marxism' – a term connoting widely divergent thinkers and practices with the only common factor being some kind of allegiance to the writings of Marx. This is different from both Soviet and Chinese communism because not only do they have very unorthodox readings of Marx, but also because most of the so-called Western Marxists operate in the domain of cultural theory and not economics and politics (Kellner 2). It may also be noted that they are primarily housed in universities and allied academic institutions in the West. Gramsci and Lukács are prominent exceptions as they were deeply involved in Marxist/communist political struggles as well. Said himself has often been seen as a Marxist critic and there have been anthologies of Marxist criticism that have included his essays on the Empire. Said, however, has expressed his strong reservations about Marx on several occasions, going to the extent of representing Marx himself as an Orientalist and even as a potential imperialist (see Chapters 3 and 6 for further discussion). As suggested earlier, it must be noted that Marx has been the most influential forerunner of the culture of reading against the grain, seconded by Freud. And without Marx in the background, Said as we know him would not have been possible at all. The same is true to an extent about Foucault's reception of Marx as well.

Further, the figures Said finds himself often drawn to – Gramsci and Williams – have always held working on Marxism to be their critical and ideological forte. In spite of his recurrent critical engagements with Lukács, Said does not find Lukács convincing beyond a point and also rejects the historical mode of analysis practised by the latter in favour of the geographical mode of analysis practised by Gramsci. Said feels that Lukács belongs to the Hegelian tradition of Marxism and Gramsci 'to a Vichian, Crocean departure from it' (*Culture and Imperialism* 57). The Hegelian tradition actually prefers to see history as a teleological process ('teleological' means something that has a goal, an end; from the Greek *telos* meaning 'end') and comes up with justifications for colonialism as a historical process. It is difficult for any anticolonial or postcolonial thinker therefore, to own and use Lukács unproblematically in their critical analyses. Comparatively, Gramscian analyses foregrounds the politics of space, is also free from any pro-imperial sympathy and is a more viable model for them. Gramsci becomes a compelling alternative, therefore, not only to Foucault but also to Lukács.

SHORT TAKES

Georg Wilhelm Friedrich Hegel

Georg Wilhelm Friedrich Hegel (1770–1831) is from the Idealism (better known as German Idealism) school of Western philosophy, but his influence has been widely felt well beyond his school of thought. Just as the terms 'poststructuralism' and 'theory' almost immediately remind one of Foucault and Derrida, for a long time Western philosophy itself was synonymous with Kant and Hegel. Karl Marx adopted Hegel's theory of history and applied it to his own end, but as Marxism was not treated as a 'philosophy' at all in elite European universities, the predominance of Hegel and Kant continued for a long time. Hegel believed, and wanted others to believe, that history was a conscious (or intentional) force which was leading humanity to the choicest goals possible. Unfortunately, his idea of 'humanity' did not quite include non-whites and the attitude he had towards them was extremely racist. While Marx took Hegel to task for being too much of a 'believer', postcolonial theory has censured him for being an imperialist as well as a racist.

In fact, as stated earlier, Said has displayed his interest in Gramsci at several places in his works, most notably as counterpoint to Foucault and Lukács. In *Culture and Imperialism*, he has referred to Gramsci's influential essay 'Some aspects of the Southern Question' (56–59) in connection with analyses of power and hegemony. In that essay, Gramsci famously argued that the opulence and prosperity of the Italian north is maintained by the poverty and labour of its southern regions. It is not difficult to see that this reading of Gramsci has been instructive for Said in his illustrations of the fact that English novels do not give due recognition to the contribution of those British colonies on whose labour the societies represented by the novels thrive (for example, Antigua in *Mansfield Park* and Australia in *Great Expectations*).

Similarly, in the essay 'History, Literature and Geography', Said finds it interesting that both Lukács and Gramsci celebrate 'dissonance as a central element in modern consciousness' (464), and yet finally shows a greater affiliation to Gramsci for the latter's more committed interventions into politics and political readings. As Said argues, Gramsci sees politics 'as a contest over territory, both actual and historical, to be won, fought over, controlled, held, lost, gained' (464). Gramsci's fascination with philology, resistance to all homogenising tendencies and his unification of theory and practice, which gives us the new idea of a 'concrete intellectual work' (466) are some of the other attributes that Said stresses. But most importantly, it is the Gramscian notion of hegemony that Said has found very useful, as is evidenced by his use of the same in *Orientalism*. Just as from the Foucauldian point of view Orientalism fits the bill of a discourse, from the Gramscian point of view it is a tool for creating and maintaining a Western hegemony over the non-West. Hegemony and discourse (and also, one would like to add, Althusser's ideological state apparatus), in fact, are correlated and can be seen as mutually reinforcing phenomena of cultural politics.

Said often saw his condition as that of an exile, over and above everything else. This has drawn scathing criticism from those who could not visualise how a widely influential professor at a prominent American university could ever be seen as an exile or as dispossessed. These critics fail to note two things. Firstly, the paramount sense of loss and dispossession that can result from the loss of one's birthplace. After the 1948 Arab–Israel war, the house that Said was born in was taken over by the Israelis. Secondly, Said always saw himself as a representative voice of his community. Consequently his musings on the exilic condition encompass things well beyond his individual life. Three figures that occur repeatedly in the Saidian oeuvre in the context of the exilic condition are Vico, Auerbach and Adorno. Vico is also important for Said as he had stressed the need for scrutinising human history as a human product, without any reference to God or divinity (unlike Hegel, as discussed above).

SHORT TAKES

Erich Auerbach

Originally a German literary critic, comparative scholar and philologist, Erich Auerbach (1892–1957) is mostly known for his *Mimesis* which has earned for itself the status of a classic text in comparative literature as well as in English and other European literatures. The text chiefly deals with the history of representation in Western literature from Homer to Virginia Woolf. The book, however, does not engage in the politics of representation to the same extent as it does with the history of representation. This is because Auerbach's book was written in a period which predated the emergence of schools like New Historicism and postcolonialism which have, perhaps irreversibly, foregrounded the political aspects of representation. Said, in his turn, implicates the text and the author in the politics of dispossession and exile. Auerbach, it must be noted here, was forced to resign from the post of Professor of Philology at Marburg University in 1935 because he was a Jew. The next year he fled to Istanbul where he stayed till 1947, before relocating to the US. Given the close parallels with regard to their exilic life and scholarly career, it is hardly surprising that Said felt irresistibly and repeatedly drawn to Auerbach's life history and oeuvre. What was very noteworthy on Auerbach's part is that he wrote his *Mimesis* without any European library at his disposal. It was written from sheer memory during his exile in Istanbul. In his posthumously published last major critical work, Said has unambiguously declared *Mimesis* to be the greatest book of general humanistic practice since World War II (*Humanism and Democratic Criticism* 6).

While Said heartily celebrates Auerbach's virtuosity and brilliance, he also hastens to add that such a work could not be written under any other circumstances than that of exile. It is precisely Auerbach's banishment from the political geography of Europe that compelled him to construct a cultural geography of Europe by way of squeezing its two thousand years of literary history into roughly three hundred pages. Said is clearly following (for want of a better word) Auerbach closely when he declares in the 'Introduction' to *Culture and Imperialism* that 'this book is an exile's book' (xxx). Another crucial common factor between Auerbach and Said was their love for philology. However, it is the bond forged by the exilic state of existence that brings Said close to Auerbach, with recurrent references to Auerbach's state of exile as prefiguring, echoing or consolidating Said's own state of exile.

The same bond of exilic existence can be seen at work in Said's admiration for Adorno whom he finds to be 'the quintessential intellectual, hating all systems, whether on our side or theirs, with equal distaste' ('Intellectual Exile' 375). In fact, apart from the intellectuals and thinkers discussed above (and in the following pages), if there is any phenomenon that has cast the longest and the strongest spell on Said it is undoubtedly that of exile – to be more precise, the Palestinian exile or Palestinian diaspora, in contemporary critical parlance (Said mostly avoided the term diaspora until the last phase of his writings). It is also interesting to note that a great number of intellectuals who Said found to have made meaningful interventions in the world were exilic figures.

Said insisted that it is imperative for an intellectual to inhabit an exilic space, at least metaphorically, whether they have been actually exiled or not ('Intellectual Exile' 377). Said frequently invoked his exilic status in almost all his significant works, primarily to foreground the loss of the Palestinian homeland. However, over the years, he also tried to give shape to the concept of the exilic as a critical device on its own. His 1984 essay 'Reflections on Exile' is arguably the most important piece in this regard, where Said attempts to show how being in exile can be both a disabling as well as an enabling condition. The essay begins with the assertion that the terrible sadness and losses of an exilic life can never be made up for: 'It is the unhealable rift forced between a human being and a native place, between the self and its true home' (172).

This leads him to the immediate question that if the exilic state is one of 'terminal loss', why is it such a recurrent and powerful motif of modern culture? For Said, 'Modern Western culture is in large part the work of exiles, émigrés, refugees' ('Reflections on Exile' 173). The chief reason behind this privileging of the figure and the status of the exile is related to transcendence. Since exiles have lost their homelands and cannot become insiders to the new societies and cultures to which they are often exposed, they become acutely aware of the provisional and transient nature of human realities. It is because they know that homes are provisional; 'Exiles cross borders, break barriers of thought and experience' (185). In other words, they become more universal, less parochial. By the same token, an exile has the ability to assess cultures more comparatively, more neutrally. To quote Said's own words 'Most people are principally aware of one culture, one setting, one home; exiles are aware of at least two, and this plurality of vision gives rise to an awareness of simultaneous dimensions, an awareness that—to borrow a phrase from music—is contrapuntal' (186). As we will see in the following pages, it is this 'contrapuntal awareness' which is at work in all of Said's formations and formulations.

For all his seemingly irreversible state of exile visibly caused by the theory and praxis of Zionism, Said, surprisingly enough, does not seem to identify Jews or Israel as his prime target. His nuanced point of departure is that it is not the state of Israel itself, but the US and its allied forces which are responsible for the current Palestinian predicament; just as the origin of the problem lies with British colonial policies. America and its allies are engaged in a proxy war against Palestine and the Arab world using Israel and Zionism as their tools. The radical othering, inferiorisation and even demonisation of the non-Western world that Orientalism engaged itself with are being continued far more deftly and effectively by Israeli–American strategic alliances. Almost all, if not all, of Said's works are best seen as an unrelenting opposition to this inhumane politics and poetics of dispossession.

In other words, while Said's epistemological rigour appears to be largely a continuation of Western intellectuals like Marx, Gramsci, Adorno and Foucault, the ethical as well as the ontological concerns of his writings are almost exclusively related to the question of Palestine. Just as I have tried to foreground the significance of his work on the politics of Palestine in my discussion of Said's important texts, I want to stress the Palestinian component while discussing his intellectual lineage as well.

While there have been numerous figures who Said found inspiring so far as the Palestinian cause is concerned, three figures that deserve special attention are his Aunt Nabiha, Ibrahim Abu-Lughod and Yasser Arafat. It was his Aunt Nabiha's dedicated service to dispossessed Palestinians that made Said experience the severe suffering and deprivation of Palestinian refugees for the first time. As he puts it,

> It was also she who communicated to me the desolations of being without a country or a place to return to, of being unprotected by any national authority or institutions, of no longer being able to make sense of the past except as bitter, helpless regret nor of the present with its daily queuing, anxiety filled searches for jobs, and poverty, hunger, and humiliations. (*Out of Place* 119)

While Nabiha was the strongest early influence on Said so far as his Palestinian consciousness is concerned, as an adult he often found himself drawn to the charismatic political scientist Ibrahim Abu-Lughod who rekindled his conviction for the cause. In an obituary written for the *London Review of Books* in 2001, Said referred to Ibrahim as his 'Guru', and said that 'Ibrahim introduced me to the subject and the experience, as it were, of Palestine' ('My Guru'). In addition, Said was also considerably influenced by Yasser Arafat until they parted ways (a detailed discussion on Said's chequered relationship with Arafat can be found in Chapter 6). Though he categorically stated more than once that he did not espouse violence as a strategy of liberation, Said also tried to understand and contextualise the activities of militant groups such as Hamas.

What should be apparent by now is that his scholarship and academic achievements notwithstanding, the crucial source as well as force of Said's writings lie in the lived world of real politics. It would be sheer injustice to Said as well as his scholarship to only place his works under the rubric of a study in textual representation. The political dimension of Said's works and his recurrent emphasis on the urgent need for the intellectual to speak truth to power cannot but lead one to see that, in the Saidian worldview epistemological and cultural concerns are always preceded and contextualised by overt or covert political acts. Intellectuals should be constantly dedicated to the uncovering of this unholy nexus between knowledge and culture on the one hand and political and exploitative motives on the other – this is the secular religion of the intellectual, as Said sees it.

A key signifier of the intellectual's commitment to society for Said is the use of a transparent and lucid language: 'The net result in terms of my writing has been to attempt a greater transparency, to free myself from academic jargon, and not to hide behind euphemism and circumlocution where difficult issues have been concerned' ('Between Worlds' 565). Said is well aware of the possibility that the convoluted arguments and abstruse constructions often used by intellectuals may be used to camouflage a lack of honest commitment to ethics and politics.

Further, his commitment to values – humane, secular and democratic – makes him 'oppositional' to authority and authoritarianisms of all hues and colours, be it academic, imperial, statist, cultural or religious. Said argues that it is the intellectual's responsibility to explore all human institutions – cultures and literatures included – and show that they are not eternal authorities handed down to us by some unchallengeable power like God, but are human constructs generated against spatial and temporal specificities of various kinds. Authorities, norms, laws and institutions need constant challenging and change, even overhauls, if necessary for the greater good. And all these are to be done with an abiding love for and faith in a human destiny where all have access to the ways and means of making their lives a little more dignified, a little more liveable.

NOTES

1. According to Timothy Brennan, the 'W' in Edward W. Said stands for William, not Wadie (Brennan 3, 18); but it is not agreed upon by all scholars.

REFERENCES

Ahmad, Eqbal. "Introduction". *The Pen and the Sword: Conversations with Edward Said.* Monroe, Common Courage Press, 1994, pp. 7–22.

Bayoumi, Moustafa, and Andrew Rubin, editors. *The Edward Said Reader.* Vintage, 2000.

Brennan, Timothy. *Places of Mind: A Life of Edward Said.* Farrar, 2021.

Chomsky, Noam. "The Unipolar Moment and the Culture of Imperialism". Columbia University Edward Said Memorial Lecture, Columbia University, 3 Dec 2009, https://chomsky.info/20091203-2/. Accessed 24 August 2021.

Hitchens, Christopher. "Whose Life Is It Anyway?". *The Nation Company* LLC, 4 Oct. 1999. *The Free Library*, https://www.thefreelibrary.com/Whose+Life+Is+It+Anyway%3f-a056982827. Accessed 23 December 2021.

Kellner, Douglas. “Western Marxism”. *Modern Social Theory: An Introduction*, edited by Austin Harrington, Oxford UP, 2005, pp.154–174, https://pages.gseis.ucla.edu/faculty/kellner/essays/westernmarxismfinal.pdf. Accessed 22 December 2021.

Macey, David. *The Penguin Dictionary of Critical Theory.* Penguin, 2001.

Said, Edward. “Between Worlds”. *Reflections on Exile and Other Essays.* Penguin, 2001, pp 554–68.

---. *Culture and Imperialism.* Alfred A. Knopf, 1993.

---. “History, Literature and Geography”. *Reflections on Exile and Other Essays.* Penguin, 2001, pp. 453–73.

---. *Humanism and Democratic Criticism.* Columbia UP, 2004.

---. “Intellectual Exile: Expatriates and Marginals”. *The Edward Said Reader*, edited by Bayoumi Moustafa and Andrew Rubin, Vintage, 2000, pp. 368–81.

---. “My Guru”. *London Review of Books*, vol. 23, no. 24, 13 Dec. 2001, https://www.lrb.co.uk/the-paper/v23/n24/edward-said/my-guru. Accessed 22 December 2021.

---. *Orientalism.* 1978. Penguin, 2001.

---. *Out of Place: A Memoir*. Granta, 1999.

---. “Reflections on Exile”. *Reflections on Exile and Other Essays*. Penguin, 2001, pp. 173–86.

---. *Reflections on Exile and Other Essays.* Penguin, 2001.

---. *The World, the Text, and The Critic.* 1983. Vintage, 1991.

Spivak, Gayatri Chakravorty. “Thinking about Edward Said: Pages from a Memoir”. *Critical Inquiry*, vol. 31, no. 2, 2005, pp. 519–25.

St. Clair, Jeffrey and Alexander Cockburn. “Commentary ‘Scholar’ Deliberately Falsified Record in Attack on Said”. *Counterpunch*, 1 Sept. 1999, https://www.counterpunch.org/1999/09/01/commentary-scholar-deliberately-falsified-record-in-attack-on-said/. Accessed 23 December 2021.

Veseer, H. Aram. *Edward Said: The Charisma of Criticism.* Routledge, 2010.

Walcott, Derek. “A Far Cry from Africa”. *An Anthology of Commonwealth Poetry*, edited by C.D. Narasimhaiah, Macmillan, 1990, p. 200.

Weiner, Justus Read. "'My Beautiful Old House' and other Fabrications by Edward Said". *Commentary*, Sept. 1999, https://www.commentary.org/articles/justus-weiner/my-beautiful-old-house-and-other-fabrications-by-edward-said/. Accessed 23 December 2021.

Williams, Patrick. "Nothing in the Post?: Said and the Problem of Postcolonial Intellectuals". *Edward Said and the Post-Colonial*, edited by Bill Ashcroft and Hussein Khadim, Nova, 2001, pp. 31–56.

Chapter Two

Said Unread

JOSEPH CONRAD AND THE FICTION OF AUTOBIOGRAPHY & BEGINNINGS: INTENTION AND METHOD

Based on Said's first two books, *Joseph Conrad and the Fiction of Autobiography* and *Beginnings: Intention and Method*, this chapter focuses on ideas like the relation between an author and their work, the construction and deconstruction of the concept of 'authority' and the centrality of the novel as a form in European culture – all of which become recurrent motifs in Said's later works. Here lies the foundational importance of these books. Additionally, *Beginnings* was one of the first books in English which introduced the so-called French Theory to the Anglo-American world, helping the transition of literary criticism to literary theory. Said himself has said that he was seeking to establish a voice of his own by using other's voices in *Beginnings.* The phenomenal success of *Orientalism* has, no doubt, led to the emergence of postcolonial studies, but there are many other sides to Said. One of the primary aims of this book is to foreground the Said that has largely remained unsaid. The present chapter is especially focused on rediscovering and foregrounding the other Saids.

The academic world has, for a long time, mostly nurtured a calculated distance from the world of action or engagement – at least direct political engagement. Noam Chomsky, Edward Said, Judith Butler and Slavoj Žižek are exceptions to a tradition of university academia which seems to be premised upon the concept of purity of knowledge and guarding itself zealously against action/interference from the outside world. The ruling spirit of academia in this regard seems to have been based on the notion that gnosis (knowledge) is antithetical to action (praxis). The idea that a contemplative person is not suitable for worldly action is a long held one, in both Oriental and Occidental traditions. In the West, the idea was famously concretised by William Shakespeare through the character of Hamlet in the eponymous play. Following the same idea, the celebrated mathematician G. H. Hardy once suggested that real mathematics is one which serves no worldly purpose: 'I have never done anything "useful". No discovery of mine has made, or is likely to make, directly or indirectly, for good or ill, the least difference to the amenity of the world' (*A Mathematician's Apology* 49).

Edward Said's life and oeuvre has constantly challenged this position. Not only was he uninterested in 'pure' academics, but he repeatedly posited the impossibility of unalloyed objectivity on the part of a scholar or researcher. Further, he acted on the belief that academicians should also be intellectuals whose primary job is to speak truth to power, to ensure greater justice and better democracy for all. Consequently, in Edward Said's lifeworld, there is no epistemology divested of ontology and ethics. According to Said's own arguments, such apparently divergent fields of epistemology and ethics or gnosis and practice are not, or have never been, separate entities. One of his seminal contributions to epistemology is the concept of 'worldliness': the embeddedness of a text, author, or theory in its sociopolitical–economic contexts. This concept counters the poststructuralist position on textuality (as famously made available by Derrida in statements such as 'there is nothing outside the text') and locates Said in the realm of socially and politically committed intellectuals. This commitment can be seen as the condition and consequence of Said's own subject position as an Arab Palestinian in the USA. For Said, the intellectual relativism of the 1980s and 90s is a consequence of the intellectual's reluctance to discern and establish truth. It is because of this that Said insists on reading texts as human products generated and bound by specific contexts. Said, in fact, refers to Vico's concept of history as a human construct to highlight a basic hypothesis in his reading strategy. As he sees it, this is the only way to interpret literature which does justice to its production and existence. In a crucial passage of his 'Introduction' to *Reflections on Exile,* Said makes the concept of 'worldliness' explicit:

> To value literature at all is fundamentally to value it as the individual work of an individual writer tangled up in the circumstances taken for granted by everyone, such things as residence, nationality, a familiar locale, language, friends and so on. The problem for the interpreter, therefore, is how to align these circumstances with the work, how to read the work and its worldly situation. (xv)

In other words, a text is the joint product of authorial intention as well the sociopolitical and historical background against which the author operates. This plea for contextual readings of texts remains the key operational strategy in his readings of Orientalist and colonial values in the so-called great works of European literature – the Western Canon, as it is now commonly known after Harold Bloom's influential publication bearing the same name. Over the years, Said's readings have offered corrections not only to the Eurocentric notions of what a great text is, his interventions have really problematised the critical practices that were in place in Western academia. He has shown the limitations of and challenged the assumptions of traditional modes of criticism (focused on aesthetics and literariness) as well as structuralist and poststructuralist tenets. In fact, Said's disagreement with nearly all major modes of criticism – aesthetic/liberal humanist, formalist and structuralist/poststructuralist – is unambiguously borne out by his almost obsessive insistence on relocating texts and authors in their contextual specificities. This is the central message that recurs throughout his oeuvre, albeit against different contexts and variegated expressions. The most important expression that he uses for the phenomenon is, of course, 'worldliness'.

JOSEPH CONRAD AND THE FICTION OF AUTOBIOGRAPHY

Published in 1966, Said's first book-length critical engagement, *Joseph Conrad and the Fiction of Autobiography*, is no exception to his overarching tendency to relate texts to their contexts. Though the book has received the least critical attention in all works published on Said, an engaged reading of it confirms the fact that Said's critical desire to relate a text to the world finds its longest sustained expression in this book. The Saidian theory of the 'worldliness' of texts was formulated much later, but the practical application of the theory is at work in the book on Conrad. Conrad, it must be remembered, is one of the four novelists identified by F. R. Leavis as 'great' in *The Great Tradition.* Said's choice of Conrad is not accidental; rather it is an implicit dialogue with Leavis's choice. This is also borne out by the fact that in many of his subsequent works, Said has often chosen to engage at length with as many as three out of four of Leavis's 'great' authors, especially Jane Austen, George Eliot and Joseph Conrad. While Said has never negated the literary or aesthetic excellence of any of these writers, thereby accepting their greatness, he has also shown these writers to be deeply political and in fact, pro-imperial; something Leavis never thought of, or perhaps, did not want to think about.

Said's *Joseph Conrad and the Fiction of Autobiography* is a critical examination of not only Conrad, but also, by implication, the contemporary prominence of structuralist modes of studying literature. In this book, Said uses phenomenology as his critical tool to relate Conrad's writings to his consciousness: 'this study attempts a phenomenological exploration of Conrad's consciousness, so that the kind of mind he had, both in its distinction and energy, will become apparent' (7–8). This desire to understand the mind of an author, it must be noted, goes against the formalist, structuralist, as well as poststructuralist dicta of seeing texts as autonomous verbal icons devoid of authorial intentions or interference. The book is not, however, methodologically rigid. While phenomenological tenets are definitely at work, Said is more interested in showing the correspondence between Conrad's letters and short stories in almost a matter of fact, common sense way. This is yet another trend which he followed till the end of his career: he never used any critic or methodology, be it Lukács, Foucault or Gramsci, to the exclusion of all else. He accepted only as much as he found acceptable in a theory or theorist, and proceeded on his own. In fact, Said has quite often alerted us against turning theories into cultural dogmas and applying them indiscriminately beyond their points of origin. This was sounded most powerfully in his influential essay 'Travelling Theory', among others. It is also useful to remember Aram Veseer's words about Said in this context: 'a restless character who could not embrace any position or idea without simultaneously pushing it away' (23).

Said's book on Conrad was originally his doctoral dissertation at Harvard University. Influenced by phenomenology, and more importantly, his own conviction about the interconnectedness of a writer and his lived world, Said unambiguously asserts that 'he [Conrad] has lived what he describes' (8).[1] It is the same conviction about a writer's 'worldliness' that leads Said to say, 'I found it difficult to believe that a man would be so uneconomical as to pour himself out in letter after letter and then not use and reformulate his insights and discoveries in his fiction' (vii).

Having set the tone in his very first book, Said's life and oeuvre can be read as a prolonged engagement with Conrad, among others. There are two sides to this engagement. At one level Said affiliates himself fully with Conrad, especially on the grounds that both were exiles, and both were writing in a language not their own. Yet on another level, Said, much like Chinua Achebe, stood against the imperialist and colonialist in Conrad. This a very intricate love–hate relation; while *Joseph Conrad and the Fiction of Autobiography* mostly showcases Said's love of Conrad, later engagements counterbalance it with criticism and resentment, if not hatred. Here it is important to note that there is a difference between Achebe's dismissal of Conrad as a racist and Said's more nuanced reading of Conrad as one who resented the 'horror' of colonialism yet was powerless to reject it or go beyond it. While it is true that in his vision of Africa as the 'Heart of Darkness' Conrad was party to the colonial and racial imaginaries of Europe, it is equally true that it was the same Conrad who also wrote,

> The conquest of the earth, which mostly means the taking it away from those who have a different complexion or slightly flatter noses than ourselves, is not a pretty thing when you look into it too much. What redeems it is the idea only. An idea at the back of it; not a sentimental pretence but an idea;

> and an unselfish belief in the idea—something you can set up, and bow down before, and offer a sacrifice to . . . (*Heart of Darkness* 13)

It was part of Said's agenda to establish Conrad as a responsible writer. Taking exception to contemporary critical receptions of Conrad that viewed him as 'a writer of "mythic" or "unconscious" fiction', Said sought to 'deepen our admiration for Conrad as an eminently self-aware, responsible, and serious artist' (ix). Said states that a reading of Conrad's letters indicate that the latter was always in the process of changing himself intellectually as well as spiritually (8). He further claims 'pain' and 'intense effort' are the chief sources as well as the profound keynotes of Conrad's spiritual growth. Conrad's life was fraught with numerous anxieties, a fact that can only be indirectly apprehended from his fiction, but directly from his letters. As an exile, Conrad was threatened by a serious existential crisis. Said notes how 'Conrad's understanding of life made it appear before him as an inescapable meaninglessness, a series of particular occurrences', divorced from any divine purpose and determined only by 'a mechanical and perverse inevitability' (6). As a creative writer writing in a language not his own, Conrad faced, what can be named after Harold Bloom, an anxiety of influence from prominent European writers. He writes in one of his letters, 'I am afraid I am too much under the influence of Maupassant' (8). According to Said, these precarious feelings and haunting understandings troubled Conrad throughout his writing career (6). Perhaps these weaknesses and limitations were also the very source of Conrad's prolific outpourings. It could also be suggested that as far as there is a direct correspondence between Conrad's word and his world, he was as much a creator as he was a creation of his world.

For writers like Conrad or Said himself, writing as an ethical practice forms the strongest part of their struggle for existence. According to Said, for Conrad the essence of the struggle for existence lies in 'the achievement of character', by which he implies the attainment of individuality through narratives and other voices (13). This character, or individuality, is to be achieved by working through the oppositions of various forces, both in life and in writing. Though Said was yet to theoretically formulate his ideas on the predicaments and perils of an exiled life, there are already sufficient indications in the present text that he had taken note of the debilitating effects of the state of exile in Conrad's life. He agrees with Gustav Morf's reading of 'Conrad's spiritual and physical exile from Poland (which contributed to the tentativeness of his place in existence) as the essential donné of his life and work' (15) though he adds that Morf's analysis is compromised by an insufficient exploration of Conrad's letters.

Said would very shortly put himself in Conrad's shoes. The Third Arab–Israeli War, that started in 1967, changed the course of Said's life forever (see the following section on *Beginnings*). In fact, it is easier to explain Said's recurrent returns to Conrad's work in terms of the former's formulations on the exilic condition – as found in his essay 'Reflections on Exile' among others – and the related issue of colonialism, which has been instrumental in forming the lives and vision of both writers in various ways. In an article published in 1998, Said has stated that,

> In the first book I wrote, *Joseph Conrad and the Fiction of Autobiography* . . . and then in an essay called "Reflections on Exile" . . . I used Conrad as an example of someone whose life and work seemed to typify the fate of the wanderer who becomes an accomplished writer in an acquired language, but can never shake off his sense of alienation from his new—that is, acquired—and, in Conrad's rather special case, admired, home. ('Between Worlds' 554)

Associated with Conrad's exile and dislocation are the several schisms between contradictory emotions and predilections that he parses and records directly in his letters, and implicitly in his fiction. There is, for instance, the linguistic schism: Conrad caught between his ex-Polish tongue and the English language that he wants to write in and write himself into. This also implies the tension and clash between two cultures.

There is one more interesting schism, according to Said: between Conrad the sailor and Conrad the novelist. Conrad terms the 'consequences of this double life *homo duplex*' (*Joseph Conrad* 38). Said argues that Conrad the novelist could only emerge at the cost of Conrad the sailor: 'Only by forgetting too well his other character as a sailor, he seems to be saying, he has been able to become a novelist' (38). This foreshadows, to a great extent, Said's twin roles as a professor of literature and a political activist upholding the Palestinian cause. The difference is Said sees both his roles as essentially the same.

Similarly, while it is rewarding and enriching to read both Said and Conrad as products of the important issue of exile, it must not be lost on us that there are significant differences between the two. A key difference between the two perhaps lies in the fact that while Conrad, much like Nietzsche and Thomas Hardy, finally emerges from his oeuvre as a person whose profound pessimism 'made him write repeatedly of life as if it were a terrible dream begging for relief' (38), Said has always been full of hope for a better world, envisioning a collective humanist future for all, present discontent notwithstanding.

The most significant difference between Said and Conrad, however, lies in their attitude to colonialism. While Said was decidedly an anticolonial thinker and writer, Conrad's attitude to colonialism was, at best, ambivalent. Though Conrad is sympathetic towards the natives 'suffering under the atrocities of colonial rule, his portrayal of natives has drawn strong criticism from postcolonial writers like Chinua Achebe. In an essay titled 'An Image of Africa: Racism in Conrad's *Heart of Darkness*', Achebe suggests that Conrad portrayed Africa and the Africans from a typically racist point of view. While not denying the presence of a Eurocentric (if not racist) bias in Conrad, Said chooses to focus on Conrad's sympathies with the colonised and his abhorrence for the act of colonialism. In fact, there are two sides to Conrad, and Said squarely foregrounds this dichotomy in a later work in a section titled 'Two Visions in *Heart of Darkness*'. As a man of his time, Conrad was not in a position to 'grant the natives their freedom, despite his severe critique of the imperialism that enslaved them' (*Culture and Imperialism* 34).

Coming back to *Joseph Conrad and the Fiction of Autobiography*, while Said seemingly accepts the canonisation of Conrad by Leavis as a great writer, his source of interest in Conrad comes from things closer to politics than aesthetics. While Leavis placed Conrad with

Austen, Eliot and James on the basis of his identifying in these writers a worldview that was primarily aesthetic and pastoral/pre-industrial with a certain kind of moral vision, Said consciously connects Conrad with a group of writers he sees as engaged with action and realism: 'His [Conrad's] professed literary heritage was composed of writers of action and realism—writers like Cooper, Marryat, and Maupassant' (43). This affiliation to the 'tradition of action and realism' also accounts for Conrad's suspicion of omniscient narration as well as the finality of authorial reporting. Said contends that for Conrad, reality could only be retrieved from action, not narration (43). Conrad's reservations against 'authorial interpretation' have an uncanny parallel in Said's opposition to authorities and authoritarianisms of all kinds, as I have argued in the following section on *Beginnings.* Further, Said quotes Conrad saying 'a good book is a good action', which is also close to Said's conviction regarding the need for the intellectuals to act for the world even as they act with the word (44). It is this commitment to action that finds reflection in Conrad's anxiety of being 'considered merely a writer of accurate details' (47). In fact, Conrad could not overcome this anxiety and saw himself as a writer whose 'fate is to be descriptive and descriptive only' (47). As Conrad feels that he is far from achieving what he wanted to achieve – that is, becoming a writer of action, and not mere description or narration – he twists the well known maxim 'Art is long, life is short' into 'Life is long and art is so short that no one sees the miserable thing' (47).

Another striking feature of Conrad's shorter fiction, as per Said's observation, is that in Conrad's works 'reflection' or 'interpretation' follows, rather than accompanies, action. It is often because reflection or interpretation is mostly possible after an event or incident occurs, not before it. While ordinary novelists or narrators would interpret an incident before it occurs – mostly through a third person omniscient narrator – Conrad prefers to represent the action–reflection chronology of real life. Said terms this 'the retrospective mode' of Conrad's shorter fiction and supports his hypothesis with evidence from one of Conrad's personal letters in which the latter categorically states that 'Men often act first and reflect afterwards' (87).

This so-called retrospective mode, however, is not without its problems. As Said puts it, 'most of Conrad's shorter fiction dramatizes the problematic relation between the past and the present, between then and now' (91). There is a time gap, for obvious reasons, between the occurrence of an incident and reflections on it which is true of real life as well as fictions that strive hard to correspond to real life. A narrative, fictional or otherwise, can only attempt to retrieve or approximate past incidents and not reproduce it as it had exactly happened: 'Between the recollecting narrator and the actual tale there is a barrier that is eternally closed' (88). Writers like Conrad, however, put this barrier to creative use in their fiction.

It is interesting to note that both Conrad's insistence on the gap between an incident and its recollection, as well as Said's elaboration of the same, closely anticipate two particularly important critical tropes that emerged in the following years: representation and cultural memory. Commenting further on Conrad's handling of the relation between the past and the present in his shorter fiction, Said says the 'characteristic ideal twist in every Conrad story is that the attempt to see a direct relation between the past and the present, to see past and present as a continuous surface of interrelated events, is frustrated' (95). Said's incisive reading of Conrad's works in the light of the latter's interweaving of the past and the present can be seen as an implicit critique of Leavis's reading of Conrad in *The Great Tradition.* While Leavis (toeing the paths of Matthew Arnold and T. S. Eliot before him) presents Conrad in impersonal and universalist terms, Said is keen on foregrounding Conrad's personal moorings and contextual specificities.

BEGINNINGS: INTENTION AND METHOD

Edward Said's first major critical work, *Beginnings: Intention and Method* (1975), marks (among other things) his shift from the phenomenological school of thought to what may be called the structures and strictures of structuralism and poststructuralism. In their comment on the essay 'Molestation and Authority in Narrative Fiction' from *Beginnings*, Moustafa Bayoumi and Andrew Rubin have suggested that 'the essay marked for Said a methodological shift from the phenomenological criticism of George Poulet, Jean Rousset, and Merleau-Ponty to the narrative theory of the structuralists like Tzevetan Todorov and Roland Barthes' (38). It is difficult, however, to decide Said's critical affiliations in such clear terms.

SHORT TAKES

Vico

Giambattista Vico (1668–1744) is one of the major figures of Western epistemology. Primarily a professor of rhetoric, Vico stood strongly against the philosophy of René Descartes that had been foundational for the development of rationalism in the West. While Descartes had tried to identify reason as the basis of all knowledge, making a strong argument for a difference between scientific and non-linear studies, Vico tried to revive faith in imagination, rhetoric and the humanities. He has also exerted considerable influence on the development of the philosophy of history, so much so that he is recognised as the founder of this discipline. Though a Roman Catholic by faith, he had anticipated the phenomenon of class struggle as well as modern secularism in his own way. Consequently, he has been a strong influence on thinkers like Karl Marx and Edward Said, among others.

As I have argued above as well as in the following chapters, Said has never adopted any critical tenet or school uncritically, in complete compliance with original theorist. While critics and schools of various hues have all attempted to co-opt Said, his writings defy and deny any such classification and induction. In fact, Said himself considers branding critics into schools like Marxist, Feminist or Structuralist as non-secular, quasi-theological and inimical to criticism's basic task of constant interrogation of all norms and assumptions. His critical genius, which is defined more by eclecticism than insularity, is at full play in *Beginnings* as well. Let me cite an instance of this eclecticism at this point. While Said has his eyes fixed almost constantly on contemporary poststructuralists like Foucault, Derrida, Barthes and Bloom in *Beginnings*, the last part of the book is dedicated to Giambattista Vico, in a chapter titled

'Conclusion: Vico in His Work and in This'. Said's putting on record the phenomenal influence that the eighteenth century philosopher exerts on him is very much in sync with the poststructuralist trend of 'self-reflexivity'. However, the fact that he looks for definitive solutions in the writings of a pre-modern philosopher after intricate analyses of contemporary critical philosophy for about 350 pages strongly contends that Said was a lot more versatile than any one particular school of thought could hope to contain.

Apart from contemporary theory and Vico, Said's *Beginnings* is also influenced by the experiences of the 1967 Arab–Israeli War as well as his divorce from his first wife. While neither of these is readily visible in the text itself, Said has confessed elsewhere that but for these two incidents he would have become a Jonathan Swift scholar only. In fact, during 1967–68, Said was at the University of Illinois on a fellowship to study and research Jonathan Swift. The Arab–Israeli War compelled him to remember his Palestinian roots, and he found himself increasingly drawn towards pro-Palestinian politics. Propelled by the defeat of the Palestinians in the war, Said felt he could not be comfortable any more with being an academic scholar only; becoming a committed intellectual and activist dedicated to the cause of Palestine was the need of the hour. In an interview given to Moustafa Bayoumi and Andrew Rubin, Said categorically declared that '*Beginnings* is really the product of 1967 war' (*The Edward Said Reader* 422) and also adds: 'Furthermore, my marriage was coming apart' (423). The book is, at a personal level at least, a reaction to 'a crisis that caused me rethink what I was doing and try to make more connections in my life between things that had been either suppressed, or denied, or hidden' (423). The things 'suppressed, or denied, or hidden' here are obviously his Palestinian roots; that despite being a brilliant professor of literature at a prestigious university, there was something about him that the larger American society and culture would never own or acknowledge. What is more interesting, however, is that Said's search for things suppressed, hidden or denied did not remain limited to his own life. In his subsequent works, Said gradually translated and transformed this personal query to a search for the imperialist affiliations suppressed beneath the so-called great monuments of Western literature and culture.

A strong sense of secularism has marked Said's oeuvre all through, befitting his ideals of the rational and free enquiry into everything that exists under the sun. The reason that he gives for his preference for the term 'beginning' over 'origin' also emanates from a commitment to secularism. Given that 'origin' almost always has a religious, divine or Biblical connotation, he finds it to be more 'passive' and uses 'beginning as having more active meaning' (*Beginnings* 6). For Said, 'beginning' implies and invokes human agency rather than divine intervention. Beginning as a concept, therefore, looks at writing as a human production generated by specific historical, political and social contexts, and not as something that Yeats once described as 'Monuments of unageing intellect'. For a better perspective on his stance, let us look at what he says in his last critical work *Humanism and Democratic Criticism*:

> For my purposes, the core of humanism is the secular notion that the historical world is made by men and women, and not by God, and that it can be understood rationally according to the principle formulated by Vico in New Science, that we can really know only what we make or, to put it differently, we can know things according to the way they were made. (11)

While these words squarely reflect the imperatives of the secular for Said and his work, they also reveal that Vico's works exerted a strong influence on Said's abiding interest in secularism at various levels.

Returning to *Beginnings*, Said displays remarkable erudition and a wide range of study in this critical work. He maintains that he has read every text that has been discussed in the book in the original, except for those that were written in Russian (xvii). Given that Said engages with texts and authors in languages as diverse as Arabic, French, German and Italian, his linguistic competence is formidable. *Beginnings* is an exploration of both the ideological ('intention') as well as technical ('method') acts of beginnings, especially the beginnings of literary and philosophical texts and traditions. The chief aim of the book is to explore 'the question of beginning in an interesting, fairly detailed, practical and theoretical way' (xii). The book, however, is not an inventory that takes stock of all beginnings. It is not a 'catalogue of infinite cases', but an in-depth study of new beginnings in writing in terms of two aspects: 'both as something one does, and as something one thinks about' (xi). While the former is the technical aspect of new writings ('method'), the latter signifies issues related to ideology and consciousness. While Said succinctly defines a 'beginning' as an act that makes a difference to the order of things already in place, he adds a rider to the definition: 'beginning is making or producing difference; but . . . difference which is the result of combining the already-familiar with the fertile novelty of human work in language' (xiii).

In other words, no new beginning can afford to have a complete, radical break with the past; past and present interact through discontinuities as well as continuities. To cite an instance from English literature, Victorian literature – especially its poetic forms – was also in certain ways a continuation of the ethos of Romantic poetry. Tennyson, Browning and Arnold would not have become what they did without Wordsworth, Shelley and Keats before them. Similarly, almost all the striking features of postmodernist writing are already present in a high modernist text like James Joyce's *Ulysses* or Samuel Beckett's *Waiting for Godot*. In fact, many informed critics consider Laurence Sterne's *The Life and Opinions of Tristram Shandy, Gentleman* (popularly known as *Tristram Shandy*), which was published in nine volumes between 1759–67, as the first 'postmodern' novel! Said's insistence on the continuity between the past and the present despite his categorical declaration that a beginning is 'a designated point of departure' (xiii) is perhaps best captured in these famous lines of T. S. Eliot:

> Time present and time past
> Are both perhaps present in time future,
> And time future contained in time past. (*Four Quartets*)

While the 'past' figures in *Beginnings* through a body of texts and authors as diverse as the Bible, the Koran, *The New Science* (Vico) and others, the new or the 'present' is provided by his engagement with contemporary theory, especially structuralism and poststructuralism. Said's closeness to poststructuralist protocols of reading becomes evident when, for instance, he seeks to do away with the distinction between the 'creative' and 'critical' thought process. A 'verbal beginning', Said says, is 'both a creative and a critical activity, just as at the moment one begins to use language in a disciplined way, the orthodox distinction between critical and creative thought begins to break down' (xi). This is visibly drafted in a Derridean fashion. Derrida does not admit of any difference between critical writing and creative writing; all writings in any given system are but different permutations and combinations of the same set of signs. Further, a beginning in writing can only take place following a thought about beginning in the consciousness: 'In language, therefore, writing or thinking about beginning is tied to writing or thinking a beginning' (xi).

This insistence on thought translating into actuality is a continuation of Said's phenomenological moorings. This is not quite in tandem with the poststructuralist pursuit of seeing books and works as verbal or linguistic structures composed by an interplay among signifiers without any reference to authorial consciousness, thought or agency. The importance of the authorial voice for Said can hardly be overstated when we see him asserting that a beginning is 'not only a kind of action; but a frame of mind, a kind of work, an attitude, a consciousness' (xi).

As far as the act of writing itself is concerned, a beginning signals a well defined departure or difference from what has already been in place. Thus, '[f]or any writer to begin is to embark upon something connected to a designated point of departure' (xii). Again, while all new writing is a beginning, it is particularly true of the novel. Said wants to show how 'forms like the novel and how concepts like the text are forms of being and becoming in the world' (xii). While Said's perspective on the novel challenges the traditional idea of the novel as realistic prose fiction, it also anticipates his further explorations of the novel form in terms of its complicity with colonialism. The second chapter of *Beginnings* titled 'The Novel as Beginning Intention', suggests that Said does not take the novel to be only a reflection of reality; rather, it creates realities of its own. Further, it is also worthwhile to enquire as to why the novel emerged in the first place, and why did it emerge in Europe only? While the explicit link between the novel and imperialism is yet to be established, Said emphasises the fact that the novel is primarily a European or Western genre (81). Pointing to the absence of novels in Arabic literature before the twentieth century, Said adds that even in the Western tradition, the novel is of recent origin. This is significant as it may tell us why the novel form has been so important in Europe, 'what needs the novel has filled and what effects it has produced' (81). Said's hypothesis is that 'a central purpose of the Western novel is to enable the writer to represent characters and societies more or less freely in development' (82). It may be noted that his comparison of the histories of the novel in Europe and the Arab world is the first moment when Said directly pits a European tradition against an Oriental one. While he does not develop the comparison beyond a point, it foreshadows the shape of things to come.

Said does not seem to favour the view held by F. R. Leavis and his followers that the novel is primarily a vehicle of aesthetic pleasure and moral values, nor is he ready to accept it as only a mimetic form. Further, the novel is also not simply an act of pure imagination. For Said, the novel is all about generating new worlds which offer a parallel to the real world, accommodating all that the real world cannot. Consequently, he argues that the main thing about novel writing, beginning a novel, is 'authority'. It is authority that a writer enjoys, enabling them to create worlds wholly as they desire. In other words, the novel is both a social formation and a social practice. To consolidate his argument, Said refers to his mentor Harry Levin who also says that 'the novel is an institution, wholly differentiated from the more generalised idea of fiction' (82–83). Said's arguments make it clear that no novel can keep away from exercising some control and authority not only inside the narrative, but on the society that it speaks to.

Nonetheless, the 'authority' of a novel or novelist to create new worlds or realities is not an unchallenged one. Every novelist also knows, no matter how complete their authority is over the narrative that is being created, ultimately that authority 'is a sham' (84). The novel as a narrative form gives much more creative freedom or authority to its writer than any other form, and yet cannot make the author a creator in a true sense for the obvious reason that novelistic creations are fictional, textual, imaginative and have no palpable existence in the real world. This leads Said to observe that the genre is 'both an enabling condition and a restraint' (83). The enabling condition that a novel provides its author as well as characters is what Said chooses to call 'authority', and the restraint on that authority (the understanding that it is after all a sham, and not a real creation) is 'molestation'.

It is interesting to observe that Said's views on the author is a fine balance between the traditional approach that sees the author as the final source of truth and the structuralist and poststructuralist ideas of 'the death of the author', as famously made available by Barthes and Foucault among others. Also, while Said engages in tacit as well as explicit dialogues with Barthes and Foucault regarding the concept of the author, he is constantly at work to shift the focus of fiction–criticism from authors and texts to their sociopolitical imbrications and implications. In fact, Said adds to our ideas of the author by suggesting a linkage between 'author' and 'authority'. For this, he draws heavily from Giambattista Vico: '*Authority,* says Vico, comes from *auctor,* which certainly comes from *autos* (*proprius* or *suus ipsius)*; thus the word's original meaning is "property". Property is dependent upon human will and upon choice; therefore, it is axiomatic for Vico that "philology observes the authority of human choice, whence comes consciousness of the certain"' (91). The human language, especially when used to generate dense social texts like the novel, also becomes 'property' made by human will and choice. It is rewarding to relate Said's Vichian reading of the novel as property owned by some authority to Pierre Bourdieu's concept of 'cultural capital' that he offered in 1977, and more specifically to his further formulation of 'objectified cultural capital'.

It is interesting to note that Said's forays into the authority of writers in *Beginnings* take him back to Conrad, the very author with whom his critical journey began. In his attempt at showing how the readers of a novel must be dependent on its author, he cites the instance of Kurtz's experience in Conrad's *The Heart of Darkness.* What Kurtz may have experienced in Africa is quite outside Marlowe's discourse. Said implies that within the ambit of its fictional narrative framework, *The Heart of Darkness* holds Kurtz's

African experiences back from both Marlow as well as the readers. The only way for the reader to learn about Kurtz's suffering is to depend on the author's voice.[2] However, even as Said says this, he also indicates that it is also possible to read a text or narrative going against the authorial or narrative voice. In fact, this is the kind of reading that almost all contemporary schools of critical reading engage with. The reading of a text against its apparent meaning, or what is 'given' at the surface level, is also what Said employs in all his literary critical works to a greater or lesser degree. In fact, all Saidian terms and tropes in this regard – 'antidynastic' reading from *Beginnings*; 'secular criticism' from *The World, the Text, and the Critic*; 'contrapuntal' reading from *Culture and Imperialism*; and last but not the least, 'democratic criticism' from *Humanism and Democratic Criticism* – are geared towards the same goal. In other words, textual authority is not final, unless we allow it to be so (84).

Said engages in detailed and subtle readings of authors like Conrad, Kierkegaard and Dickens to prove his point that the novel cannot be seen only as a fantasy or long story written and read for private entertainment. It has served, albeit not always consciously, a regulative and institutional function in Europe in shaping the minds, views and ideologies of the reading public. In doing so, it has mostly tried to keep the existing social order in place. While the novel may have originated with and thrived on characters who were rogues (the Picaresque tradition), foundlings (*Tom Jones*) or orphans (*Great Expectations, David Copperfield, Jane Eyre* and many more), it did not become a vehicle to record these marginal figures' resentments against society. On the contrary, the novel, while sympathetic to the plight of its suffering hero or heroine, also indicated that it was possible for them to become successful and climb up the ladder of social mobility while remaining within the socio-economic and political system that had led to their deprivation in the first place. However, this is not stated directly since the Said of *Beginnings* is often, in spite of himself, caught up in the labyrinth of structuralist and poststructuralist language and style. By the time he wrote *Culture and Imperialism*, after a series of denouncements of the obfuscations and abstractions of contemporary theory (most of which can be found in *The World, the Text, and the Critic*), he makes his critical agenda clear. Asserting unambiguously that the novel form is fundamentally connected to the realities and ethos of bourgeois society, Said writes in *Culture and Imperialism* that 'Every novelist and every critic or theorist of the European novel notes its institutional character' (82–83). He reasserts his belief in the sociopolitical investments of the European novel when he further states – taking cues from Frederic Jameson's *The Political Unconscious* and David Miller's *The Novel and the Police* – that 'the novel generally, and narrative in particular, [has] a sort of regulatory social presence in West European societies' (87).

For Said the oppositional intellectual however, it is not enough to point out that the novel exerts authority and influence over societies. It is more important to oppose these authorities; an opposition which is as pronounced in *Culture and Imperialism* as in *Beginnings.* Any authority, whether narrative or political, is after all man-made – products of human agency and history – and not something handed down from a suprahuman power that cannot be questioned. As Said puts is, 'One aspect of authorship, then, is its contingent authority, its ability to initiate or build structures whose absolute authority is radically nil, but whose contingent authority is a quite satisfactory alternative to the absolute truth' (*Beginnings* 86). While here his immediate focus is on narrative authority and the authenticity of the novel's narrative voice or the author, in the years that followed the publication of *Beginnings,* Said increasingly dedicated himself to interrogating authorities of all hues and variations and at all levels – from taking on the US government to opposing military interventions in Palestine. The point that I am trying to make here is that there is an uncanny reciprocity, call it intertwined affiliations if you will, between Said's literary critical works on the one hand and his political works in text and the world on the other.

Such arguments and contentions definitely indicate that *Beginnings* should be considered as a watershed book from which most of Said's later ideologies and positions evolve. Further, while Said engages in intertextual dialogues with a wide range of authors that include Vico, Valery, Nietzsche, Freud, Saussure, Lévi-Strauss, Husserl, Derrida and Foucault – especially to show the power and hold of novelistic authority – it is his insistence on a criticism that is humane and socially responsible that makes *Beginnings* not only an erudite but an ethically enabling text. Said informs *Beginnings* with formulations and contentions that relate the text to the world, prefiguring his arguments in subsequent texts. His insistence on the regulative functions of the novel/narrative (82–83; as discussed above) is a strong case in point in this regard.

Along with an intricate analysis of the growth and influence of the novel, Said's analysis and interpretation of contemporary structuralist (and poststructuralist) poetics makes the book an engaging read. In fact, *Beginnings* was one of those pioneering works which helped popularise French philosophers like Foucault and Derrida within Anglo American academia. Admittedly, Said here attempts to explore 'these French critics as making a sort of thought by which the contemporary awareness about beginnings is most deeply and typically acted upon, in method and in practice' (282). Said's explorations lead him to note four different aspects of what he has called the 'contemporary awareness about beginnings'. However, in doing so, he has in fact identified the basic critical strategies of structuralist poetics, and the fifth chapter of the book can be read as an independent introduction to critical theory as well. The four features or aspects of contemporary French criticism, as Said sees them, are as follows:

- Knowledge is no longer seen in terms of coherence, but 'as radical discontinuity' (282). Here, Said is referring to the Derridean idea of meaning being a product of difference and deferment, and language – the very medium of knowledge – being self-referential rather than referring to external objects and realities.
- 'The method is postnarrative' (282). Students of English and other European literatures would be aware of Aristotle's ideas of the beginning, middle and end, and his emphasis on an 'organic whole' that have been the guiding principles creative and critical texts in the West. Said prefers to call this model of continuity the narrative model given that thematic and chronological continuity has been the forte of novels, especially the classic realist novels. Structuralism (and poststructuralism) rejects these notions of continuity and completeness in favour of gaps, fissures and breaks.

Foucault was the chief proponent of this 'system of thought' (a phrase Foucault himself coined to designate his position at the institution he taught). As Said puts it, 'the novelistic form was displaced by the later form in which discontinuity, dispersion, and rarefaction are the essentials' (282).

It is possible to be confused over Said's use of the term 'discontinuity' in both the first and the second point; but he actually refers to two different kinds of discontinuities. To simplify further, the first discontinuity is about the medium of knowledge itself – that is language; the second one is about the breakdown of historical continuities across subjects and fields.

- The act of apprehending knowledge itself is threatened by 'a combination of uncertainty and invention' (282). Further, the very act of writing itself is no longer regarded as the expression of authorial or individual consciousness and intention. Instead, 'writing is considered a controlled play of forces dispersed in a textual space that is created by writing and that does not exist before it' (282).
- Finally, 'underlying all this discontinuity is a supposition that rational knowledge is possible, regardless of how very complex—and even unattractive—the condition of its production and acquisition' (282).

The last observation by Said, however, applies only to structuralism, if at all. The core of poststructuralism runs counter to the very idea that rational knowledge is at all possible, mostly because the very medium of knowledge – language – is highly arbitrary and nothing but a play of signs. In fact, it is precisely this aspect of poststructuralism that made Said drift away from Derrida and Foucault, his initial interest in their work notwithstanding. Even in *Beginnings* itself, it is apparent that Said's enthusiasm for the structures, signs, plays, genealogies and archaeologies of the human sciences is not all encompassing. As I have said above, his choice to conclude the book with a chapter on Vico speaks volumes in this regard. Still, of all the thinkers generally identified as poststructuralists, Said's greater sympathies lie with Foucault than anyone else, whether in *Beginnings* or any other text. This is especially because, unlike other poststructuralists whose domains are more or less purely textual, Foucault always connects to human history, events and institutions even as he subjects these to incisive academic scrutiny. Assessing the significance of Foucault's contribution to the understanding of human knowledge, history, and the very idea of the human itself, Said states,

> Of them all, it is Michel Foucault who has become, in Roland Barthes's words, the very thing his works describe: a consciousness completely awakened to and processed with the troubled condition of modern knowledge. As history is gradually unveiled in Foucault's explicitly historical investigations, we witness, not only an easy chronicle of events, but a succession of functional conditions that give rise to the existence not only of knowledge, but of man himself. (283)

This sense of history has been the guiding principle behind Said's works on politics as well as literature. And as far as history is to be seen as a human construct, Foucault and Vico inhabit the same terrain for Said. Further, while traditional protocols of critical inquiry and scholarship expects scholars to have a dynastic or 'filial' relation with their field of study and carry forward the legacy of their predecessors, the Foucauldian model of scholarship – whether in history or philology – 'is anti-dynastic, not the continuation of a line from privileged origin to present consciousness' (290).

Interestingly enough, beginning with *Orientalism* (if not earlier), Said's own relation to his fields of research and study has also been 'anti-dynastic'. While in *Orientalism*, he has categorically negated Orientalism's imaginings of the Orient, in *Culture and Imperialism* he reads the entire tradition of the English novel as a product of, as well as a producer of, colonialism. However, as I have pointed out in the previous chapter, Foucault frustrates Said beyond a point leading the latter to look for alternative models in other intellectuals such as Gramsci and Chomsky. Though Foucault's systems would remain the key theoretical model for Said's next major book on the Western representation of the Orient, the presence of Gramsci is also clearly visible. By the time Said authored the essays collected in *The World, the Text, and the Critic*, his utter dissatisfaction with poststructuralist and allied modes of studies had become clear.

NOTES

1. It is interesting to note that the book begins with the phrase 'On November 1', referring to a letter written by Henry James to Conrad on that date, which is also Said's own date of birth (*Joseph Conrad* 3). To some extent then, Said, while arguing about the connection between Conrad's works and personal life, has also implicitly left a personal mark in the beginning itself. The date, it has to be noted, comes immediately after the chapter title which is 'The Claims of Individuality'.

2. What Said suggests here is based on an assumption that the story or experience of Kurtz has an empirical existence outside the narrative framework of *The Heart of Darkness*. This is actually counterfactual, and such readings in English studies are often branded as Bradleyan, after the famous critic A. C. Bradley who analysed Shakespeare's characters as if they were real people.

REFERENCES

Achebe, Chinua. "An Image of Africa: Racism in Conrad's *Heart of Darkness*". *The Massachusetts Review*, vol. 57, no. 1, 2016, pp. 14–27. *Project MUSE*, doi:10.1353/mar.2016.0003.

Bayoumi, Moustafa and Andrew Rubin. *The Edward Said Reader.* Vintage, 2000.

Conrad, Joseph. *Heart of Darkness*. Koncept Books, 2011.

Eliot, T.S. "Four Quartets". *Cold Bacon*, http://www.coldbacon.com/poems/fq.html. Accessed 4 January 2022.

Hardy, G.H. *A Mathematician's Apology.* 1940. University of Alberta Mathematical Sciences Society. Electronic edition, 2005.

Said, Edward. *Beginnings: Intention and Method.* Basic Books, 1975.

---. "Between Worlds". *Reflections on Exile and Other Essays.* Penguin, 2001, pp. 554–68.

---. *Culture and Imperialism.* Alfred A. Knopf, 1993.

---. *Humanism and Democratic Criticism*. Columbia UP, 2004.

---. *Joseph Conrad and the Fiction of Autobiography.* Harvard UP, 1966.

---. *Reflections on Exile and Other Essays.* Penguin, 2001.

---. *The World, the Text, and the Critic*. Vintage, 1991.

Veseer, H. Aram. *Edward Said: The Charisma of Criticism*. Routledge, 2010.

Yeats, W.B. "Sailing to Byzantium". *Palgrave's Golden Treasury*, edited by John Press, Oxford UP, 1976, pp. 425–26.

Chapter Three

Orientalism and the Cultural Politics of Representation

BEGINNING *ORIENTALISM*

'What is Orientalism?' is perhaps best answered by a counter question: 'What is not Orientalism?' This has been possible chiefly because of Edward Said's seminal book *Orientalism*. Europe's colonisation of the other parts of the world has been such a durable and momentous event that till date human aspirations and formations remain largely Eurocentric (that is, centred on the norms set by European or Western nations). Drawing from a wide archive of Western knowledge, Said states that Eurocentric ideologies have infiltrated every field of European knowledge, even the ones perceived as objective such as philology, anthropology and cartography. Due to the realities of colonialism and neocolonialism, many non-Western countries, too, carry on the legacy of Eurocentric ideas at different levels. Consider, if you will, an example from cardiology. Till date, most cardiologists in the non-Western world fall back on one of two sets of guidelines for the management and treatment of various cardiac ailments and hypertension: the American College of Cardiology/American Heart Association and the European Society of Cardiology guidelines. This is despite the fact that some of these countries have their own cardiology societies. Even international responses to the pandemic caused by the COVID-19 virus, it has been alleged, 'has paid insufficient attention to the realities in the Global South, making the response Eurocentric in several ways' (Evans n.p.). Similarly, almost all non-European countries are reliant on an American search engine to use the World Wide Web. There are many such instances. All these imbalances, as already mentioned, are the direct results of colonialism. *Orientalism*, therefore, is a significant text because it argues that the logic and philosophy of colonialism was (and is) heavily reliant on the tenets of Orientalism. These are some of the reasons why *Orientalism* has remained widely influential, not only among the victims and survivors of colonialism, but to anyone with a sense of justice and humanism. As Said himself puts it, 'If this book has any future use, it will be as a modest contribution to that challenge, and as a warning: that systems of thought like Orientalism, discourses of power, ideological fictions—mind forg'd manacles—are all too easily made, applied and guarded' (*Orientalism* 328).

The success of reception apart, even those who oppose Said cannot underestimate the book's value. As Moore-Gilbert maintains: 'Even among those who are essentially hostile to Said, like John MacKenzie or Aijaz Ahmad, *Orientalism* is recognized as a seminal text, the influence of which must be undone before what are considered to be more adequate modes of analysis. . . can be elaborated' (35). The apologists for the Empire too return to it frequently, perhaps more frequently than others. Their aim is to find faults and gaps in Said's arguments. However, few have been successful in denying the charges Said brought against Orientalism, though there have been criticisms in terms of what Said leaves out. Interestingly, a book-length critique of *Orientalism* was published only in 2007, five years after Said's death.

Coming to the more commonly accepted definition of Orientalism, it can be said that it is a field or discipline of study of the non-West by the West. Since the beginning of colonialism, a group of scholars and experts from the European countries, especially Britain, Germany and France, have been studying and writing books about 'oriental' cultures, countries, religions and so on. More often than not, these studies were taken to be a matter of great pride by Oriental people themselves. The very fact that the dominant or ruling powers of Europe studied the cultures, customs and texts of the colonised was intriguing to the latter, to say the least. The trend of 'rediscovering' India set by scholars like William Jones, Richard Burton and Max Müller is an example of this particular form of Orientalism. Max Müller was considered so influential that even conservative Brahmins and allied upper castes of India considered his editions of the Vedas as the most authentic. Not only that, the honorific title of *Bhatta* – reserved for highly accomplished Brahmin scholars – was added before Max Müller's name and he was often referred to as 'Bhatta Mokshamular' by certain Indian thinkers. For instance, Bankim Chandra Chattopadhyay, one of the leading intellectuals of nineteenth century India, refers to Max Müller as 'Bhatta Mokshamular' in his widely acclaimed Bengali treatise on the life of Krishna titled *Krishnacharitra* (801). Even Vivekananda, one of the most influential religious and cultural figures of late-nineteenth century India, compared Max Müller and his wife with the Vedic sage Vasistha and his wife Arundhati, after meeting them in London in 1896: 'all these sent me back in imagination to the glorious days of Ancient India, the days of our Brahmarshis and Râjarshis, the days of the great Vânaprasthas, the days of Arundhati and Vasishthas' (Vivekananda).

At the same time, along with the image of the spiritual India or Orient that these scholars projected to the world, works like Richard Burton's translations of *The Arabian Nights* and the *Kamasutra* helped build an image of the Orient as a land of endless erotic promises. Similarly, a pioneer in the field of Orientalist Sanskrit studies, William Jones's translation of the Sanskrit play *Abhijnanashakuntalam* (1789) earned the text a prominent place in the Western imagination. Jones's English translation of the play led to a series of translations and re-translations in other European languages like French and German. The renowned German writer Goethe was so enamoured of the play that he praised it as the most beautiful creation on earth:

> Wilt thou the blossoms of spring and the fruits that are later in season,
>
> Wilt thou have charms and delights, wilt thou have strength and support,
>
> Wilt thou with one short word encompass the earth and the heaven,
>
> All is said if I name only, [Shakuntala], thee. (Müller 1)

There was (read is) yet another category of texts which engaged themselves in the project of painting the Orient as primitive, irrational and barbaric, or at the very least, diametrically opposed to the Western world. Such projects continued under the garb of 'scientific' studies of the languages, races and cultures of Oriental peoples and nations. All these scholars and their work constitute the core of what Said means by Orientalism. The two most influential Orientalists Said subjects to critical scrutiny in great detail are Antoine Isaac Silvestre de Sacy and Ernest Renan.

Published in the year 1978, Edward Said's *Orientalism* is a blatant rejection of the tendency to see knowledge and power as two distinct categories, especially European knowledge and European power. By drawing examples and evidence from literary, cultural, political and allied texts and documents produced over a period of almost two thousand years, Said has convincingly(if not conclusively) argued that Orientalism or the study of the Orient by European scholars was never a purely academic or politically neutral project. On the contrary, the aim of Orientalism has been to 'know' the Orient in such a manner that it can be ruled.

It is a fairly well established precept of current critical thought that the better one knows something (such as a region, idea, discipline, person, and so on), the easier it is to rule or control that. In fact, the idea can be traced back to Francis Bacon in the European epistemological tradition, if not earlier. Bacon's famous dictum in this regard is 'Knowledge is power' which has been rephrased by Foucault as 'Power is knowledge'. While Bacon and Foucault look at the connection somewhat differently from each other, both acknowledge the connection. Further, Foucault's critical reformulation of the Baconian equation foregrounds the overarching hold of power on human society which shapes all aspects of human life, including knowledge. Put simply, no knowledge is ideologically or politically innocent; the search for knowledge is always driven by what Friedrich Nietzsche termed the 'will to power'. This is precisely what Orientalism, according to Said, was (read is) about. Orientalist studies and discourses about particular peoples and regions often preceded the invasion of the land by European colonisers. Napoleon's conquest of Egypt, for instance, was preceded by discourses and writings on Egypt that Napoleon had followed from his childhood. While Said substantiates his claim about Orientalist discourses preceding, motivating or expediting the conquest of Oriental lands by using this example, there are many more such cases. It is a never ending process which, according to Said, is continued by the United States of America, though without actual geographical hold over other territories in most cases.

Running into approximately 400 pages, the first edition of *Orientalism* comprises an introduction and three, rather long, chapters titled 'The Scope of Orientalism', 'Orientalist Structures and Restructures' and 'Orientalism Now'. While the first chapter is a broad overview of the entire field of Orientalism locating its beginnings in the classical Greece of Homer and Aeschylus (see pages 55–57), the second and third chapters give a more or less chronological account of the field implicating well- known people such as Napoleon, Renan, Flaubert, and Marx.

Like George Bernard Shaw, Said includes in many of his books long, explanatory introductions and prefaces. This is especially true of *Orientalism*, *Culture and Imperialism* and *Covering Islam.* In all these books, the introduction clearly spells out the hypothesis and central arguments of the work to the extent that the following pages mostly become examples or instances of the hypotheses and arguments introduced in the introduction. The present discussion, therefore, has been divided into several sections. In the first section, we will examine the 'Introduction', followed by a critical survey of the major signposts of the following chapters in the subsequent sections.

Reading Said's Introduction to *Orientalism*

The third line of Said's 'Introduction' to *Orientalism* sets the tone of the entire book, and possibly all the works that were to follow: 'The Orient was almost a European invention, and had been since antiquity a place of romance, exotic beings, haunting memories and landscapes, remarkable experiences' (1). The fifth line adds, 'Perhaps it seemed irrelevant that Orientals themselves had something at stake in the process' (1). The two sentences together generate the sense of the Orient being a creation of European fantasy, and that the 'Orientals' themselves hardly had any stake in that game of representation. This in itself would not have been much of a problem if such thoughts and ideas about the Orient had not been used to dominate and restructure the Orient in such a manner as to configure authority over it (3).The idea that the Orient, especially as represented in the works of the Orientalists, is more a European fantasy than an actual place, is reinforced when Said adds that the Orient not 'an inert fact of nature' (4) and that it has its own histories and traditions of thought (7). The book attempts to show how and why the idea of the Orient does not remain only an imaginative fantasy but grows into a well-structured or institutionalised knowledge system over a long period of time, with its own 'paradigms' of research, societies and its own 'Establishment' (43). Most importantly, he attempts to explicate what the consequences of this knowledge system were. The overarching argument of the book is that Orientalist studies have always preceded the actual colonisation of the Orient. This points to an associated function that Orientalism performed: to supply arguments, materials and 'proofs' of the inferiority of Oriental races so that their subjugation and rule by Europeans may be justified.

In other words, behind and along with this coercive or 'power' aspect of colonialism, there is an equally strong, or even stronger, 'knowledge' aspect – the gathering and creation of knowledge about something to possess it and control it better. Orientalism is the embodiment of such 'knowledge'. The physical/administrative/military control of the East or the 'Orient' by European powers is preceded by a long history of a conscious or unconscious misrepresentation of the Orient. These misrepresentations, taken together, can be said to construct the discourse of Orientalism. Building on the Foucauldian idea of discourse, Said has extensively argued that the entire body of European knowledge about the Orient is a discourse. Said also makes it clear in the 'Introduction' itself that in the work, he would study not so much the correspondence between the actual Orient and its description in Orientalist texts, but 'the internal consistency of Orientalism and the ideas about the Orient' (5). This might look confusing to one who is not fully conversant with poststructuralism, but what Said is attempting here is actually a deconstruction of the concept of the Orient as well as the Orient–Occident binary. Interestingly enough, while Derrida is not invoked directly in *Orientalism* (Said's preferred poststructuralist is Foucault), it is not difficult to see his spirit looming large behind these formulations.[1]

The Orientalist discourses, Said argues, strive to represent the Oriental or non-European races, places and cultures as the 'Other' of the European self; an inferior and 'despicable' other. Along with Foucault and Derrida therefore, Jacques Lacan – the third of the so-called holy trinity of poststructuralism and arguably the most influential theorist on the question of the other – is also an invisible presence in the text. Said states that the Orient for Europe is 'one of its deepest and most recurring images of the Other' (1). It is also useful to remind ourselves at this point that Foucault was not the only one in the Western epistemological tradition who asserted the deep relation of knowledge with power; there are at least two equally powerful predecessors in Nietzsche and Bacon. Foucault's line of argument is closer to Nietzsche than Bacon in so far as their equation of power and knowledge emanates from a deep distrust of both power and knowledge. *Orientalism*, among other things, confirms the postulations of Bacon, Nietzsche and Foucault about the inextricable linkage between knowledge and power/politics (27).

To connect Said's endeavours in this book to his previous works, it would be useful to remember that the interrogation of power, authority and subjugation constitutes one of the core concerns of *Beginnings* (as discussed in the previous chapter). However, while *Beginnings* was mostly a critique of narrative authority or the author's voice, in *Orientalism* the critique of authority becomes explicitly connected to the sordid realities of colonialism. In fact, Said's opposition to Orientalism and its experts as a body of authority is premised on his resistance to authorities of all hues and colours. In *Orientalism,* he makes the point clearly when he says that no authority is 'mysterious' or 'natural'; all authorities are human constructs, constructed by a group of human beings to rule over others. Any given authority establishes standards of various kinds, 'canons of taste and value' (19). And precisely because authorities are man-made, they can be questioned and should be brought under scrutiny (20).

Tracing the genealogy of his writing *Orientalism,* Said presents three aspects of what he chooses to call his 'contemporary reality' (9). First, he resists the difference usually made between pure and political knowledge; this is visibly based on the linkage between politics and knowledge that his predecessors and contemporaries like Marx, Gramsci and Foucault have suggested in various ways. The entire book is an attempt to show that Orientalism was not only an academic field of knowledge, but but also one that was deeply implicated in the cultural politics of European imperialism. This point recurs throughout the book. The repetitions, one must understand, are not mechanical iterations but reinforcements of a single point with a panoply of examples so that the point is established beyond reasonable doubt. A glaring case of Orientalist scholarship influencing political decisions about the colonies may be found in John Stuart Mill, for instance. While Mill passionately advocated for both greater individual liberty and representative government, he added a rider that his views on this could not be applied to India 'because the Indians were civilizationally, if not racially, inferior' (14).

In continuation of this line of argument, Said avers that pure or full objectivity can never be expected in the production and consumption of knowledge. Owing to the fact that the very agents of the 'production' of knowledge (and, one may add, those who consume that production) are subjective human beings, it seems rather obvious that some amount of subjectivity would creep into the acts of production as well as dissemination of knowledge. This is possibly truer in case of what may be called humanistic knowledge – the humanities and social sciences – where the subjective involvement of the scholar seems to be more than that of the physical sciences like mathematics, chemistry or physics.[2] In fact, thinkers like Thomas Kuhn and Bruno Latour have argued that the objectivity of even these physical or hard sciences are also disputable, and their meanings can often be understood only within a given paradigm. Interestingly, by staking such a claim about the subjective dimension of knowledge, Said jeopardises his own position as well. But then he has hardly shown any discomfort with admitting the possibility of the influence of his own background, preferences and circumstances in his works, hypotheses and formulation. The Saidian argument, in fact, is that it is precisely because all knowledge is subjective that no knowledge tradition can claim superiority over competing knowledge traditions. As he says, 'no production of knowledge in the human sciences can ever ignore or disclaim its author's involvement as a human subject in his own circumstances' (11). Consequently, Said argues, a European or American studying the Orient 'comes up against the Orient as a European or American first, as an individual second'(11). Said hastens to add, however, that this emphasis on the subjective dimension does not preclude or rule out the possibility of some degree of objectivity (11). In continuation of his insistence on the subjective dimension of knowledge, he argues that Orientalism too, as a field of study, is 'a kind of *willed human work*—not of mere unconditional ratiocination—in all its historical complexity' (15).

The second point of his contemporary reality is 'The methodological question': the critical or research methodology that he has used in writing *Orientalism* (15). Starting with his idea that every new beginning is a point of departure (an idea he theorised elaborately in *Beginnings*; see the previous chapter), Said goes on to systematically define both his field and his tools. The field is not the entire range of European discourses about the Orient, but specifically 'the Anglo-French-American experience of the Arabs and Islam, which for almost a thousand years together stood for the Orient' (17). He candidly admits that this eliminates a large part of the Orient – India, Japan, China and other Asian countries, for instance. Consequently, the subsequent charge by a group of critics that Said does not talk about significant Oriental countries like India is somewhat misplaced. Nonetheless, there are occasional references to India (for instance, Mill on India, cited above) as well as other European authors and traditions. Dante's misrepresentation of Islam (see *Orientalism* 68–70) is an important instance. So far as the critical methodology of the book is concerned, it is primarily based on the Foucauldian concept of discourse combined with the Gramscian notion of hegemony. This shall be discussed it in greater detail in the next section.

The third point that has been instrumental in shaping the book is Said's 'personal dimension' – his experiences of hostility towards Arabs and Islam in the West, particularly in America. This is closely linked with the history of colonialism as well as the history of Orientalism, combined with the increasing support for Zionism or Jewish causes by America and its allies. It may be noted that some arguments in favour of the 'personal dimension' has already been made in his elaboration of first point itself: that is, there is no 'pure knowledge' free from political undercurrents. Analogously, (according to Said), there cannot be any objective knowledge independent of its producer's personal realities.

Foucault and his Concept of Discourse

It is important at this point to look at the concept of discourse which is a foundational concept in *Orientalism*. While in the common parlance 'discourse' usually means any serious or formal discussion in speech or writing, Said's use of the term is more in sync with Michel Foucault's definition. Discourse or discursive formations, in the Foucauldian sense, implies a set of rules and regulations which decides what can and cannot be said in a particular period and particular age. As Julian Wolfreys puts it, '[Discourse is] Defined by Michel Foucault as a language practice; that is, language as it is used by various constituencies (the law, medicine, the church, for example) for purposes to do with power relationships between people' (298).

To give a simple example: a student cannot speak on their own in a class unless and until asked to by the teacher. Similarly, a lawyer, while arguing in a courtroom, cannot share jokes that they may share with their friends. Even how a lawyer would address a judge is strictly codified. Addresses such as 'Sir', 'Your Lordship' and 'Your Honour', for instance, are not interchangeable within the discourses of the Indian judiciary. There is a well-defined hierarchy, and the appropriate honorific for addressing a judge depends on whether the court in question is a District Court, High Court, or the Supreme Court. Since courts are among the most obvious sites of the operations of power and legality – sites which decide the permissibility or the validity of discourses (in the ordinary sense) – the rules or contours of its discourse are quite clearly laid out. But such codes are at play in every area of human experience. To cite another example, in the post-Independence India largely built on the Gandhian–Nehruvian ethos, the word 'secular' was a highly sought after word and a much cherished ideal. In recent years, political and public discourses have changed and 'secular' seems to have lost its earlier appeal. The public ethos these days seems to be more in tune with religious nationalisms, cleanliness drives, sustainable development and eco-friendly projects.

Foucault's major purpose behind redefining the word 'discourse' was to show how knowledge is always related to power. In other words, there is nothing called pure knowledge. This knowledge, in its turn, would help us see through the subtle designs of the authorities and powers that be. Authorities and powers, Foucault strongly believes, do not operate only through force or direct coercion. Along with a direct application of force or power, authorities also rule through knowledge. Each power or regime presents truths or even falsehoods favourable to them as 'the truth'. Foucault has explored and exposed the nexus between power and knowledge at various levels in a series of works characterised by incisive and dense scholarship – *Madness and Civilisation*, *The Birth of the Clinic*, *The Archaeology of Knowledge*, *The Order of Things* and *A History of Sexuality* (3 vols.), to name the more prominent ones. He has shown how sites like hospitals and schools are highly political in their origins as well as current function, even though they do not appear to be so.

A glaring instance of the power of discourse can be clearly seen in the rise of Hitler. Hitler's rule was successful, for instance, more due to the fact that he convinced a majority of Germans that going against Hitler meant going against Germany. He even wrote a pseudo-autobiography titled *Adolf Hitler: His Life and his Speeches* (1923) using a pseudonym, attempting to show that he was the new Christ come to deliver the Germans from their miseries, especially from the Jews. All these fortified his image as the unchallenged leader of Germany till his fall. He could never have had that kind of hold on people only with military power. The Hitler phenomenon is not unique to him, but applies to the operational strategies of all powers and regimes – religious, political, social or otherwise – and applies more so to fascist rulers like him.

According to Said, colonialism succeeded in a very similar fashion, by way of proliferating various textual representations of the East through Orientalist discourses. Orientalism was dedicated to proving that Orientals were far inferior to Europeans as people and hence the former, for their own development, needed to be ruled by the latter. This narrative was bought into by a majority of Europeans as well as the people belonging to the Orient. It is useful at this point to invoke Gandhi's critique of the Indians who desired to be 'civilised' by the British in his *Hind Swaraj* (1910). Gandhi counterintuitively argues that the British Empire had been kept in place for such a long period in India because Indians themselves adopted British education and culture willingly. The desire to be 'civilised' as per the norms of Western civilisations, according to Gandhi, was the root cause of India's servitude. This was augmented by colonial institutions of law and medicine as well as mediums of communication and travel such as the newspaper and the railway. It is interesting to note that Gandhi's arguments anticipate the Foucauldian conceptualisation of discursive formations as agents of power, the Gramscian concept of hegemony, as well as Althusser's concept of the ideological state apparatuses. Said's reading also makes one see Orientalism as performing all these functions.

While Foucault's contribution in making us see power as knowledge, reversing the Baconian idea of knowledge as power, has been phenomenal, a significant issue that Foucault leaves out, or engages at best by way of implication, is colonialism. Further, although the visible oppressions and exploitations of colonialism are available in books on history and political science, what were its invisible tentacles that helped it maintain its hold over such a large section of people for such a long period of time? This is what Said is particularly interested in exploring in *Orientalism*.

Said takes on the task of uncovering the invisible power politics of colonialism and finds the academic field of Orientalism to be a major culprit behind the institutionalisation of colonialism and imperialism. Taking his cues from Foucault, Said suggests that Orientalism is not an objective field of study where scholars presented realities about the actual Orient. It was rather a discourse or discursive field primarily built around the idea of a 'good Orient' and a 'bad Orient'. The good Orient is the Orient of great sages; of fabulous poetry; of all kinds of abundance and opulence; the Orient of *Zend Avesta* and *Shakuntalam*. This, nonetheless, was a thing of the remote past, the memories of which can only be cherished. On the other hand, the bad Orient was the contemporary Orient which was regressive (contra a progressive west); superstitious (contra scientific Europe); full of morally decrepit people (contra European men of character); and so on and so forth (*Orientalism* 98–99).

However, Orientalism is not the only discursive agent of colonialism, though Said identifies it to be the primary one. In his 1993 book *Culture and Imperialism*, Said establishes the novel as the second most important agent of colonialism; an issue that shall be dwelt on in a later chapter.

As has been pointed out in quite a few of his works, and consequently in more than one place in my book, Said does not find Foucault useful beyond a point. Unlike Foucault and other poststructuralists who undermine the individual agencies of authors as well as other human beings, for Said individual investments are as important as the networks of power (like colonialism and Orientalism) that they create. He therefore qualifies the Foucauldian idea of discourse by claiming that, unlike Foucault (to whose work he acknowledged he was greatly indebted), he strongly believes in 'the determining imprint of individual writers on the otherwise anonymous collective body of texts constituting a discursive formulation like Orientalism' (23).

This undermining of individual agency in Foucault coupled with his calculated distance from contemporary politics moves Said closer to Antonio Gramsci, the Italian Marxist critic of the early twentieth century.[3] The Gramscian concept of 'hegemony' famously claims that modern authorities and powers rule not only by force, but by convincing the subject that to be ruled by those authorities is the best possible option for them. In other words, rule is maintained not by coercion but consent. Said uses this notion closely along with the Foucauldian concept of discourse to suggest that Orientalism facilitated the cultural hegemony of the West over the Orient. In other words, what Said does in combining Foucault and Gramsci is that he attempts to show Orientalism as a 'discourse' that helps in the creation and maintenance of a Western 'hegemony' over the Orient. The following rewording of the Gramscian notion of hegemony is helpful in understanding Orientalism from that point of view: 'In any society not totalitarian, then, certain cultural forms predominate over others, just as certain ideas are more influential than others; the form of this cultural leadership is what Gramsci has identified as hegemony, an indispensable concept for any understanding of cultural life in the industrial West' (7).

While critics and scholars looking for theoretical nuance have faulted Said for conflating Foucault and Gramsci[4], Said has made his point. Further, given that both Gramsci and Foucault formulated their theories based on the cultural and power politics of Western societies, Said's application of these in understanding the rule and the role of the West in the Orient also extends the scope of these theories and enables them further. This is an illuminating instance of Said's own formulation of 'travelling theory' (see the next chapter). The two cases cited earlier in this chapter, namely the acceptance of Max Müller as an authority (perhaps 'the authority') on Hinduism in India and Indians' willing cooperation with the British Raj (as suggested by Gandhi), are instances of successful cultural hegemonies. The point that Said is trying to make – and does get across – is that more than a field of academic scholarship or knowledge, Orientalism was a cultural and ideological tool of imperialism, especially after the eighteenth century. As he puts it,

> My idea is that European and then American interest in the Orient was political according to some of the obvious historical accounts of it that I have given here, but it was the culture that created that interest, that acted dynamically along with brute political, economic, and military rationales to make the Orient the varied and complicated place that it obviously was in the field I call Orientalism. (12)

Critics and readers who have not studied Said thoroughly, often miss presenting the fact that Said never stated that the imperial investments of European culture makes it a despicable thing altogether. His is a nuanced position on the cultural politics of Orientalism and other forms of European imperialism. In the Saidian worldview, cultural artefacts do have aesthetic merit, but the political investments also exist and must be acknowledged as such. Unfortunately, readers sympathetic to Said also often miss this point. But as Said states very directly and unambiguously in the 'Introduction' itself, his assertion that literature, scholarship, historiography, social theory and other such cultural productions of Europe have been closely connected with imperialism is 'by no means equivalent to saying that culture is therefore a demeaned and denigrated thing' (14). What he expects is a double vision, or a contrapuntal awareness as he would formulate it later: a simultaneous awareness of the value and validity of culture as well as its political implications. Said foregrounds these dual aspects of culture so that people stop short of recycling the cultural politics of imperialism or any other form of cultural domination even as they continue to appreciate the aesthetic aspects of culture. His expectation in this regard is not only from the Europeans, but the victims of colonisation as well: 'My hope is to illustrate the formidable structure of cultural domination, and specifically for formerly colonized peoples, the dangers and temptations of employing this structure upon themselves or upon others' (25). *Orientalism,* thus, is not a case for 'anti-racist racism' but a passionate plea for humanism, human rights and human values. His humanism, understandably, is not the Eurocentric humanism that has been the cultural logic of imperialism itself, but a truly inclusive one. His ideas about inclusive humanism are fully developed in *Humanism and Democratic Criticism*, which has been discussed at length in the last chapter of this book.

Critics of *Orientalism* have quite often found it problematic that while Said contests the misrepresentation of the Orient by the West, he himself does not come anywhere near giving an account of the 'real' Orient. But that is not something he is interested in doing, nor does he believe in the existence of a 'real' Orient. What Said takes as a given premise is that since no representation can capture the living reality in totality or actuality, it is always important to counter and contest misrepresentations. In this regard he is somewhat closer to Foucault in particular, and poststructuralism in general. For poststructuralist thinkers like Foucault and Derrida, the duty of the thinker or the intellectual is to 'problematise' (simply put, to raise issues, doubts; point at the fissures of any given system or set of systems) and not to give 'solutions', which they see as more of prophet's job than a thinker's. However, it may also be argued that by pointing out the problems inherent in issues, cultures and systems, steps towards their solution have already been initiated.

THE SCOPE OF THE CULTURAL POLITICS OF ORIENTALISM: AESCHYLUS TO PRESENT

In the process of unmasking the colonial undertones in Western concepts of selfhood, *Orientalism* traces the discriminatory representation of the Orient by the West from the days of classical Greek literature to the twentieth century. While evidence of the prejudicial othering of the people of Orient is available in the Western tradition from the days of Aeschylus (if not earlier), the consolidation of studies on the Orient into a systematic body of knowledge with its own codes and conventions happened during the eighteenth century, the so-called Age of Reason in Europe. According to Said: 'Taking the late eighteenth century as a very roughly defined starting point Orientalism can be discussed and analyzed as the corporate institution for dealing with the Orient—dealing with it by making statements about it, authorizing views of it, describing it, by teaching it, settling it, ruling over it' (3).

The first definitive and systematic encounter of the West with Oriental textual and cultural traditions was facilitated, according to Said, by Abraham-Hyacinthe Anquetil-Duperron (1731–1805). French by birth, Anquetil-Duperron translated the *Avesta* in 1759 and the *Upanishads* in 1786 into his native tongue. By this very act of translation, '*For the first time, the Orient was revealed to Europe in the materiality of its texts, languages, and civilizations*' (77, emphases added). Anquetil's tradition continued till the first climax in terms of the consolidation of Orientalist knowledge that happened in the eighteenth century, materialised and realised by the founding of the Asiatic Society. The central figure in this context was the

British (Anglo-Welsh) Orientalist William Jones (1746–94). Jones was a judge of the newly founded Supreme Court of Judicature at Fort William, Calcutta, which had been established in 1774 by the Regulating Act of 1773, and was the highest court of British India till the establishment of the Calcutta High Court in 1862. Apart from his juridical profession, or rather along with it, Jones had developed commendable competence in a wide range of languages including Hebrew, Greek, Persian and Arabic (in addition to his mother tongue English). During his tenure in India, he took a deep interest in the Sanskrit language and Vedic traditions, and educated himself under the orthodox tutelage of the Brahmins of Navadvipa in West Bengal (which was often referred to as 'The Oxford of the East'). This is how Jones expresses his wonder at the 'discovery' of Sanskrit:

> The Sanscrit language, whatever be its antiquity, is of a wonderful structure; more perfect than the Greek, more copious than the Latin, and more exquisitely refined than either, yet bearing to both of them a stronger affinity, both in the roots of verbs and in the forms of grammar, than could possibly have been produced by accident; so strong indeed, that no philologer could examine them all three without believing them to have sprung from some common source. (qtd. in *Orientalism* 79)

On 15 January 1784 (the same year that saw the publication of Kant's 'What is Enlightenment?') Jones founded the Asiatic Society at Calcutta, which went on to become widely acclaimed as a high seat of knowledge. After *Orientalism,* it is now seen as the first institute that systematically disseminated Orientalist knowledge.

While Said locates the official 'beginning' of Orientalism in the eighteenth century, it must also be pointed out here that this has its antecedents in Foucault's identifying the eighteenth century as the key period when the collaboration of knowledge and power intensified in Europe like never before. According to Foucault, even the 'modern' concepts of identity and selfhood were formulated and consolidated in the eighteenth century. This was done especially with reference to sexuality and rationality. In his *History of Sexuality* (Vol. 2), for instance, Foucault writes, 'In any case, it seemed to me that one could not very well analyze the formation and development of the experience of sexuality from *the eighteenth century* onward, without doing a historical and critical study dealing with the desire and the desiring subject. In other words, without undertaking a genealogy' (5, emphasis added). Similarly, in his *Madness and Civilization*, Foucault has argued that the modern idea of madness as a clinical category that needed only medical attention, has its origins in around the same period.

It is useful to remember here that the eighteenth century is also a period of consolidation of values, tastes and literary canons in several European cultures like Italian, French, German and British. The critical, creative and cultural ethos of the time is generally known as neoclassicism and it largely coincided with the phenomenon called the Enlightenment. While in other European nations the most visible effects of neoclassicism are to be found in art, music, culture and architecture, English neoclassicism found its fullest articulation in literature. Authors and intellectuals like Alexander Pope and Samuel Johnson tried to define and fix literary standards once and for all. Johnson attempted to construct a canon of English literature through his *Lives of the Poets* and to standardise the English language by compiling a dictionary. While these are well known to students of English or other European literatures and histories, Foucault and Said's critical engagements with the eighteenth century or the so-called Age of Reason go deeper by studying the more problematic aspects of the times.

In the annals of European history in general, and English, French and German histories in particular, the eighteenth century is also known as the Age of Reason or the Age of Enlightenment. While Immanuel Kant had famously defined enlightenment as humanity's journey towards rationality, later critics like Foucault have stressed the fact that this emphasis on reason was disabling and harmful for people who did not belong to or were not thought of as belonging to the domain of rationality: the insane, for instance. It is not difficult to see that there is a close parallel between Foucault's reassessment of madness as the product of the discourses of the Enlightenment and Said's reclamation of the Oriental by re-reading Orientalism as a political discourse of imperialism. In fact, the postulation of the rational man (read 'European rational man') as the ultimate model of humanity by Enlightenment philosophy and Orientalism's insistence on the racial inferiority of the non-Western were practically two sides of the same coin – one reinforcing the other. As a result, the logic of the Enlightenment seamlessly translated into the logic of colonialism. The linkage between the Enlightenment and Orientalism has been clearly spelt out by Said when he brings both under the ambit of 'discourse'. (3). It was not possible to think, say or write anything about the actual Orient without reference to the 'whole network of interests' that Orientalism was (3).

SHORT TAKES

What was Enlightenment?

The year 1784 saw the publication of Immanuel Kant's classic essay 'What is Enlightenment?' ('*Was ist aufklärung?*' in German). Few other essays have been as influential in charting the subsequent course of human history as this. Kant famously defined enlightenment as man's progress from immaturity to maturity. For Kant, 'immaturity' implies man's inability to use his understanding without guidance from others (and yes, the practice then was to use 'man' to refer to humanity). The reverse of this, that is the ability to use one's own intelligence or reason to understand the world and making decisions for oneself, is maturity. While the definition is simple and obvious, the matter was far from easy. In spite of the Renaissance having taken place, people's life revolved around instructions from the Church and the Bible, without whose guidance few dared to do anything. Kant's essay was a clarion call to come out of this 'self-imposed immaturity'. The document as well as its message, therefore, has had a lasting significance for humanity.

It is good to remember, however, that Kant was not so much dictating a new way of life and philosophy as he was systematically articulating the tenets of a turn to rationalism that had been taking place in Europe for quite some time. In fact, the Renaissance was the first catalyst of this turn. And as early as 1733 (fifty-one years prior to Kant's pronouncement), we find the neoclassical English poet, Alexander Pope, writing in his 'An Essay on Man': 'Know then thyself, presume not God to scan,/The proper study of mankind is man.'

This couplet can be taken to be a perfect synopsis of Kant's essay without much difficulty. As has been discussed above, however, the fervour for Enlightenment came under severe strain after the interventions of poststructuralists and postmodernists like Foucault and Lyotard. There have been counter arguments as well, especially from Jürgen Habermas.

Napoleon invaded Egypt in 1798. This, for Said, is the key moment when the linkage between Orientalism and European colonialism was finally solidified. Napoleon had been an avid reader of books and works on the Orient from his childhood which, according to Said, incited his imperial interest in Egypt. He was particularly influenced by a French traveller named Comte de Volney, whose travelogue titled *Voyage en Egypte et en Syrie* ('Travel to Egypt and Syria') was published in two volumes in 1787. In fact, Said was the first thinker to draw attention to the fact that European travel writing also served the purposes of European colonialism, willingly or unwillingly.

SHORT TAKES

Travel Writing and Imperialism

Along with the works of European scholars, litterateurs and philologists on the Orient, there is an impressive body of writing by European travellers who visited the Orient from time to time. Before *Orientalism*, these were largely read as politically or ideologically innocent accounts of travel. Said alerted us to the Orientalist biases and imperial aspirations of these writings and their writers. Section four of the second chapter titled 'Pilgrims and Pilgrimages, British and French' dwells on this issue at length. The prime example is that of Edward Williams Lane who found the Orient to be a place of 'threatened hygiene' and deviant or dangerous sexual practices with 'an excessive freedom of intercourse' (167). This obsession of portraying the Orient as a place of exotic romances and deviant sexualities, among other things, are endemic to accounts of actual travel as well as the fictional ones, whose writers include figures as famous as Hugo, Byron, Chateaubriand and Lamartine. Following Said's lead, extensive research and readings on the travel writings of European travellers and writers have been taken up. This has led to the emergence of the study of 'travel writings' as an important branch of postcolonial studies. Of late there are indicators which may lead one to believe that it has become an academic specialisation on its own (something that Said would never agree with, given his resistance to reifying knowledge and academics into closed compartments; see the following chapter of this book; also Brennan xiv). The most influential of all these works is Mary Louise Pratt's *Imperial Eyes: Travel Writing and Transculturation* (1992).

Napoleon's reliance on Volney is borne out by his memoir on the Egyptian invasion titled *Campagnes d'Egypte et de Syrie, 1798–1799,* where he refers to Volney's prescribed strategies for spreading 'French hegemony in the Orient' as an authoritative text (*Orientalism* 81). Further, in his conquest of Egypt Napoleon was accompanied not only by an army of soldiers but an army of scholars too, 'several dozen savants' as Said calls them (81). They were well versed in Islamic culture and religion and Napoleon made optimal use of that. Based on these resources, he succeeded in convincing the Islamic population of Egypt that he was fighting for Islam, not against it: 'everything he said was translated into Koranic Arabic, just as the French army was urged by its command always to remember the Islamic sensibility' (82). Understanding that the actual strength of his French army was insignificant before the Egyptian resistance, Napoleon tried to persuade the local Islamic priests and clerics to interpret the Koran in his favour. As many as sixty *ulemas* (Islamic scholars) were invited by Napoleon to meet him personally, whom he greeted with full military honours, and he flattered them with seeming admiration for the Prophet Mohammed and his (Napoleon's) own knowledge of the Koran 'with which he seemed perfectly familiar' (82). This had a magical effect on the Egyptians, and soon the people of Cairo seemed to lose their distrust of the French occupiers (82). This is perhaps the most direct, tell-tale instance of how Orientalist knowledge about an Oriental people on the part of a European helped him subjugate those very people with ease and aplomb.

However, Napoleon did not stop there. He furthered the causes of Orientalism (and hence, imperialism and colonialism) by subjecting Egypt – its languages, cultures, religions, antiquities – to more intensive study and research 'to make it totally accessible to European scrutiny' (83). Given that most of the concerned scholars and allied experts were French, 'Egypt was to become a department of French learning' (83).You could more easily relate to European and Western fantasies about Egypt if you recall the setting and plot of the 1999 American movie *The Mummy*, and its sequel *The Mummy Returns* (2001). Consider, if you will, the differences between the presentation of Western and non-Western characters in these movies. While most of the former are highly individualised, the latter are not; they exhibit a group behaviour in their costumes, expressions, and so on. This is what Orientalist representations achieve. In fact, all Hollywood movies about the non-West continue, overtly or covertly, the Orientalist politics of representing the non-West and non-white in a poorer light in comparison to the West.

Having said that, it is also important to point out that Said does acknowledge what may be called the positive, regenerative aspects of Orientalism. During its heyday in the nineteenth century, Orientalism produced great scholars; familiarised the West with many non-Western languages; valuable manuscripts were collected and archived which may, otherwise, have been lost or remained unknown beyond closed groups. In fact 'in many cases, it provided the Orient with sympathetic European students' (96). This is comparable to Said's stance on European culture in general, as discussed earlier. Unfortunately, all these activities also reinforced what Said has called the 'textual attitude', the tendency on the part of the West to see the Orient more as an archive of past traditions to study, than a living reality. That is, even in cases where Orientalist scholarship was not in the direct service of European imperialism, it failed to take into account the actual, living Orient. Hence Said's regret: 'Yet—and here we must be very clear—Orientalism overrode the Orient' (96).

'Crisis in Orientalism'

While Edward Said's *Orientalism* has been unparalleled in terms of its influence, it is definitely not the first work of its kind (much less the only one). Resistance to Western misrepresentations of erstwhile colonies abound in the writings of figures as famous and diverse as Vivekananda, Tagore, Aurobindo, Gandhi, Fanon, Achebe and Ngũgĩ (who started his anticolonial writings before Said and continues to write till date) – to name but a prominent few. For Said however, a more direct precursor was Anwar Abdel Malek, an Egyptian–French scholar and a kindred spirit. It can be said without much disagreement that *Orientalism* builds on and consolidates the arguments of Malek to a great extent, especially the ones made available in Malek's essay 'Orientalism in Crisis' (1963). The section titled 'Crisis in Orientalism' makes it clearly visible.

It begins with Said's formulation of the concept of 'textual attitude', by which he means the attitude of approaching a living reality on the basis of texts or books (93). This attitude is promoted by two situations: encountering something new or unknown which compels one to draw analogies or knowledge from texts one has read; the second situation is the success of such an attitude itself. Said uses an example here: if one has read in a book that lions are fierce and then somehow encounters a lion which happens to be actually fierce, the person will not only greatly believe the author of the book he or she has read, but would be interested in more books on the topic. A chain of demand and supply for books on lions or the fierceness of lions would thus be generated, perpetuating the myth of the fierce lion. This, in other words, is all about the generation and success of *discourses.* Said uses the analogy of a fierce lion possibly because the fierceness of lions, or tigers for that matter, are more a matter of human perception than factual truth about lions. It is widely known now that lions and other beasts of prey attack others only when they are hungry, or feel threatened. In a similar fashion, discourses about the Orient and its people ('the fierce lion') continued because the fierce lion/Orientals could not speak for itself/themselves.

The crisis in Orientalism refers to the fact that the Orientals have begun to speak for themselves for quite some time. (Said's

Orientalism itself is such an example, perhaps the most prominent one.) As Said sees it, from approximately the 1920s onwards, the relationship between the coloniser and the colonised became 'dialectical' and by the time of the Bandung conference, the entire Orient had become politically independent of its European colonial masters. Confronted with this shock, Orientalism seems to have suffered a setback. But the setback was so temporary that it hardly made any difference: Orientalism made its way into the new media and social sciences, particularly in the US, and continued the same politics of misrepresentation as had been done during or under the high tide of Anglo-French colonialism. In other words, decolonisation just made Orientalism change its fields of operation, but not the methods; much like the mutation of a virus. (Said has not used that analogy though.) In this regard, it is interesting to note a similar observation that V. S. Naipaul has made in his classic novel *The Mimic Men*: 'The empires of our time were short lived, but they have altered the world for ever; their passing away is their least significant feature' (32).

Orientalist Structures and Re-structures: Philology and Racism

The second chapter of *Orientalism*, titled 'Orientalist Structures and Restructures', engages in an in-depth analysis of how Orientalism was given its full academic shape by two Orientalists in particular: Antoine Isaac Silvestre de Sacy (1758–1838) and Ernest Renan (1823–92). Silvestre de Sacy had a brilliant and distinguished academic career. He taught as a professor in renowned French institutes of learning like the School of Oriental Languages and the Collège de France; and was also made a Baron in 1814. Widely known as the pioneer of Arabic studies in France, de Sacy was also the first president of the Société Asiatique (a French Society founded in 1822 for studying Asia). He is extremely important as a scholar 'whose work virtually put before the profession an entire systematic body of texts, a pedagogic practice, a scholarly tradition, and an important link between Oriental scholarship and public policy' (*Orientalism* 124). In other words, he transformed the field of Oriental studies, which had started as individual academic explorations, into a highly systematised and methodical field of enquiry. To use a Foucauldian trope, de Sacy disciplined Orientalism into a discipline. In de Sacy's works, as Said sees it, 'there was a self-conscious methodological principle at work as a coeval with scholarly discipline' which was nearly unprecedented in Europe (*Orientalism* 124). However, while Said appreciates de Sacy's hard work and academic rigour, what de Sacy finally did was to focus, rather arbitrarily, on 'a relatively small set of powerful examples [that] delivers the Orient to the student' (125). This is the essentialist tendency in Orientalism which originated with de Sacy and has continued ever since.

The Orient can and should be known only in parts, and it is the job of the Orientalist to select the parts that they feel are essential and present them before the European audience: 'So if the Orientalist is necessary because he fishes some useful gems out of the distant Oriental deep, and since the Orient cannot be known without his mediation, it is also true that Oriental writing itself ought not to be taken in whole' (128). While de Sacy compiled several anthologies on Arabic prose, poetry and even Arabic grammar, he also suggested in various ways that it is best for Europeans to access these things only through the mediations of Orientalists like him. Thus, while Napoleon's project was to know the Orient in its entirety, de Sacy started the trend of selective (mis)representation. The difference comes obviously from the fact that Napoleon's purpose was the immediate and direct subjugation of the East. Silvestre de Sacy and other scholars like him also served the imperial purposes of Europe, but more indirectly and less immediately than Napoleon. Sacy's philological pursuits saw further interesting transformations in the other influential French Orientalist Ernest Renan, who may be seen as a direct disciplinary successor to de Sacy.

It is a widely held notion that the Judeo-Christian idea of God and religion received the strongest challenge from Darwin's *Origin of Species* (1851) and *The Descent of Man* (1871) which led to an overpowering sense of loss of faith among believers. However, what is not generally known is that philology, reinvigorated by Orientalism, led Orientalist scholars to the same condition in the late eighteenth and early nineteenth centuries. In the second chapter of *Orientalism*, Said argues that it was the very difference between the theological history of humanity offered by Christianity and the secular history that resulted from the early Orientalist Sanskritist studies which 'made modern philology possible' (135). While philology as a subject has been around in Western scholastic traditions since antiquity, it became much more secular and aware of multiple language traditions beyond the Hellenic and the Hebraic when Western philologists encountered Oriental languages, particularly Sanskrit. This is what Said calls 'New philology' (135) whose core characteristics are the comparative and the secular dimensions that were missing in the old scholastic philology. Based on the scholarly work of William Jones and his successors, it was not difficult for one to see that the hitherto held Judeo-Christian belief about Hebrew being the oldest language with a divine origin (God gifted it to Adam in the Garden of Eden) was no longer tenable. Consequently, 'A new historical conception was needed, since Christianity seemed unable to survive the empirical evidence that reduced the divine status of its major texts' (136).

The new historical conception was a renewed form of Orientalism – Orientalism 'restructured' through the mediation of new or comparative philology based on the study of Sanskrit. Language families were created or imagined (see 'filiation' and 'affiliation' in the next chapter) to bring all languages of the globe under a common umbrella of the philological paradigm of a so-called 'language tree'. In that new family structure, Sanskrit was closely associated with European languages such as Greek, Latin, German and French which were named Indo-European Languages, while Arabic and Hebrew were clubbed together as 'Semitic'. The Indo-European tag was also based on the ideology of the racial purity of Europeans, whose purest form was the Aryan race (a purely imaginary race according to most contemporary scholars). In fact, the name Indo-Aryan was often used interchangeably with Indo-European, and the obsession with the purity of the so-called Aryan race finally resulted in one of the most heinous crimes against humanity itself in the form of the Holocaust.

One immediate result of classifying Oriental languages (and people) into Indo-European and Semitic was that there was an intense othering of 'Semitic' peoples, especially the Arabs. Here is Said's statement on the arch-Orientalist Renan in this context:

> Whenever Renan wished to make a statement about either the Jews or the Muslims, for example, it was always with his remarkably harsh (and unfounded, except according to the science he was practicing) strictures on the Semites in mind . . . It should by no means be lost on us that Semitic was for Renan's ego the symbol of European (and consequently his) dominion over the Orient and over his own era. (141)

This inhumane othering of Semites, especially the Arabs, is what is contested by Said in the third chapter titled 'Orientalism Now'.

There are those who say that Said has generalised the Orientalist study of the Orient without addressing the field's divergent contours and constituents. It might be worthwhile to read *Orientalism* (135–48) where the specificities of the different strands of Orientalism have been squarely addressed. In fact, one of the major contributions of *Orientalism* lies chiefly in its charting the development of Orientalism temporally (over a large period of time, from Aeschylus to Bernard Lewis) as well as spatially (French versus British Orientalism). Said's engagement with the differences between French and British Orientalism goes well beyond *Orientalism* and continues with equal fervour in *The World, the Text, and the Critic*. The overall conclusion is (and I have to essentialise once again, for obvious reasons) that the French Orientalists seemed to be better scholars and greater intellectuals; they were more academically oriented than the British. The British Orientalists seemed to have more of a non-academic and pragmatic approach to the matter.

The nuances, differences and divergent trajectories of different types of Orientalisms notwithstanding, they were all united in the project of 'knowing' the East and domesticating and dominating it. Said has underscored the futility of studying the internal divergences of various kinds of Orientalisms pointing out the fields' 'proclivity' to constantly divide its own subject matter without changing the way in which the Orient is seen 'as being always the same unchanging, uniform and radically peculiar object' (98).

REREADING 'ORIENTALISM NOW': RACE, RELIGION AND OTHERING

The structures and re-structures of Orientalism are not a thing of the past, they continue well into contemporary times, even after the colonies have gained independence from European nations. For instance, the structures of Orientalism are continued and reinforced in effective ways by the American government and media. This is in line with what has often been called 'neocolonialism', after Jean-Paul Sartre and the Ghanaian politician and thinker Kwame Nkrumah.

SHORT TAKES

LATENT AND MANIFEST ORIENTALISM

In the first section of the third chapter of *Orientalism,* Said builds further on his thesis of Orientalism being an all-pervasive phenomenon of Western epistemology. He introduces the twin concepts of 'latent' and 'manifest' Orientalism to that end (there is an obvious intertextual connection with Freudian psychoanalysis here). By 'latent Orientalism', Said refers to those widely held beliefs and assumptions among the Orientalists which led to the othering of the Orient in the first place: 'the separateness of the Orient, its eccentricity, its backwardness, its silent indifference, its feminine penetrability, its supine malleability' (*Orientalism* 206). Said argues that these ideas were commonly held by writers and thinkers as diverse as Ernest Renan, Edward Lane, Silvestre de Sacy, Gustave Flaubert, Gérard de Nerval, and even Karl Marx. 'Manifest Orientalism' is the actual act of representing the Orient through writings, 'stated views', or Orientalism in practice. The writings of various Orientalists differed only 'in form and personal style, rarely in basic content' (206). In fact, it is 'latent Orientalism' which manifests itself till date in phenomena such as neo-Orientalism, green Orientalism or techno-Orientalism. All these terms refer to how the Orient continue to be oppressed and misrepresented by Euro-American cultural politics in domains as diverse as ecology, technology, cyberspace and the public sphere.

The continuation of the Anglo-French Orientalist project by American authorities and media is the theme of the third chapter titled 'Orientalism Now'. Said's special focus is on the dehumanising misrepresentation of Muslims and Arabs, especially the Palestinians. The misrepresentation and marginalisation of Palestinians by the Western, especially American, media and governmental powers is the most recurrent theme in Said's oeuvre. He sets the tone for this chapter in the 'Introduction' itself when he says that 'One aspect of the electronic, postmodern world is that there has been a reinforcement of the stereotypes by which the Orient is viewed' (26). Television, cinema, newspapers and other media resources (including social media now, we may add) have joined hands in intensifying 'the hold of the nineteenth-century academic and imaginative demonology' of Orientalism (26).

This observation is also informed by Said's own dispossession and exile from his homeland due to Zionism – the ideology and operational strategy of Israeli statehood – of which America is the strongest supporter. In fact, much like European colonialism, the interventionist politics and policies of America have complicated matters for many peoples, including America itself. For instance, America finally withdrew its military forces from Afghanistan in 2021 almost offering the place on a platter to the Taliban after embittering and complicating the fight between factions there for decades in various ways. It is now widely recognised that many such forces were nurtured, even created, by successive American governments to keep the former USSR and now Russia under tactical and practical pressure. Such policies and politics, however, bring untold suffering to common people, especially those whom Fanon famously named 'the wretched of the earth'. The life of an Arab Palestinian in America, therefore, is precarious and perilous, as his or her image is always tarnished for a greater part of the American public.

One just has to remember the spurt of xenophobic violence against the Sikh community in the US after the heinous attack on the World Trade Centre on 11 September 2001. The attacks, which continued for years together, stemmed from the fact that the appearance of Sikhs resembled that of Arabs/Muslims in popular

American imagination.[5] The 'Arab' portrayed by American media, thus, has a cascading effect going well beyond its primary target (which, too, is based on essentialist and stereotyped representations). The term neo-Orientalism is being used increasingly in critical writings to refer to this renewed phenomenon of America's othering of the Islamic and the Arab world. However, there is hardly anything 'new' as such in it, if we care to read *Orientalism* minutely. As Behdad and Williams have rightly put it, 'neo-Orientalism should be understood not as sui generis, but rather as a supplement to enduring modes or Orientalist representation' (n.p.). Perhaps the most useful words in *Orientalism* that can help us contextualise these otherings are the following: 'The life of an Arab Palestinian in the West is disheartening. There exists an almost unanimous consensus that politically he does not exist, and when it is allowed that he does, it is either as a nuisance or as an Oriental' (27).

There is, thus, a nefarious link between Orientalism, colonialism and neocolonialism on the one hand and racism on the other. Ironically enough, while Said's critique of Orientalism is predominantly against racist philosophies and ideologies, some critics have indicated that *Orientalism* is lacking in formulations on racism. This allegation, however, is more imaginary than real and appears to stem from a lack of deep reading on the part of those critics. After all, what is Said challenging in his protests against misrepresentations of non-Western people if not racism? In other words, racism and colonialism are the proverbial two sides of the same coin, and so are racism and Orientalism too. In fact, the word 'race' does occur in numerous places in the book in connection with figures like Balfour, Gibb, Renan and Schlegel among others, along with foregrounding the politics and poetics of Semitism as well as anti-Semitism.

In spite of the fact of his belonging to the side of the colonised, however, Said demonstrates catholicity in admitting that he does not believe in the 'privilege of an "insider" perspective over an "outsider" one', nor is it his thesis that 'there is such a thing as a real or true Orient (Islam, Arab or whatever)' (322). While Said does not contend the fact that there are peoples, races and cultures that inhabit the place that is geographically called the Orient, what he definitely discredits and debunks is the idea that the very fact of living in a particular region or practising a particular religion can be seamlessly translated into rigid classifications of humanity. In his own words, his final goal is not limited to reclaiming Palestinian rights, but challenging 'the notion that there are geographical spaces with indigenous, radically "different" inhabitants who can be defined on the basis of some religion, culture, or racial essence proper to the geographical space' (322). The goal of his book, therefore, is to liberate humanity and the humanities from the pernicious and persistent tendency to essentialise others, mostly motivated by a 'will to power'; a desire to rule. The point is often badly missed or ignored by those who choose to read *Orientalism* as an anti-European or anti-Western book.

ORIENTALISM AND ITS CRITICS

Orientalism and its author earned a huge number of followers, both inside and outside of academia; and, not unsurprisingly, an equally formidable number of not only critics and detractors, but even enemies. While the book was held in very high esteem, both critical and personal, by leading scholars and intellectuals like Noam Chomsky, Partha Chatterjee, Gayatri Spivak, Bill Ashcroft and Homi Bhabha, opponents like Bernard Lewis and Stanley Kurtz went to the extent of suggesting that Said was part of a treacherous conspiracy against Zionism and the US government. In fact, so numerous are Said's followers and detractors that to make even passing references to all those who matter would constitute material enough for a complete book in itself. Since this book is meant to be an introduction to Said's works and not to works written on his works, I would like to present some of the broader outlines of the basic arguments for and against *Orientalism*.

While recognising the laudable contributions of *Orientalism*, one may begin by pointing to the fact that it led to the creation of at least three fields of studies directly, while inspiring and transforming many others. The three fields of scholarship that *Orientalism* led to are postcolonial studies (and postcolonial theory), subaltern studies and studies in travel writing. While initially the latter two were included within the former, by the early years of the twenty-first century they had become independent fields in their own rights. Acknowledging the phenomenal contribution of *Orientalism*, Gayatri Spivak in *Outside in the Teaching Machine*, for instance, identifies it as 'the source book in our discipline' (61). She further adds, 'The study of colonial discourse, directly released by work such as Said's, has, however, blossomed into a garden where the marginal can speak and be spoken, even spoken for' (62). Partha Chatterjee, arguably the most representative figure of the subaltern studies group, similarly argues that *Orientalism* provided him with the language to talk about 'things I felt I had known all along but never had the language to formulate with clarity' (194). Chatterjee's reading of Said, more importantly, makes him realise how Orientalist thoughts formed a part not only of British colonialism 'but also of the nationalism which was my own heritage' (194). Furthermore, fields like geography, history and political science have been modified by the insights and arguments of the book to a great extent. The unprecedented and transformative changes that Said brought into academia have been captured with remarkable precision by Timothy Brennan who says, 'More than anyone, he [Said] moved the humanities from the university to the centre of the political map' (xiii).

Said's detractors and opponents – who ranged from hard core Orientalists to pro-Zionist thinkers and writers (in most cases these attributes coexisted in the concerned opponent) – had their own reasons. Given that Said had demolished the premises of innocent scholarship and intellectual impartiality on which Orientalism thrived, it was natural that there would be backlash, as there was from scholars like Bernard Lewis. In a riposte titled 'The Question of Orientalism', Lewis unleashed a barrage of allegations against Said, accusing him (and a few others) of 'poisoning' the field of Orientalism. Lewis tried his best to discredit the book's authenticity with sweeping generalisations stating that it showed an 'arbitrary rearrangement of the historical background' and was 'a series of reckless accusations' rather than actual scholarship. He was actually countering Said's incisive criticism of 'Lewis's sarcastic scholarship' in *Orientalism* (315–21). In his 1995 'Afterword' to *Orientalism*, Said pointed out – in continuation of his arguments against Lewis in the original book – that Lewis's allegations are symptomatic of the very Orientalist mode of thought that his book had exposed in the first place. As late as twenty-five years after the publication of *Orientalism*, a contributing editor to the *National Review*, Stanley Kurtz, reported to the US legislature that '*Orientalism* was somehow behind a nefarious hatred of the West and [was] hindering efforts of the Bush administration to fight terrorism' (Bayoumi and Rubin xl). These mindless oppositions only reassert the bitter truths that *Orientalism* contains. Such Eurocentric and Orientalist oppositions to Said continue till date, despite the fact that a thinking and humanist audience have increasingly sided with Said over the years.

Leaving such polemicists aside, let us now concentrate on the relatively unbiased criticisms of *Orientalism* that have come from serious scholars and academicians like Gayatri Spivak or Homi Bhabha, who have also upheld the merit of the work. These criticisms mostly cluster around three issues: gender, class and essentialism. The critics who focus on gender issues have tried to point out that *Orientalism* is not sensible to the nuances of gender, neither in relation to the colonisers nor the colonised. Reina Lewis has written an entire book on it titled *Gendering Orientalism,* while Lata Mani, Ruth Frankenberg and Spivak herself have highlighted this issue in various articles and research papers, directly or indirectly. In fact, Spivak's most famous and influential essay 'Can the Subaltern Speak?' is an implicit dialogue with *Orientalism,* trying to bring to the fore the plight of oppressed women in colonial India who were often subjected to colonial as well as indigenous patriarchy. Partha Chatterjee's previously discussed essay also does the same job, focusing on Bengali womens' lives and life-writings in colonial India.

Additionally, Spivak is mindful of the class identities of colonial subjects, which is absent in Said's oeuvre in general. This failure to address the class issue in Said has led some Marxist thinkers to critique him for weakening the Marxist and Communist movements of the world. Aijaz Ahmad's *In Theory: Classes, Nations and Literatures* can be seen as representative of the Marxist critique of Said. Indeed, Said's repeated emphasis on what he identifies as the Eurocentric biases of Marx himself has deeply problematised the claims made in favour of Marxism as a liberating philosophy universally applicable across cultures and tradition. As Leela Gandhi argues, for Said, 'the radical failure of Marxist categories arises from his perception of their inability to accommodate the specific political needs and experiences of the colonised world' (71). However, it must be admitted that class or economic difference is a crucial variable and identity marker, and must be recognised as such.

There is a third group of critics who often suggest that in his attempt at countering the European essentialist representations of the Orient, Said himself falls into the same trap. He presents Europeans and Orientalists as homogenous entities. While a facile reading of *Orientalism* can generate such a view, it is far from being true. Said is quite nuanced in dividing Orientalists as well as European colonisation across the coordinates of time and place. The three chapters of the book are precisely divided on the principle of growth of Orientalism over time, while in each of these chapters he has categorically pointed out the differences between British and French Orientalism, and then their differences from the American mode of Orientalism. It is another matter that the subtle differences among their operational strategies notwithstanding, they collectively contribute to the othering of the Orient and Orientals all the same.

A related issue is Said's silence on German Orientalism. This is something that Said has himself admitted, saying such a silence 'needs to be reproached, and I freely reproach myself' (18). This absence, along with the charge about gender blindness, can be squarely addressed if one keeps in mind the fact that no given book on any subject can cover all its aspects, and it is very difficult to be comprehensive beyond a point when the field of study is as vast as Orientalism. Said has candidly admitted in the 'Introduction' itself that he would be focusing on certain aspects only; it would be 'foolish to attempt an encyclopaedic narrative history of Orientalism'. Further, it would not 'suit my [Said's] descriptive and political interests' (16). In fact, Said admitted beforehand many of the lacks and absences that critics pointed out later. It is to his credit that these absences have been academically productive; critics like Spivak, Bhabha and Chatterjee started their key works in their attempts to address these gaps. Said's promise that 'this book is one installment of several' (24) has been a prophetic one, fulfilled by many, including himself.

NOTES

1. Said devoted a substantial part of his writings to comparisons between Foucault and Derrida both before and after *Orientalism* (*Beginnings* and *The World, the Text, and the Critic* respectively), hence their influence on him can hardly be overemphasised. He also increasingly moved away from them as his work and thinking progressed (see the next chapter for a more detailed discussion).
2. It may be argued, contra Said, that since these days computers and other associated devices can produce knowledge objectively, his postulation regarding all knowledge being subjective is flawed. But computers work on data fed to it by human agents. And more importantly, Said is talking about a field of study whose scholars and practitioners had no idea about computers or digital humanities simply because it did not exist then. Said, interestingly, wrote most of his works with a fountain pen (see Brennan xviii).
3. Said's allegation that Foucault was not politically committed is not acceptable to all. Please see a detailed discussion of this in the next chapter.
4. The details of Said's preference for Gramsci over Foucault have been discussed in the next chapter. Also see the first chapter for some introductory remarks on the topic.
5. https://edition.cnn.com/2016/09/15/us/sikh-hate-crime-victims/index.htm

REFERENCES

Bayoumi, Moustafa and Andrew Rubin, editors. *The Selected Works of Edward Said:1966–2006*. Bloomsbury, 2021.

Behdad, Ali and Juliet A. Williams. "On Neo-Orientalism, Today", https://web.archive.org/web/20150928220441/http://www.entekhabi.org/Texts/Neo_Orientalism_Today.htm. Accessed 1 January 2022.

Brennan, Timothy. *Places of Mind: A Life of Edward Said.* Farrar, 2021.

Césaire, Aimé. *Discourse on Colonialism*. Translated by Joan Pinkham, Monthly Review Press, 1972.

Chatterjee, Partha. "Their own words? An essay for Edward Said". *Edward Said: A Critical Reader*, edited by Michael Sprinker, Blackwell, 1992, pp. 194–220.

Chattopadhyay, Bankim Chandra. "Krishnacharitra". *Prabandha o Anyanya Rachana*. Kolkata: Sahityam, 2007, pp. 569–810.

Evans, Hayley. "A Critical Analysis of the Eurocentric Response to COVID-19: Western Ideas of Health". *Bill of Health*, https://blog.petrieflom.law.harvard.edu/2021/06/11/eurocentric-response-covid-western-ideas-health/. Accessed 1 January 2022.

Foucault, Michel. *Madness and Civilisation: A History of Insanity in the Age of Reason*. Translated by Richard Howard, Random House,1965.

---. *The Archaeology of Knowledge and the Discourse on Language.* Translated by A.M. Sheridan Smith, Pantheon Books, 1972.

---. *The Birth of the Clinic: An Archaeology of Medical Perception.* Translated by Alan Sheridan, Vintage, 1994.

---. *The History of Sexuality: The Use of Pleasure*. Translated by Robert Hurley, vol. 2, Vintage, 1985.

---. *The Order of Things*. Routledge, 2001.

Gandhi, Leela. *Postcolonial Theory: A Critical Introduction.* Oxford UP, 1998.

Gandhi, M. K. *Hind Swaraj.* Navajivan Trust, 1938.

Lewis, Bernard. "The Question of Orientalism". *The New York Review of Books*, 24 June 1982, pp. 49–55.

Mani, Lata and Ruth Frankenberg. "The Challenge of Orientalism". *Economy and Society*, vol. 14, 1985, pp. 174–92.

Max Müller, Friedrich. *A History of Ancient Sanskrit Literature.* Williams and Norgate, 1860.

Moore-Gilbert, Bart. *Postcolonial Theory: Contexts, Practices, Politics*. Verso, 1997.

Naipaul, V. S. *The Mimic Men.* Picador, 2002.

Pratt, Mary Louise. *Imperial Eyes: Travel Writing and Transculturation*. Routeldge,1992.

Said, Edward W. *Beginnings: Intention and Method* . Columbia UP, 1985.

---. *Humanism and Democratic Criticism*. Columbia UP, 2004.

---. *Orientalism*. Penguin, 2001.

---. *The World, the Text, and the Critic*. Vintage, 1991.

Spivak, Gayatri. "Can the Subaltern Speak?". *Postcolonial Studies: A Reader*, edited by Bill Ashcroft, Gareth Griffiths and Helen Tiffin, 2nd ed., Routledge, 2006, pp. 28–37.

---. *Outside in the Teaching Machine.* Routledge, 1993.

Vivekananda, Swami. "On Professor Max Muller", https://www.ramakrishnavivekananda.info/vivekananda/volume_4/writings_prose/on_professor_max_muller.htm. Accessed 27 August 2021.

Wolfreys, Julian. *Introducing Literary Theories.* Edinburgh UP, 2001.

Chapter Four

Said between the Text and the World

The World, the Text, and the Critic is a sincere and urgent attempt on Said's part to restore the world to the text. As he puts it, 'My position is that texts are worldly, to some degree they are events, and even when they appear to deny it, they are nevertheless a part of the social world, human life, and of course the historical moments in which they are located and interpreted' (*The World, the Text, and the Critic* 4).

In the West from the 1960s, there has been an increasing focus on the text as the sole guarantor of the meaning of the text itself, leaving aside any consideration of its author; sociocultural, historical or political contexts; the history of the literary tradition to which the text belongs; and so on. The phenomenon had Anglo-American antecedents in critics of the 1930s and 40s like T. S. Eliot, I. A. Richards, John Crowe Ransom and Cleanth Brooks, most of whom were associated with the school called New Criticism. Similarly, the highly influential F. R. Leavis practised a critical method very close to the 'close reading' technique used by the New Critics, though he focused primarily on the British literary tradition. His *Great Tradition* and the journal *Scrutiny* bear ample evidence of this. The crux of their methodology was perhaps best expressed by Eliot: 'Honest criticism and sensitive appreciation is directed not upon the poet but upon the poetry' (Eliot 297). The immediate origin of the radical and exclusive turn to textuality in the 1960s, however, was the rise of poststructuralism in Western philosophical and critical traditions. Scholars of this field such as Roland Barthes, Jacques Derrida, and to some extent Michel Foucault, finally 'killed' the already ailing figure of the author who had been suffering from the onslaughts of formalism, New Criticism and structuralism. The climax was perhaps reached in Barthes' classic essay 'The Death of the Author', and Foucault's 'What is an Author?' helped the author's burial.

Edward Said, with his strong roots in both academics and political/worldly investments, found this trend to be uncommitted, terribly disheartening and utterly debilitating. His contention was that a text is always produced in the world and can only be fully understood in relation to the world. Further, it is the critic's ethical and critical obligation to mediate between the text and its world. This belief constitutes the core of *The World, the Text, and the Critic*. Additionally, the book is also a sustained critique of the aesthetic or liberal humanist approach to the study of literature.

Issues and Contentions

The World, the Text, and the Critic begins quite directly, without recourse to any anecdote, abstruse formation, or abstract generalisation: 'Literary criticism is practiced today in four major forms' (1). Perhaps this matter-of-fact beginning aims to highlight Said's dissatisfaction with literary theory's excessive engagement with verbal jugglery. These four major forms, according to Said, are:

- practical criticism, generally found in book reviews and what Said calls 'literary journalism'
- 'academic literary history' (more commonly known as history of literature)
- literary appreciation (commonly known as critical appreciation)
- literary theory (also known as theory, critical theory or – especially these days – critical and cultural theory).

While Said exemplifies the features of all these in the essays he puts together in this book, the book is also an attempt on his part to 'go beyond the four forms as defined above' (1–2).

In fact, *The World, the Text, and the Critic* is Said's second book-length take on literary theory or critical theory, *Beginnings: Intention and Method* being the first. But the enthusiasm and the celebratory mood of *Beginnings* is visibly on the wane here. The fascination for French theory that *Beginnings* is rife with is counterbalanced in *The World, the Text, and the Critic* by a sharp attack on what Said reads as the escapist strategy of theory. The book, consequently, is his desperate (and one may add, successful) attempt to go beyond all the four forms of 'literary criticism' mentioned above and add a fifth dimension: 'worldliness'. Worldliness is the key theoretical and practical position that Said operates from and upholds. To delve deeper into the poetics and politics of Said's worldliness, it is necessary to take stock of the conditions of theory against which he formulated the concept. Though it is not always explicit in this book, it would be useful to keep in mind that Said's repeated insistence on worldliness is a direct result of his experiences as a Palestinian exile in America. The materialist underpinnings of classical Marxist criticism are also at work, though he finds it left out by contemporary American leftist criticism.[1]

SAID AGAINST CANON AND THEORY: FILIATION AND AFFILIATION

The urgency to locate texts within and against the conditions of their production and proliferation is propelled by Said's anxiety about the loss of worldly engagement in traditional literature studies as well as contemporary theory. At this point, a rough outline of the traditional schools of literary criticism that existed before the advent of theory will help us place the matter in perspective. The traditional schools of literature and criticism can be primarily divided into three classes: aesthetic, moral and historical (the latter a development beginning with figures like Dr Johnson – also a 'moral' critic – and culminating, arguably, in Taine). While the aesthetic schools of writing as well as criticism have always maintained they are apolitical, the moral and historical schools of thought expected literature to have some ameliorative functions. However, these 'schools' were not often consciously organised, having centres or departments in universities and often working on the basis of spontaneous affiliations and influences. Things took a different turn with the institutionalisation of literature in modern university departments. Here we are talking about English literature and criticism to be specific.

In his attempt to ideologically situate the development of modern literature departments in Europe, Said gives us an interesting history of what he calls 'the passage from nature to culture' (20) in modern Europe. He does this by introducing two tropes: 'filiation' and 'affiliation'. By 'filiation' Said means relations that are based primarily on biological markers – father–son, mother–daughter and so on. Late-nineteenth and early-twentieth century European writers, however, record a strong protest or resentment against biological 'filiations' and exhibit 'the failure of the generative impulse – the failure of the capacity to produce or generate children' (16). *Ulysses*, *The Waste Land, Death in Venice* and *The Way of all Flesh*, according to Said, are some of the major texts that express strong notes of dissent against the idea of family and procreation. This is the first part of his schematic history.

The vacuum created by the real or ideological annihilation of families, however, was closely followed by an attempt to forge solidarities based on common interests which would eventually fill the vacuum. In other words, the alternative seems to have been provided by institutions, associations, and communities whose social existence was not in fact guaranteed by biology, but by '*affiliation*' (17, emphasis added). This is the second part. Said's leading example here is Eliot, who gradually comes to adopt the Church of England as his 'family' amidst the barrenness of modern life, 'the waste land' (18). Eliot's case, however, is not unique, but a highly representative one. Consider, for example, the fact that an average person today, especially in a metropolitan set up, is more likely to be known by their job, profession, business or institutional affiliation than their family lineage.

Thus, especially in modern times, there has been a massive movement from identity based on 'filiation' to 'a kind of compensatory order that, whether it is a party, an institution, a culture, a set of beliefs, or even a world-vision, [that] provides men and women with a new form of relationship, which I have been calling affiliation, but which is also a *new system*' (19, emphasis added). Said's contention is that the modern university system, especially departments of literature therein, are a part of this 'new system' of affiliation. Prima facie, Said (and most other intellectuals) would seem to prefer things based on affiliation to those based on filiation as the former is, by definition, more liberal and democratic. However, that unfortunately is not the entire truth. According to Said, the new systems based on cultural, religious, or ideological affiliations implicitly replicate 'the kind of authority associated in the past with filiative order' (19). This is the third axis of his schematic history of the development of a modern cultural ethos in Europe.

According to Said, this tripartite development has left strong imprints on the study of literature today (20). He very briefly outlines the development of English studies with references to Eliot, Richards and Leavis – people who were central to the institutionalisation of English. The idea behind a literary education was to create a band of people who became affiliated members of the discipline by devoting themselves 'to the study of great monuments of literature' (20) and perpetuated the pattern by passing it on to the following generations in an unbroken line of succession. This closely parallels the protocol of inheritance in families, the only difference is that here the succession is disciplinary, not biological. Consequently, literature departments and courses in contemporary Europe seem to be more interested in exclusion than inclusion at various levels. One must remember that the book under discussion was published in 1983 and subsequently many changes have taken place, though the overall picture is still not fully egalitarian. This is evident from Said's posthumously published *Humanism and Democratic* criticism, which has been discussed in the last chapter.

Said particularly stresses two exclusions from what may now be called 'the Western canon' and its teaching in Western universities. Firstly, texts and authors from non-Western traditions are systematically excluded, making the canon reflect 'only a fraction of the real human relationships and interactions now taking place in the world' (21). Students are taught to read and revere texts and authors from the Western tradition only. Secondly, 'they are taught that such fields as the humanities and such sub-fields as "literature" exist in a relatively neutral political element', disconnecting them from their worldliness (21). Secular criticism, as Said proposes it, is an antidote and corrective to both these quasi-religious trends of venerating select cultural texts as universal, apolitical and sacrosanct.

The 'turn to theory' offers no better alternative to the aesthetic and quasi-religious tradition of literature studies. It may be noted that while Marxist and feminist modes of readings had emphasised the sociopolitical imperatives of literature even before Said did, things changed to the opposite direction with the advent of structuralism and poststructuralism. As stated above, the so-called linguistic turn became increasingly concerned with texts as verbal artefacts only, without any consideration for the larger sociopolitical contexts that produced those texts. This move did not find favour with Said, who saw his precarious position as an Arab intellectual in the West as more or less determined by cultural stereotypes propagated by Orientalist and other such texts. That texts are generated in the real world, and subsequently affect and intervene into the world, was always a living truth for Said. Therefore, he was dissatisfied with a mode of reading that attempted to see texts only as verbal (or, for that matter, aesthetic) structures. He resents and laments the withdrawal of critical theory (especially as practised in America) from the real world of action, its initial radical promises notwithstanding. While critical theory or theory had begun with signs of transformative changes across disciplines, 'American literary theory of the late seventies had retreated into the labyrinth of "textuality"' (*The World, the Text, and the Critic* 3). Said faults Foucault and Derrida for not only initiating this retrograde move, but also for encouraging their 'trans-Atlantic canonization and domestication' (3). Consequently, theories and theorists have withdrawn themselves from any interference, let alone meaningful interference, in the real world. Their gospel is '*not* to appropriate anything that is worldly, circumstantial or socially contaminated' (3) and to operate within a very safe zone of textualities without any regard for actualities.

Said is also not appreciative of the traditional mode of aesthetic reading either. The tradition of an aesthetic mode of reading literature and culture, currently called the liberal humanist tradition, also suppresses crucial facts about the material conditions in and against which texts have been produced. They try to extract some 'universal' values from these texts, avoiding any kind of cultural or social politics that go into their making. So, while the passive and anti-humanist attitude of theory is greatly detrimental to humanity, the traditional aesthetic or liberal humanist tradition is no better. *The World, the Text, and the Critic*, therefore, is a rejection of both these trends. Its core thesis, as pronounced by the author, is that texts 'are always enmeshed in circumstance, time, place, and society—in short, they are in the world, and hence worldly' (35).

In much the same way, criticism too must be worldly. In fact, criticism for Said has a great responsibility: that of enlightening and liberating humanity. Such a responsibility cannot be carried out by criticism that is merely literary, philosophical, aesthetic, or epistemological. Nor can it be done by criticism that has limited itself by adopting qualifications such as 'Marxist', 'feminist', 'poststructuralist', or even 'postcolonial' for that matter.[2] Instead of developing a particular school of thought where members talk to each other in obscure jargon, Said has constantly and consistently stressed that criticism must be oriented towards the transformation and betterment of society.

While he objects to qualifying criticism by any adjective, there are two exceptions to this general rule: 'secular' and 'oppositional'. Both reinforce the idea of criticism as an open-ended and sustained opposition to power, politics and oppressive authorities. Furthermore, secular criticism is also opposed to the parochial, dogmatic and fractional nature of specialisations of various kinds for the reasons stated above and it is 'worldly' – not detached from political, historical and economic considerations:

> Criticism, in short, is always situated; it is sceptical, secular, reflectively open to its own failings. This is by no means to say that it is value free. Quite the contrary, for the inevitable trajectory of critical consciousness is to arrive at some acute sense of what political, social and human values are entailed in the reading, production and transmission of every text. (26)

What is clear is that for Said, criticism is nothing if it does not interrogate prevailing beliefs, orthodoxies and dogmas; in its ideal form it is also acutely self-reflexive and self-critical. This is a trait Said himself exhibits when he couples his criticism of Israel and America with an equally strong interrogation of Palestinian leadership in his works on the question of Palestine. More importantly, the true glory of 'critical consciousness' lies in its ability to see the social, political and human values behind the writings as well as reception of every text.

Said finds his contemporary critics more interested in avoiding these sociopolitical and human connections between text and authors. Their overriding concern with textualities leads Said to conclude that 'Textuality has therefore become the exact antithesis and displacement of what might be called history' (3–4). It is focused almost exclusively on illuminating the disjunction between a text's 'formal characteristics' and its 'ideological or thematic surface', which is done by way of 'deconstructing the contradictions woven into a text's formal being' (87). This is the procedure adopted by 'the Derridean school, the school of Marxist readers, of Foucault's disciples, the semioticians, of the so called Yale school' (87). For Said, such moves are indicative of avoiding political and ethical responsibilities on the part of the critics who practice them. The British Marxist critic Terry Eagleton, interestingly, has argued in a very similar vein that the absolute textual engagement of the poststructuralist obsession with texts, signifiers and signifieds is also a strategy to evade criticism's greater responsibilities to the world. As Eagleton argues, the poststructuralist mantra of the impossibility of truth 'frees you from having to assume a position on important issues, since what you say of such things will be no more than a passing product of the signifier and in no sense to be taken as "true" or "serious"'(125).

Returning to Said, there is another important point here. He argues that these poststructuralist critics do not apply their theories to any and every text, but only to texts that easily lend themselves to such interpretations. Jonathan Swift is a perfect example who cannot be readily subjected to such an approach, precisely because his writings directly correspond to his ideological positions (*The World, the Text, and the Critic* 87). In fact, Swift comes closest to Said's idea of the committed intellectual; Swift's writings exhibit what Said and Chomsky (a significant ally) see as the responsibilities of the intellectual to society as well as art. Such commitments, according to Said, are mostly conspicuous by their absence in contemporary criticism, especially in Foucault and Derrida. Said's analysis of their strategies is an instance of his 'worldliness', erudition and critical vision.

BETWEEN FOUCAULT AND DERRIDA/CULTURE AND SYSTEM

The longest essay of the book, 'Criticism Between Culture and System' (178–225) is an exploration and evaluation of two formidable contemporaries: Michel Foucault and Jacques Derrida. As discussed earlier, Said's *Beginnings* is replete with his enthusiasm for both. By the time he writes *The World, the Text, and the Critic*, his enthusiasm has been replaced by a critically evaluated distance from both. This is not synonymous with either an instinctual rejection or a knee jerk reaction at all. What Said finally resents in both is their lack of commitment to the world as he sees it. In this regard, Foucault still has some redeeming features. Unlike Derrida, he is not fully caught up in texts, signs and signifiers, but also sees and foregrounds the operations of power behind all texts, knowledge systems and cultures. This is a theme that is close to Said's heart. What he finds problematic, however, is that while Foucault is quite right in linking knowledge and culture to power, he does not offer ways out of the vast network of what he calls the 'microphysics of power'. Both the Derridean obsession with an overarching textuality (made famous by his own pronouncement 'there is no outside-text') and the Foucauldian concept of a 'microphysics of power' leave little room for human agency – the ability of human beings (both individually and collectively) to bring about meaningful changes to life and reality. This is where Said finds Antonio Gramsci to be more liberating and rewarding than both Foucault and Derrida. Having stated the crux of Said's arguments regarding Foucault and Derrida as made available in *The World, the Text and the Critic*, we shall now look into the matter in a little more detail.

As Said rightly states, despite their differences, disagreements and even debates, Foucault and Derrida are closer to each other then they would admit precisely because their common goal is 'to make visible what is customarily invisible in a text, namely the various mysteries, rules and play of its textuality' (184). Said suggests that Derrida's definition of the text as something that constantly tries to hide 'the law of its composition and the rules of its game' also works for Foucault's idea of the text (184).

However, there is a nuance between their apparently similar understandings of text. While Derrida's reading of the things that a text hides is primarily concerned with a text's formal, verbal, structural or grammatical features, for Foucault, what a text hides is that it is 'part of a network of power whose textual form is a purposeful obscuring of power beneath textuality and knowledge'(184). Both challenge the foundational assumptions of Western metaphysics and epistemology (185), which has made it easier for critics like Said, Bhabha and Spivak to engage in further explorations in this regard. It is generally agreed that while poststructuralists like Derrida, Foucault and Lacan interrogated (or 'deconstructed', to use the Derridean term) Western epistemology from within, postcolonial critics carried the job further by relating it to Western colonialism and cultural imperialism over the non-West. As has already been argued in the previous chapter, the central text of postcolonial studies – Said's *Orientalism* – is methodologically an application of the Foucauldian concept of discourse to the field of study known as Orientalism. And though Said has not explicitly acknowledged his debt to Derrida, it takes little effort to see that *Orientalism* is also a deconstruction of the binary between the Orient and the Occident. In any reading of Said (or other postcolonial thinkers) therefore, the formative influences of Foucault and Derrida can hardly be overemphasised. Nonetheless, there are significant disagreements between the two schools of thought – poststructuralism and postcolonialism – and any attempt to subsume the latter under the former (as, for instance, Pelagia Goulimari has done in her *Literary Criticism and Theory: From Plato to Postcolonialism*) can only be seen as a continuation of Western cultural imperialism. It is therefore important to take note of the differences between the two schools, and one of the best ways of doing it is to engage with Said's objections to Derrida and Foucault as recorded in *The World, the Text, and the Critic.*

Said finds it ironic that Derrida's writing is often full of terms like 'source' or 'origin', despite the latter's 'insistent criticism of such terminalistic or barrier ideas' (189). Even more paradoxical is the fact that Derrida's constant emphasis on doing away with the concept of [authorial] intention in the reading of texts is suggestive of his own intention to rule out intentionality. In other words, what Said is suggesting is that Derrida's attempts at eliminating volition ('voluntarism') and 'intention', in favour of 'what he [Derrida] calls infinite substitution', in reading texts, are more suggestive of an agenda on Derrida's part than a sincere effort to understand texts or writing (191). The intention is to institute 'a new interpretive opportunity associated with the name of Derrida' (191). While criticism and intellection should be essentially secular activities that do not subscribe to any totalitarian or overarching philosophy, Said seems to believe that Derrida has implicitly built a 'negative theology' placing himself at its centre (184). With its plethora of jargons like 'aporia', 'absence', 'presence', 'écriture', 'double' and so on, the Derridean project of deconstruction is as good as a religion or cult whose main interest seems to be perpetuating its own reading strategies rather than showing any real interest in deciphering texts, let alone social commitment. In all these analyses, Said wants to argue that Derrida's profound silence over the worldliness of the writers he examines, coupled with his obsession with the metaphysical, logocentric world, is indicative of his lack of commitment to society and humanity. For Said, what matters more is the real, empirical world in relation to which the texts must be read, interpreted and located by the critic. This is the critic's job: relating the text to the world, and vice versa.[3] Said seems to be rather amused by the fact that both Derrida and Foucault have come to be widely known as literary critics (thanks to the rise of poststructuralism which they themselves facilitated), while neither of them is one. While Derrida is a philosopher, Foucault is a 'philosophic historian', and their field is a hybrid of things 'quasi-philosophical, quasi-literary, quasi-scientific, quasi-historical' (185). While such phrasings may seem to indicate that Said is a purist, that is not his real intention. In fact, he stood for non-professionalism (*not* un-professionalism) or amateurism of all kinds. In Said's view, all intellectuals, in fact everyone, should have the right to enquire into and speak about as many matters as they choose – this is the hallmark of Said's amateurism. This must be differentiated from the 'amateurish'. Said's dig at Foucault and Derrida's canonisation as literary critics is actually the result of his objection to their (as well as contemporary criticism's) lack of political commitment as discussed above.

Said's problem with Foucault lies in the latter's negative suggestions about human agency and will. There is a close parallel here with Said's critique of Derrida for the latter's dismissal of intention and volition. In much the same way, Foucault also limits or negates 'the whole category of intention' (186). While he has adeptly analysed the intricate and subtle operations of power through the 'regularizing collectivity' that he calls discourse, 'Foucault's thesis is that individual statements, or the chances that individual authors can make individual statements, are not really likely' (186). Thus, while Foucault's linking of texts and knowledge systems to power is in the same vein as Said's own critical and intellectual agenda, the former frustrates the latter in so far as he does not provide any escape from power.

In a 1986 reassessment of Foucault, titled 'Foucault and the Imagination of Power', one can see Said reinterpreting Foucault's concept of power along with 'his highly wrought presentation of the order, stability, authority, and regulatory power of knowledge' (239). He is visibly impressed by the absence of the Hegelian concept of history in Foucault's work. Said also identifies an inclination towards studies of actual spaces, territories, domains and sites which is attributed to Foucault's 'geographic bent'. However, in these readings too, what Said finds problematic is Foucault's lack of interest in resistance to dominant powers. Attempting a 'genealogy' of this 'lack', Said offers a conclusion that seems to rob Foucault's thought of its highly radical appearance: 'Foucault's imagination of power is largely with, rather than against it' (242). This utterance makes it clear that, at least for Said, the apparent radical fervour of the Foucauldian critique of power is finally ineffective. Foucault's 'microphysics' of power, brilliant and insightful as it is in detecting the operations of power in zones and ways that are not visibly related to power, suffers from the lack of any inspiration or strategy for contesting that power.

Foucault, Said feels, neglects the movements and attempts on the parts of the marginalised, oppositional or eccentric groups of the society, to inscribe themselves into the mainstream. It should be noted, however, that Foucault's involvement in and contribution to struggles against authority was much more pronounced than Said would have us believe. While there are important points in Said's critique of Foucault, it would be counterfactual to claim, as Said did, that Foucault's imagination of power often went with power, and not against it.

Said's disenchantment with Foucault leads him to Antonio Gramsci and Raymond Williams who, Said feels, leave enough space for opposition and contestation in their envisioning of power. Though chronologically Gramsci is Foucault's predecessor, for Said, Gramsci begins where Foucault ends. Said parts company with Foucault and joins hands with Gramsci as he sees the latter as providing viable strategies to overpower and alter oppressive power structures. This choice is clearly stated in an essay of the volume titled 'Travelling Theory', where Said says that while Gramsci would appreciate Foucault's intellectual and analytical skills, he too 'would find it odd that they [Foucault's theories] make not even a nominal allowance for emergent movements, and none for revolutions, counterhegemony, or historical blocks' (*The World, the Text, and the Critic* 246). Said and Gramsci both believe (much like Marx, Tagore or Gandhi) that no matter how corrosive or powerful the structures of authoritarian oppression are, the power of humanity can outgrow oppression and liberate itself: 'In human history there is always something beyond the reach of dominating systems, no matter how deeply they saturate society, and this is obviously what makes change possible, limits power in Foucault's sense, and hobbles the theory of that power' (246–47).

SHORT TAKES

Travelling Theory: Theory at its Limits

The essay 'Travelling Theory' in *The World, the Text, and the Critic* charts the limits of theory, by pointing out that all theories are generated against specific historical and geographical contexts, and hence no theory can be universally applicable without modifications and riders. In fact, no given theory can exhaustively represent even the problems or issues of the very situation from which it arises, let alone other situations. This nuanced and logical argument from Said alerts us against indiscriminately using theories outside their contexts. For example, let us consider the application of Foucault in literary and cultural research. The Foucauldian theory of power has often been used as theoretical frameworks to read African or Indian texts, especially those by writers like Chinua Achebe, Ngũgĩ wa Thiong'o or Mahesh Dattani. Often these frameworks are applied predictably – as if the writers wrote their works to prove Foucault's hypothesis – and hence, such acts of reading often generate an illusion of theoretical veracity. More importantly, such 'methodologies' are often oblivious of the fact that Foucault's formations are based on his research on and study of European societies – particularly French societies, with occasional inputs from other histories and cultures. Even within the framework of Western society and history, Foucault's theories have a disabling affect, as pointed out by Said, among others. The idea, therefore, is not to reject theory – which is of deep significance – but to customise it to new situations; to interrogate and test its limits.

In other words, theories, especially when they have 'travelled' or have been 'borrowed' from a different context, must be used and applied with a simultaneous awareness of their specific origins and limitations. As Said puts it, 'What we also need, over and above theory, however, is the critical recognition that there is no theory capable of covering, closing off, predicting all the situations in which it might be useful' (*The World, the Text, and the Critic* 241). Critical consciousness, which for Said must be always already oppositional, should act against the ossification of theories into monoliths and dogmas.

As Said reiterates in 'Foucault and the Imagination of Power', Foucault's lack of interest in resistance 'provokes allusion to the formation in writers like Gramsci and Raymond Williams of an emergent or alternative consciousness' who insisted on the possibilities of resisting power by emphasising its contingent and provisional nature (244). Said reinforces the same point in yet another essay published almost a decade after *The World, the Text, and the Critic*. The 1995 essay 'History, Literature and Geography' once again presents Gramsci as more complete and competent than Foucault in his conceptualisation and analysis of power (467). Said's movement from Foucault to more politically committed intellectuals like Gramsci indicates that Said's faith in a human being's ability to change systems of power and authority was a long held belief. This is a secular faith. Its strength lies in the understanding, after Giambattista Vico, that all human systems of oppression and authority are human constructs, and can therefore be resisted, changed, and annihilated by human will or human agency.[4]

In his Gramscian and Vichian faith in human abilities, Said finds a great ally in Chomsky, who committed 'himself to description of power and oppression with some intention of alleviating human suffering, pain, or betrayed hope' (*The World, the Text, and the Critic* 247). It is Said's abiding faith in these humanist goals of criticism and intellectualism that led him to formulate 'secular criticism' as the central concept of *The World, the Text, and the Critic*. As Said states with certitude, the only word that he would allow as a qualifier of criticism is not Marxist, feminist, poststructuralist or postcolonial, but 'oppositional'; he further clarifies that by the use of the term 'oppositional', he would like to foreground how 'criticism must think of itself as life-enhancing and constitutively opposed to every form of tyranny, domination, and abuse' (29). Along with its constant opposition to tyranny and oppressions of all kinds, criticism's 'social goals are noncoercive knowledge produced in the interests of human freedom' (29).

It is perhaps not difficult to see that Said's recurrent assertion of the importance of the 'worldliness' of texts and critics is also a vindication of what he has already done in *Orientalism*. It is also perhaps important to remember that Said was a professor of literature who wrote an erudite and persuasive book on politics and history: the Penguin edition of *Orientalism* that I am using classifies it as 'Penguin History', and not 'literary criticism'. While this has drawn criticism from scholars of literary as well as political studies, Said's emphasis on the critic's worldly involvement in the book under discussion as well as other works is a vindication and consolidation of his stance. After Said, forays into political and historical analyses have become more a trend than an aberration for professionals of English and other literature departments.

THE INTELLECTUAL'S RESPONSIBILITIES

It can be posited that the quest for truth (truth understood both at individual and universal levels) has been fundamental to all great thinkers from the East and West alike. In the Western tradition, this has haunted figures as diverse as Socrates, Plato, Aristotle, Christ, Bacon, Shakespeare, Descartes, Heidegger and Sartre, to name only some of the more well known figures. In the contemporary world, it has been the key concern of thinkers like Foucault, Chomsky, Derrida and Said, either directly or indirectly. Among these again, the closest parallel can be found between Chomsky and Said who are in favour of intellectuals intervening in the real world. Said's writings and interventions indicate that he wanted intellectuals to play a central role in bringing about positive changes in human society. The fact that most of his works relate to pressing issues of colonialism and the precarious Israeli–Palestine conflict proves that he was never in favour of scholars, critics and intellectuals pursuing academic goals in isolation. He believed in the argument of Julien Benda that throughout human history, it is the intellectual ('clerc' in Benda's words), 'who has stood for values, ideas and activities that transcend and deliberately interfere with the collective weight imposed by the nation-state and the national culture' (*The World, the Text, and the Critic* 14). While this belief has been the key motivation behind *Orientalism* as well as *The Question of Palestine* and *Covering Islam*, Said gives it an incisively nuanced theoretical shape in *The World, the Text, and the Critic*. In fact, the expectations that he has from secular or oppositional criticism can be fulfilled by their practitioners only when they are responsible intellectuals and not just academic or professional critics. The arguments regarding the role of the intellectual presented in *The World, the Text, and the Critic* was further developed in his 1993 Reith lectures titled *Representations of the Intellectual* which became widely popular and influential. The two key ideas developed in the Reith lectures have already been included in the discussion above: the worldliness of texts (and hence of knowledge) and the consequent need of the intellectual to be worldly, material and political.

Exploring these ideas further, Said claims that the most important aspect of an intellectual is their impartiality. This would appear to be paradoxical: how can an intellectual, for example, speak for the oppressed or the downtrodden in a given situation without taking their side? However, what Said means by not taking sides is that no intellectual should profess perpetual allegiance to the views of any one standpoint only. Otherwise one ceases to be an intellectual and becomes a devotee, votary or an acolyte: 'Indeed the notion of a side is, where cultures are at issue, highly problematic, since most cultures aren't watertight little packages, all homogenous, and all either good or evil. But if your eye is on your patron, you cannot think as an intellectual, but only as a disciple or acolyte' (*Representations of the Intellectual* 119).

The fight against the dehumanising marginalisation and dispossession of the oppressed can happen without upholding the worldview or ideology of the oppressed uncritically. Said himself is an example of this critical commitment of the intellectual. While his works and words are primarily directed against the European and American domination of the Arab world, he has never promoted 'Arabism' or 'Islam' as wholly viable alternatives to Eurocentrism Not many may understand this and Said has often been seen as a defender of Arabism or Islam – a far cry from his thoughts. What he actually defended was that just because one happens to be an Arab or Muslim or Palestinian, it should not follow that others, especially American authorities, have the right to control, marginalise or misrepresent them. To this end, Said finds that the state of exile can be an enabling factor. An exile is at least aware of two cultures, by definition, and hence can aim at greater objectivity in their analyses and interventions.

To speak against authority, in turn, implies 'speaking truth to power', arguably the most meaningful phrase in *Representations of the Intellectual*. Power or authority is always more interested in continuing and consolidating its rule, causing untold suffering to people both under its direct control and beyond. It is the role of intellectuals like Socrates and Sartre, Chomsky and Said, to compel the authorities to see the truth; acknowledge their wrongdoings so that things change for the better. Though this line of thinking has antecedents in religion as well as philosophy (Christ or Socrates, for instance), Said is careful to distinguish his strategy from religious and philosophical idealism as well as obscurantism. This is in consonance with his idea of secular criticism. As he makes it clear, 'The intellectual does not climb a mountain or pulpit and declaim from the heights' (*Representations of the Intellectual* 101). The truths that an intellectual sees do not come from divination, prophesy or romantic imagination; 'it has resonance only because it associates itself freely with the reality of a movement, the aspirations of a people, the common pursuit of a shared ideal' (102). In other words, the truth that an intellectual sees and represents comes from the ground realities of a lived world.

Similarly, while he has high hopes for the intellectual, Said knows that for an intellectual to be effective, they would have to be strategic about their moves. He does not advise a Christ- or Socrates-like self-sacrificing gesture. For Said, it is more important to live for a cause than die for it. Also, he feels that the truth need not be represented everywhere at every point of time, but at the right moment and place. Said's model intellectual is an adroit hybrid of a passionate humanist who would stand for the oppressed, as well as a calculated strategist who would choose their moves effectively: 'Speaking the truth to power is no Panglossian idealism: it is carefully weighing the alternatives, picking the right one, and then intelligently representing it where it can do the most good and cause the right change' (102). However, like most other intellectuals, Said has also often suffered at the hands of authorities, in the US as well as in the Arab world. Most people may not be aware that Said was spied upon by the FBI since 1971, and his phone was in all probability tapped by them until the day he died. David Price, a professor of anthropology and activist has used the Freedom of Information Act to obtain 147 pages of Said's 238-page FBI file. Further, 'Large sections of the file remain blacked out, with stamps indicating they remain Classified Secret until 2030, twenty-five years' (Cockburn n.p.). It implies, among other things, we will have to wait till 2030 to have a complete understanding of what FBI was up to. It is also not difficult to understand the amount of pressure Said was working under, though he never compromised with his cherished ideal of 'speaking truth to power'.

As we will see, Said has recurrently returned to his formulations on the intellectual in his subsequent works, most explicitly in *Culture and Imperialism* and *Humanism and Democratic Criticism.* The relevance of Saidian formulations on the role and responsibility of the intellectual cannot be overstressed at a time when authoritarianism and oppression seem to be on the rise.

NOTES

1. It should be noted that the *The World, the Text, and the Critic* was published in 1984, and Said's 'contemporary American left' must be understood as indicative of the period preceding 1984.The same logic would apply to his critique of what he sees as Derrida's overarching concern with textuality.
2. Though generally regarded as one of the founders of postcolonial theory, Said has not been very enthusiastic about the term or the school as such, even though his works uphold possibly the most important concern of postcolonial theory – the criticism of colonialism and colonial discourses.
3. The influence of Said and other influential thinker's (such as Eagleton's) criticism of Derrida seems to have had a strong effect on his later works. Five years after the publication of *The World, the Text, and the Critic*, Derrida published *Force of Law* (1990), followed by widely read works like *Spectres of Marx* (1994) and *Politics of Friendship* (1994). In these works, there is a visible shift in Derrida's focus from textual issues to actual issues.
4. These elaborations on why he prefers Gramsci to Foucault, or in fact, the entire book itself, is also an attempt on Said's part to answer the charges of methodological inconsistency that had been levelled against *Orientalism* (see Chapter 3).

REFERENCES

Cockburn, Alexander. "The FBI and Edward Said". *The Nation*, https://www.thenation.com/article/archive/fbi-and-edward-said/. Accessed 6 March 2023.

Eagleton, Terry. *Literary Theory: An Introduction.* 2nd ed., Maya, 2000.

Eliot, T.S. "Tradition and the Individual Talent". *English Critical Texts: 16th Century to 20th Century*, edited by D.J. Enright and Ernst De Chikera, Oxford UP, 1962, pp. 293–301.

Goulimari, Pelagia. *Literary Criticism and Theory: From Plato to Postcolonialism*. Routledge, 2015.

Said, Edward. W. "Foucault and the Imagination of Power". *Reflections on Exile and Other Essays*, Penguin, 2001, pp. 239–45.

---."History, Literature, and Geography". *Reflections on Exile and Other Essays*, Penguin, 2001, pp. 453–73.

---. *Reflections on Exile and Other Essays.* Penguin, 2001.

---. *Representations of the Intellectual.* Vintage, 1996.

---. *The World, the Text, and the Critic.* Vintage, 1991.

Chapter Five

The Cultural Politics of Imperialism

LITERATURE AND BEYOND

In more ways than one, *Culture and Imperialism* is a continuation and consolidation of the arguments offered in *Orientalism.* While both these classic works explore the linkage between European colonialism and European knowledge traditions, there are a few significant differences between them. These differences, however, make them complementary to each other and not contradictory. *Culture and Imperialism* differs from *Orientalism* on at least three significant counts, as detailed in the following paragraph.

First, there is a shift in focus in terms of the choice of texts. In *Culture and Imperialism*, Said chooses to focus primarily (though not exclusively) on literary texts, especially those that are considered major works of Western literature. We may do well to remind ourselves at this point that *Orientalism* was more concerned with what may be called non-literary texts, from disciplines like anthropology, philology, history, and so on. Second, the book is an elaborate attempt on Said's part to take note of the resistance to the politics and poetics of imperialism. The acknowledgment of resisting voices from the colonies makes the work more nuanced and inclusive. In fact, in doing this, Said was also responding to the charges levelled against *Orientalism* that it did not take note of the resistances put up by the colonised or Oriental cultures. *Culture and Imperialism,* therefore, has been seen as 'a departure from Said's earlier and disablingly one sided account of the colonial encounter' in his previous works, especially *Orientalism* (Gandhi 81). Third, it was also pointed out by many that the very title of Said's *Orientalism* was rather misleading as in that book he spoke mostly about the Middle East, leaving out the Indian subcontinent altogether, which was arguably the most significant place where Orientalist epistemological and imaginative fantasies were played out. In *Culture and Imperialism*, this has also been addressed to a great extent, by including almost chapter-long analyses of two novels on India as well as critical engagement with thinkers from India like Rabindranath Tagore, M. K. Gandhi, Aniket Seal, Ranajit Guha and Partha Chatterjee. Similarly, key anticolonial thinkers from other parts of the world have also been included who were not taken into account in *Orientalism*. It is, however, not a fixed commandment that every book has to talk about everything or engage with every expert of any given field, and what *Orientalism* offers is certainly more important than what it excludes. Nonetheless, keeping these contexts in mind will enable us to appreciate *Culture and Imperialism* in a more engaged fashion.

It is useful to note at the outset that Said does not bother much with the technical distinction generally made between 'colonialism' and 'imperialism' (as is most often the case with him so far as terms and jargon are concerned) – the former term being used for actual territorial occupation and the latter for economic and cultural control from a distant land without actual geographical possession. At one point in *Culture and Imperialism*, he defines the two terms seemingly maintaining the difference between the two. Said says, for instance, '"imperialism" means the practice, the theory, and the attitudes of a dominating metropolitan centre ruling a distant territory; "colonialism", which is almost always a consequence of imperialism, is the implanting of settlements on distant territory' (8). From this definition, it appears that for Said, 'imperialism' is the theoretical aspect and 'colonialism' is the practical aspect of the same phenomenon. The nuance notwithstanding, Said can be seen as using the terms interchangeably in the book, arguably suggesting that the distinction between the two is too thin to merit a meticulous maintenance. In fact, the definition of imperialism given earlier in the book combines both the phenomena: '[I]mperialism means thinking about, settling on, controlling land that you do not possess, that is distant, that is lived on and possessed by others' (5). In other words, 'settling on, controlling land' which are actually features of colonialism proper is included within the meaning of imperialism here. This is how Said actually uses the terms, and I shall also have to use them interchangeably depending on his usage.

Following these definitions, Said provides relevant data establishing the fact that nineteenth century (and early twentieth century, we may add) European empires left all imperial processes of history far behind in terms of their sheer size. By 1914, Europe held almost eighty-five per cent of the earth's surface 'as colonies, protectorates, dependencies, dominions and commonwealths' (6). This is an important point, especially for those who might not understand why postcolonial studies concerns itself mainly with European imperialism and is often silent about the empires and colonies of other cultures and nations. However, mindful of the criticisms of his earlier work, Said often pauses here to reiterate that he has 'kept in mind the idea that the earth is in effect one world' (6) or that '[t]here is in all nationally defined cultures, I believe, an aspiration to sovereignty, to sway, to dominance' (15). It none the less remains the case that these aspirations have found their fullest manifestation in Western countries, particularly England, France and America. The meticulous presentation of factual data related to the process of colonisation also adds to the authenticity of the book from the perspective of social sciences, which is not a very characteristic Saidian style. While he can hardly be faulted for giving wrong information or facts, Said's works have focused more on arguments and ideas. *Culture and Imperialism*, at least its introductory pages, are an exception to this. In the following paragraphs, we will discuss Said's re-reading of the English novelistic tradition, followed by an exploration of his take on the prominent anticolonial thinkers of the world.

THE EMPIRE AND THE NOVEL FORM

The rise of the novel in English literature (and other European literatures too) has been variously related to factors such as the breakdown of the feudal system, the emergence of the middle class, the rise of realism, the industrial revolution and women's autobiographical writings by critics and thinkers like György Lukács, Ian Watt, Arnold Kettle and Juliet Mitchell, among others. In *Culture and Imperialism* however, Said unequivocally identifies colonialism as the chief factor leading to the emergence and the popularity of the novel form. Novelistic representations, in other words, are primarily colonial or imperial representations. Drawing on a large number of novels and novelists from the English literary tradition, he shows how the growth of the novel has a direct parallel in the growth of the empire. While one finds allusions to 'the facts of empire' in almost all nineteenth and twentieth century artefacts of British and French cultures, it appears most prominently in the British novel (73). For instance, the text that is commonly agreed upon as the first novel is Daniel Defoe's *Robinson Crusoe*. It is unmistakably 'about a European who creates a fiefdom for himself on a distant, non-European island' (xiii). Similarly, the wealth that sustains the novelistic worlds of Jane Austen and Charles Dickens, to cite two prominent examples, is clearly generated from maintaining colonies or empires and exploiting the subjects there. More significantly, novelists like Daniel Defoe, Jane Austen, George Eliot, Charles Dickens or Rudyard Kipling never raise doubts over the legitimacy of imperial exploitation or imperialism itself. To the contrary, they attempt to justify the ways of the empire, overtly or covertly.

Charles Dickens, whose works are often preoccupied with representing the plight of the poor, the orphaned and the dispossessed, never condemned the onslaught of British colonialism in India or Africa. In fact, subsequent research has revealed that Dickens was not only a shareholder of the East India Company, but had gone to the extent of suggesting that Orientals should be wiped out as a race.[1] Such research has been the result of Said's tireless efforts to expose the linkage between European colonialism and European or Eurocentric knowledge and culture that began with his *Orientalism,* if not earlier. The tendency to legitimise imperialism that we find in Austen and Dickens continues through the works of writers as diverse as William M. Thackeray, Rudyard Kipling, Joseph Conrad, Arthur Conan Doyle, Rider Haggard,

R. L. Stevenson, George Orwell, Joyce Cary, E. M. Forster, and T. E. Lawrence. As Said summarily observes, 'the empire is everywhere a crucial setting' (74).

Said's reading of politics into culture can be seen both as a continuation of the Marxist tradition of materialist readings of cultural artefacts (his discontent with Marxism as a political philosophy notwithstanding), as well as its modification. The same applies to two of Said's contemporaries: Michel Foucault and Raymond Williams. Foucault and Said have, however, tried to suppress or downplay their affinity with Marx (and Freud as well, in Foucault's case). The same is not true of Raymond Williams who exhibits no discomfort with foregrounding Marx and Marxist tenets in his cultural analyses. All three (and most theorists dealing with the oppression of minority groups by majoritarian ideologies) could be broadly clubbed together as theorists of cultural politics. However, both Williams and Foucault have been largely silent about the cultural politics of colonialism; a point that Said takes note of in *Culture and Imperialism* while acknowledging his debt to their 'genealogical discoveries' (47).

In much the same manner, while Said takes note of the fact that the central concern of most schools of theory and criticism is 'representation', he laments the fact that the problematic nature of representation is rarely seen in its 'full political context, a context which is primarily imperial' (66). This observation was valid when the book was being written in the late 1980s and the early1990s; however, this has been counterbalanced now by interrelated critical and theoretical schools of reading like postcolonial studies, African American studies, Critical Race and Ethnic studies, and so on. Said's works must be fairly credited for this change, though he was never quite in favour of adding labels such as feminism, poststructuralism or even postcolonialism for that matter, to the work of criticism. As discussed in the previous chapter, Said felt such labels create fiefdoms of critics and specialists engaged in insular conversations in obscure jargon with members of the same group, leaving them largely cut off from the world of real politics. For Said, an intellectual or a critic could not be labelled as one if they did not contribute, not only to a better understanding of the world, but a better life for the world, especially for oppressed people. In Said's continuous engagement with the world and 'worldliness', there is an echo of Marx's pronouncement on the urgent need to change the world instead of merely interpreting it (see Marx). The only difference between them in this regard is that while class-based economic exploitation is the key factor for Marx, Said prioritises colonial exploitation as the most important frame of reference. This is, however, not to say that the two are mutually exclusive, though it is also not true that (as Marxist critics like Aijaz Ahmad would have us believe) that Marxism itself squarely addresses all issues related to colonialism as well.

In Said's view, the subtlest and most persistent reinforcement of imperialist ideologies seems to be achieved through its various cultural forms, and not so much through its administrative or directly political apparatuses. Said formulates and advocates the strategy of contrapuntal reading to uncover this nexus.

SHORT TAKES

Contrapuntal Reading

The term 'contrapuntal' which Said repeatedly uses to refer to his readings of the empire and its texts is borrowed from Western music. Etymologically, it derives from the Italian *contrapunto* which actually means 'counterpoint'. In music, the term implies that 'various themes play off with one another, with only a provisional privilege given to any particular one' (*Culture and Imperialism* 59). In critical readings too – as Said formulates it – the term implies not privileging any particular kind of reading. More importantly, it seems to suggest reading a text against its obvious meaning. For instance, in his reading of Jane Austen's *Mansfield Park,* Said goes against the apparent themes of the text which appear to be related to love, marriage and social mobility, and reads the novel as deeply implicated in imperial politics.

Though Said gives this type of reading a specific name – contrapuntal reading – the process is endemic to almost all contemporary schools of criticism, especially those dealing with oppressed or marginalised groups. Each of these schools read texts to see and show how a particular community is marginalised, misrepresented or not represented at all in spite of its key significance. For instance, a feminist critic would highlight the misrepresentation of women, Marxist criticism would focus on the marginalisation of the working class and a queer theorist would explore how non-heteronormative persons are marginalised in a given text. Said's speciality in this regard of course lies in foregrounding the colonial underpinnings of English and other European literatures.

So far as English literature is concerned, contemporary critics usually focus on the 'great' books or authors and attempt to show how traditional readings of the same books or authors ignored crucial issues such as discrimination based on race, gender, class, sexuality and colonisation; issues which these texts uphold, consciously or unconsciously. These readings are often collectively called political reading, oppositional reading or reading against the grain. Said chooses to 'read and interpret English novels, for example, whose engagement (usually suppressed for the most part) with the West Indies or India, say, is shaped and perhaps even determined by the specific history of colonization, resistance, and finally native nationalism' (60).

Theory to Practice: Contrapuntal Readings of Jane Austen, Charles Dickens, Rudyard Kipling and E. M. Forster

A year after India gained independence, the formidable and highly influential British critic F. R. Leavis published his single most important volume of critical work, *The Great Tradition*. In this book, he dwells on and promotes the image of a pristine and primarily pre-Industrial English past (which perhaps never existed) and selects a handful of English authors in whose works that cultural past is reflected. His select four are Jane Austen, George Eliot, Henry James and Joseph Conrad. Idiosyncratic and contentious as the claim is, it is amusing to note that even though they wrote in English, Henry James was an American and Joseph Conrad an immigrant from Poland.

In addition to their being 'English' novelists, Leavis identifies what he sees as 'a reverent openness before life' in these writers (9). Leavis's readings stem from a tradition which is primarily aesthetic and is unlike those schools or theories of criticism that promote political or oppositional readings of literature. Interestingly, Said identifies in these writers (especially Austen, Eliot and Conrad) themes, issues and ideologies that are highly political, especially in terms of their affiliations with imperialism (or 'Zionism' in the case of George Eliot). In *Culture and Imperialism,* Said goes back to Raymond Williams's materialist reading of the English novel form as a take-off point for his contrapuntal reading of these authors. Said reinvents Williams's concept of 'structures of feeling' as 'structures of attitude and reference' in the context of the study of metropolitan cultures, especially in their relation to imperialism. He uses the term 'structures of attitude and reference' to refer to the attitude to imperialism, geographical location or space shown in metropolitan discourse (*Culture and Imperialism* 89–91).

Said does not categorically say that the English novels were the chief factor that caused British imperialism; that is too simplistic and reductive a thought. But at the same time, it is also simplistic to read English novels in complete isolation from their sociopolitical realities, especially the realities of imperialism. By invoking Williams's idea of 'the structure of attitude and reference', Said wants to point to the attitudes of English novels and the novelists towards imperialism and colonialism and also the ways in which the colonies have been represented by them. Said indicates certain major trends amongst the diversity of 'structures of attitude and reference' in the tradition of the English novel. One of his important observations is that there is an organic continuity between earlier novels like *Mansfield Park* and the later ones like *Kim* or *A Passage to India.* Within the general trend of historical study and research on the English novel, these authors and texts are not seen as related except as forming part of the same novelistic tradition. Said, however, finds thematic similarities and continuities between them: 'the Imperial theme', to be precise. While earlier generations of novelists often dealt with it through implications, the later generation of writers delved into it with certitude and confidence. In both cases, what is interesting is that the writers do not question the legitimacy of imperialism and colonialism and seem to be rather happy with Britain's domination and exploitation of its colonies. As Said says, 'it is genuinely troubling to see how little Britain's great humanistic ideas, institutions and monuments, which we still celebrate as having the power ahistorically to command our approval, how little they stand in the way of accelerating the imperial process' (*Culture and Imperialism* 97).

Mansfield Park ***and the Empire***

The novel and other allied art forms are, more often than not, seen as representative of humanist values. However, as Said alerts us, the humanism of English novelists was meant for the English, or at best, Europeans only. As he puts it, 'It is striking that never, in the novel, is that world beyond seen except as subordinate and dominated, the English presence viewed as regulative and normative' (89). The crucial point for Said is that European novels, particularly English novels, reinforce and legitimise the political and cultural supremacy of Europe in the colonies. In other words, these novels continue the trend of Orientalist misrepresentations in a more subtle and therefore, more corrosive way. These readings lead Said to observe what he chooses to call the 'consolidation' of an imperial vision in Jane Austen's *Mansfield Park* (100). For Said, Fanny Price is as much an agent in a larger pattern ('both device and instrument') as she is a full-fledged character (101).

Instead of focusing on issues such as marriage, love and the social mobility of the protagonist Fanny Price – issues that are read as central to Austen's novels – Said's reading of *Mansfield Park* foregrounds the issue of colonialism: 'What sustains this life materially is the Bertram estate in Antigua, which is not doing well' (101). There is an implicit parallel between Sir Thomas Bertram's control of his colonial plantation at Antigua and Fanny Price's insistence on morality and discipline. If Sir Bertram is a colonial master, Fanny is a colonialist in the making. Fanny's moral presence and voice in Sir Thomas' absence and her inability to relate to the play *Lover's Vows* (by Elizabeth Inchbald based on August von Kotzebue's *Das kind der liebe*) to be staged by friends and cousins of the Bertrams are, for Said, indicative of her metamorphosis into a colonial being. Equally interesting is the return of Sir Thomas to Mansfield Park. He returns just in time to stop the 'libertinage' at Mansfield Park and re-establish his authority at home. Said sees these two as apparently disparate but actually convergent processes of 'the growth of Fanny's importance to Bertram's economy, including Antigua, and Fanny's own steadfastness in the face of numerous challenges, threats and surprises' (102). Further, Austen's imagination 'works with steel like rigour' and exerts equal narrative authority on both these processes, exhibiting 'a mode that we might call geographical and spatial clarification' (102).

It would be interesting to pursue a reading of *Mansfield Park* in terms of the politics of presence and absence as Said has recommended. At one level, the colony in Antigua whose wealth sustains the metropolitan setting of Mansfield Park is absent from the novel's representational canvas. At another level, there is the profound absence of Sir Thomas Bertram from the metropolitan setting which, interestingly, enhances Fanny's metamorphosis into a potential coloniser. As suggested by Said, Bertram's corrective measures at Mansfield Park can be seen as an intertextual repetition of Crusoe's setting things in order in *Robinson Crusoe.* In both cases, order and colonialism exist in close collaboration, though it is more explicit in Defoe than Austen. Taking a cue from Bertram's imposition of order in his home, Said goes on to suggest that Bertram regulates his colony in a similar manner at Antigua. Bertram's return from Antigua also coincides with the narrative's return to authority and discipline. For Said, this is also the moment of Austen's synchronisation of domestic and international authority. Further, the novel is implicated in issues like ordination, law, and propriety associated with the actual rule and possession of territory. For a character like Fanny, spaces like Mansfield Park cannot be inherited but only acquired in much the same way as an Englishman can acquire overseas property only by becoming a coloniser: 'I think Austen sees what Fanny does as a domestic or small-scale movement in space that corresponds to the larger, more openly colonial movements of Sir Thomas, her mentor, the man whose estate she inherits. The two movements depend on each other' (105).

While Jane Austen cannot be said to be concerned with the empire the same way that Conrad or Kipling are, the fact remains that she too considers British colonies as the empire's rightful possessions. In fact, by the time Austen was writing this novel colonial investments in the Caribbean and South America had become crucial to British politics and culture. Sir Thomas Bertram's trips to Antigua, therefore, are 'absolutely crucial to the action' of the novel (106). To use another Saidian formulation discussed previously, the 'worldliness' of *Mansfield Park* includes the existence of an English estate dependent on overseas sustenance. Given that the estate is maintained by slavery, the 'humanist' and 'aesthetic' stature of the text is further strained. In other words, given that *Mansfield Park* as a novel presupposes the complete subordination of Antigua (which is represented through its absence), the novel can no longer be seen as ideologically innocent. Traditional critics like Leavis have avoided this aspect of Austen's novels. Therefore, Said is right in suggesting that 'interpreting Jane Austen depends on *who* does the interpreting, *when* it is done, and no less important, from *where* it is done' (111).

Said's reading of imperialism in *Mansfield Park* has invited criticism on the grounds of wilful misreading and gross generalisations. Moore-Gilbert, for instance, objects to Said's 'use of this one work by a single author to generalize about the existence of a wholly developed system of ideas about empire across the entire range of nineteenth-century literature' (68). But Moore-Gilbert seemingly misses the fact that in *Culture and Imperialism*, Said does refer to the workings of a colonial consciousness in quite a few nineteenth-century novels such as *Dombey and Son* (13–14), *Hard Times* (88), *Lord Jim* (198) and *Nostromo* (28), though he has not gone into detailed explications for each of these. Further, there are detailed explorations of other novels by Dickens, Kipling, Conrad and Forster, as we shall see in a moment. Moore-Gilbert's criticism of Said therefore does not seem to be unbiased. Additionally, Said's interpretive strategy is quite inclusive. He goes to the extent of saying that his readings can be seen as 'completing or complementing others, not discounting or displacing them' (114).

Said is also aware of the fact that to expect Jane Austen to treat slavery as 'an abolitionist or a newly liberated slave' would, just be counterfactual (115). Further, Said's critique of Austen does not imply the dismissal of Austen's merit as a writer at all, nor does it contest the excellence of the novel. Rather, he resents the fact that 'subaltern, minority or disadvantaged voices, attack her [Jane Austen], and others like her, retrospectively, for being white, privileged, insensitive, complicit' (115). In Said's view, therefore, the novel's ideological complicity with imperialism is not antithetical to its excellence – literary, aesthetic, or otherwise. Its colonial complicity has, in fact, made the worldliness of *Mansfield Park* a complex one: 'A lesser work wears its historical affiliation more plainly, its worldliness is simple and direct' (116).

Representation of the Colony in Great Expectations

The Saidian strategy of interrogating the canonical texts of English and other European literature entails re-reading, not replacing. While it partially stems from his belief in the artistic and aesthetic merits of great texts even as he stresses their political underpinnings, Said is also acutely aware of the fact that a mere replacement of a given canon by any other would ultimately replicate many of the orthodoxies of what it seeks to replace. In fact, Said saw a similar thing happening with poststructuralism which led him to write *The World, the Text, and the Critic.* Therefore, he insists on the twin prerogatives of historic–political reading of texts as well as avoiding the tendency to turn knowledge into watertight compartments of academic fiefdoms. Ania Loomba, an important postcolonial critic, has expressed a similar concern: 'Do we [as postcolonial critics] end up over-emphasising cultural/racial difference and alterity, albeit from a different ideological standpoint than those of colonial discourse?' (91). Said's re-readings of colonial discourses provide a better model, precisely because it stops short of upholding any essentialist or idealist image of the colonised even as it exposes the atrocities and imperialist designs of those discourses.

Said's strategy of reading the empire in the novel and the novel in the empire leads to yet another original interpretation: that of *Great Expectations* by Charles Dickens. In *Culture and Imperialism,* Said provides his critical reading of the Dickens novel in the 'Introduction' itself (see xv–xvii), but I have chosen to discuss it after *Mansfield Park*, keeping in mind the chronological development of the English novel. Drawing on research works on the formation of Australia as a penal colony, Said argues (in much the same way as in his reading of Antigua into *Mansfield Park*) that the novel is heavily reliant on Australia for the very construction and movement of its plot. And yet Australia is something that is never explicitly represented in *Great Expectations*.

The basic theme of *Great Expectations* is quite similar to many other Dickensian novels, including the quasi-autobiographical *David Copperfield*: a poor or economically disadvantaged boy desires to become a gentleman. In *Great Expectations,* the boy is named Philip Pirrip, or Pip – the more frequently used name. Pip's dream of doing well in life is realised on the basis of generous grants periodically awarded by a benefactor who remains unknown and unnamed for the greater part of the novel. This benefactor finally turns out to be a criminal called Abel Magwitch. Pip had, as a child, once met Magwitch when the latter had escaped from prison and helped him with food and other crucial supplies. While the Pip–Magwitch relationship does not take centre stage in *Great Expectations*, it is the moving force behind the narrative. Pip believes his benefactor to be a rich, idiosyncratic lady called Miss Havisham, while in reality it is the criminal Abel Magwitch. Immediately after their first encounter, Magwitch is caught again, convicted by a court and transported to Australia, which was then a penal colony. Eventually, he makes a lot of money there. However, Magwitch remembers Pip's help, which is why he keeps sending Pip money. Magwitch's reappearance in London and revealing himself to Pip frustrates the latter, as he resents having accepted money from a criminal, albeit unknowingly. There is a reconciliation however, but the protagonist's rejection of Magwitch (and consequently Australia) is far stronger than the token acceptance he is given. Magwitch, as Said says, is 'in fact unacceptable, being from Australia, a penal colony designed for the rehabilitation but not the repatriation of transported English criminals' (xv). Thus, though Magwitch is allowed a grudging return to England, the spirit of the novel and the novelist is against giving any space or representation to Australia whose wealth sustains the novel's narrative world. As in the case of *Mansfield Park,* traditional readings of *Great Expectations* prefer to read the text in relation to its metropolitan location only: England, or Great Britain by extension. Said argues that it is time we read the text from the view of what it refuses to represent: the colonisation of Australia. What connects Dickens and Magwitch to Australia is not an incidental or fanciful setting; they are actually 'participants in it, through the novel and through a much older and wider experience between England and its overseas territories' (xvi).

Said also foregrounds the imperial ethos of another Dickens novel, *Dombey and Son*, in a crisp but effective reading. The opening lines where Dickens emphasises the significance of the birth of Dombey's son reads, 'The earth was made for Dombey and Son to trade in, and the sun and moon were made to give them light' (qtd. in *Culture and Imperialism* 13). Taking a cue from Raymond Williams, Said stakes that such assertions were possible and 'specific to British novelists in the 1840s' only because of the existence of the British empire which every British person could claim as their rightful possession (14). Said puts forward valid evidence and arguments in favour of his theses on the inextricable linkage between imperialism and the novel form.

Since critics like Moore-Gilbert have tried to argue that Said's observations are based on a reading of only one novel (*Mansfield Park*, discussed above), I have chosen to highlight his readings of almost all significant novels in *Culture and Imperialism.* I also want to reiterate another important aspect of Said's reading that is often lost sight of: these are, according to him, great texts of literature. Their greatness exists despite, or perhaps because of, the colonial complexities they inhere in. As Said says, 'understanding that connection does not reduce or diminish the novels' value as works of art: on the contrary, because of their *worldliness,* because of their complex affiliations with their real setting, they are *more* interesting and *more* valuable as works of art' (13).

Kim *and Colonialism*

While writers like Austen and Dickens portray the colony marginally or by implications or absences, later writers like Kipling, Conrad and Forster reveal a more detailed, direct and confident engagement with Britain's colonial territories. This is hardly surprising given the greater consolidation of British imperialism by the time Conrad, Kipling and Forster were writing. Said suggests, to remind ourselves once again, that there is a correspondence between the growth of the English novel and the growth of British imperialism. Rudyard Kipling's *Kim* can be rightly seen as the most detailed novelistic representation of the India of its time. However, the fact that it is detailed does not mean that it is comprehensive or authentic. Said's chief argument is that Kipling's *Kim* represents only the white man's view of India and miserably fails in recording acts of resistance to British imperialism, which were widely prevalent in India by the time *Kim* was written (1902).

Kipling, as Said suggests, attempts to portray India as a place that resists both time and change. Kipling's India, in fact, is a textbook example of how the Orientalists were happy to portray the Orient as sterile, traditional and resistant to change. Perhaps Kipling's imperial mindset is most clearly visible in his assumption of 'a basically uncontested empire' (162). As argued above, by the time *Kim* was written India had started registering strong protests against British imperialism. The Sepoy Mutiny or Rebellion of 1857 was arguably the strongest protest till then and is often read by historians and political analysts as India's first war for independence from the British Raj. Kipling, however, does not display any sympathy for the Mutiny at all; nor does he register the fact that there was growing resentment against the Raj almost everywhere in the Indian subcontinent by then.[2]

Instead, Kipling chooses a loyal Indian soldier to represent his own view of the Sepoy Mutiny as sheer, unmitigated madness. What Kipling wilfully suppresses in his representation of the mutiny is that most Indians, including the soldier's compatriots, would 'regard him as (at the very least) a traitor to his people' (*Culture and Imperialism* 178). Said argues that the world represented in the novel was split into two major worldviews – pro- and anti-imperial. While Kipling does all that he can do as a writer to represent the pro-imperialist view, anti-imperialist or anticolonial views are conspicuous by their absence: 'So far is Kipling from showing two worlds in conflict that he has studiously given us only one, and eliminated any chance of conflict appearing altogether' (179).

This is, by no means, a singular occurrence in the novel; *Kim* is rife with such representations and incidents privileging the coloniser's view to the extent that all anticolonial voices are banished from its narration. At another point in the novel, one encounters the 'Old Widow' who suggests that the British judicial model and knowledge of India makes them better rulers than the natives themselves. Commenting against such colonial biases, Said points to the total absence of the representation of resistances to the empire in the novel (179–80). Said's foregrounding of the imperial aspirations of certain novels sacrosanct to the English literary canon can be seen as an act of resistance in itself. In this light, his reading of *Kim* is an exposé of imperialism in a novel that usually passes for a classic adolescent adventure story.

More interestingly, Said finds that while contemporaneous novels set in England or Europe exhibit disillusionment and disenchantment, *Kim* is full of ambitions and aspirations. Here, Said is building on Lukács's *The Theory of the Novel* where Lukács argues that the novel is the epic of the modern world. However, while ancient (and medieval) epics describe a 'happy, satisfied world', the world of the novel, consequent upon the advent of modernity, industrialisation, and so on is the world of the 'fallen, unhappy state, its "lost transcendence"' (*Culture and Imperialism* 189). Novels like *Jude the Obscure* or *Great Expectations*, for instance, show their protagonists' understanding the futility of their ambitions and their consequent acceptance of failures in life. This trend has led to certain overarching critical formulations such as Hardy's 'tragic vision' and, subsequently, disillusionment and fragmentation in modernist literature.

But while Kipling's contemporaries in England talk about the evils of industrialisation and modernisation in their works, *Kim* does not dwell on any of these possibly because Britain was enjoying nearly unchallenged supremacy in its colonies and was increasingly engaged in the annexation of lands and kingdoms. Said remarks, 'Because he gets beyond this paralyzing, dispiriting impasse, Kim O' Hara is so remarkably optimistic a character. Like those other heroes of Imperial fiction, his actions result in victories, not defeats' (190).

Kim also repeatedly betrays the Orientalist outlook of its writer. Despite the fact that Kipling was born in India and had worked there for a considerable period of time, he seems to present Indians as stereotypes in conformity with the structures and strictures of Orientalism. For instance, the trope of the 'Bengali babu', which is almost always a source of humour and irony, has its origins in Kipling's racist attitudes. Kipling's babu is called Hurree Chunder Mukherjee, but he is hardly ever addressed by that name in the novel and Kipling seems to be more interested in making him a representative of all educated Bengalis serving the British government. Similarly, while the piousness of the Tibetan Lama is portrayed with sympathy, there is no deep engagement with Buddhist spiritual philosophy. The Lama appears more as a representative of 'Oriental' spirituality, a subject that is fascinating to Orientalists. More particularly, the Lama represents what Said has termed the 'good Orient' in *Orientalism.* In much the same way, almost all the Indian characters exist as types, without any nuance or variations; in his penchant for 'Orientalising', Kipling does away with both reality and individuality. Said cites various statements from the novel to establish his point that *Kim* is more indicative of Kipling's colonial and racial prejudices than it is an authentic account of the India of that time (181).

Kipling's partial and biased representation of India is neither unique nor an aberration. This forms part of the general Orientalist attitude towards India and other parts of the Eastern world. The imperial powers used these (mis)representations to legitimise their subjugation and exploitation of the colonised while claiming they were carrying out a civilising mission – such being 'the white man's burden' – and using it to uphold 'the basic superiority of the white European male who should always retain the upper hand' (182). Further, while debates were already emerging as to the legitimacy of colonialism, very few Europeans were ready to counter the belief that the Europeans were inherently superior to the Oriental races and religions. As Said argues, 'Statements like "The Hindu is inherently untruthful and lack moral courage" were expressions of wisdom from which very few, least of all the Governors of Bengal, dissented' (182). In other words, Rudyard Kipling remained undisturbed or even untouched by the rhetoric and praxis of anticolonialism. Said maintains that 'for him [Kipling] it was India's best destiny to be ruled by England' (176).

India in A Passage to India

Published in 1924 during the heyday of British imperialism in India as well as the intense resistance to it, E.M. Forster's *A Passage to India* has frequently been listed as one of the best English novels ever written. Unlike Austen, Dickens or Kipling, however, Forster shows a deeper sympathy with the Indian ethos, yet something holds him back from envisioning a complete unification between the British and Indians. Said's reading of Forster's *A Passage to India* posits the cultural exchange between the coloniser and the colonised as the central concern of the novel. According to Said, Forster was interested in exploring the 'cultural grounds on which both native and liberal Europeans lived and understood each other', and also in knowing, if possible, 'How much could they grant each other?' (241). Said's reading leads him to a feeling that Forster's attitude towards India, at best, is ambivalent.

Further, Said feels that India in the novel does not represent India as such; rather it is a trope or symbol representing all that is generally found to be beyond representation about the Orient according to the Anglo-European novelistic tradition. This novelistic tradition, as suggested earlier, was also a continuation of the Orientalist tradition in many ways. The un-representable, according to Said, comprises 'vastness, incomprehensible creeds, secret missions, histories and social forms' (241). In other words, while Forster is arguably less of an imperialist than Kipling, he too is caught up in the alluring idea of an exotic yet static and timeless India. Similarly, in spite of his deeper sympathy for the Indians in contrast with his novelistic forebears, Forster too is unable to envision even a democratic equality between the British and the Indian, let alone a union of the two. Thus Forster's familiarity with India and her ethos remains superficial, and the lens through which he understands India is largely in congruence with the Orientalist imaginary which has always sought to design and designate India as an incomprehensible, mysterious, spiritual and unsystematic country (243).

It is interesting to note, in this context, how Fielding (the protagonist of the novel), and hence Forster, perceives Hinduism and Islam in India. While the European mind is baffled by the polymorphous pantheon of Hindu gods and devotees, it finds Islam easier to apprehend given its monotheistic tenets. As Said sees it, 'Hindus, according to the novel, believe that all is muddle, all is connected, God is one, is not, was not, was. By contrast, Islam, as represented by Aziz, apprehends order and a specific God' (244). However, though 'Forster is slightly nearer Islam than Hinduism in *A Passage to India*, but the final lack of sympathy is obvious' (244).

Despite his relatively closer exposure to the cultural, social and political realities of India, Forster's India remains a place of colonial fantasy as well as subjugation, much like Kipling's. Fielding, for instance, is highly disappointed by Aziz's nationalist spirit and thinks it is only 'posturing' (244). This, interestingly, is a repetition of Kipling's attitude towards the Sepoy Mutiny of 1857. Said cites Francis Hutchins's statement that the Indian 'nationalist movement, to an astonishing extent, drew no response from the British imagination in India' (244) in support of his argument that Forster's (or Kipling's, for that matter) attitude to Indian nationalism was not unique, but representative of the general British attitude. Consequently, Said argues that 'The novel's helplessness neither goes all the way and condemns (or defends) British colonialism, nor condemns or defends Indian nationalism' (245).

For Said, Forster's ambivalence towards Indian nationalism strengthens the worldview and morale of British colonialism in India. While Forster's ambivalence makes him perhaps less sure of his affiliations to imperialism than Kipling, he is unable to accept India as an independent political entity. Such an acceptance would act against British imperial ideology, and Forster does not seem to be ready to do that. Forster makes his disapproval of Indians engaging in politics remarkably clear when he says 'He was glad that Aziz, whom he *loved* and whose family was with his own, took no interest in politics' (qtd. in *Culture and Imperialism* 246, emphasis added). The possibility of a homoerotic relationship between Fielding and Aziz has been posited by theorists but the visible common factor inducing their love for each other is Aziz's apolitical nature. Fictional nature aside, the author's ideology in this case is certainly pro-imperial if not imperialist. While Forster does not appear to be hesitant in portraying the English as racists and as aggressive rulers, by the same token, he cannot appreciate India's aspirations towards nationhood. The novel rejects India's nationalist aspirations as merely anti-British sentiment, often in language that is derogatory as well as counterfactual. For instance, while describing an anti-British/nationalist group comprising 'Hindus, Moslems, two Sikhs, two Parsis, a Jain and Native Christian', Forster declaims 'As long as someone abused the English, all went well, but nothing constructive has been achieved, and if the English were to leave India, the committee would vanish also' (qtd. in *Culture and Imperialism* 246). Said's in-depth reading of *A Passage to India* goes against the general trend of seeing Forster as a compassionate intermediary between two civilisations.

Said's reading of Forster has been corroborated by other influential postcolonial critics such as Benita Parry and Sara Suleri. Their readings have also added issues of gender and sexuality, issues that are generally missing in Saidian analyses. In her *Postcolonial Studies: A Materialist Critique,* Benita Parry closely follows Said in claiming that the novel grossly misconstrues India as only a mythical and mystical land; 'the novel also construes an obfuscated realm where the secular is scanted, and in which India's long traditions of Mathematics, Science and technology, history, linguistics and jurisprudence have no place' (163). This is a vindication of Said's long standing contention that Western epistemological traditions (and aesthetic and cultural traditions too) do not represent the Orient per se, but an 'Orientalised' Orient. Sara Suleri's reading of Forster in *The Rhetoric of English India* chooses to focus on the tension generated by the homoerotic undertones of the novel, with an acute awareness that the novel operates within the ambit of colonial discourse. The homoerotic undertones seemingly provide an alternative space of friendship where Aziz and Fielding can meet, in spite of the colonial hierarchy separating them. Suleri seems to suggest that the only way Fielding and Aziz can get closer than they are is through the performance of gestures. The hierarchies of British imperialism, in other words, have no protocols under which a native and a British person can be equal to each other. This interpretation reinforces Said's reading of the novel as one that keeps the colonial hierarchy very much in place, its occasional wavering to the contrary notwithstanding. In fact the novel cannot show this interracial homoeroticism growing into a full-fledged homosexual bonding due to the existing colonial rules prohibiting the equality of races as well as same sex relationships.[3] Thus, the empire cannot give recognition to this male bonding either racially or sexually, and consequently, neither can Forster. As Suleri says,

> While the exchange between Fielding and Aziz is represented in resolutely heterosexual terms—Aziz plans to visit brothels in Calcutta, Fielding marries Stella—their friendship plays out a subterranean homoeroticism that functions as a figure for the limits of colonial epistemology. . . . Fielding's desire for intimacy, in other words, can register only as a violation of Aziz's space within the colonial world: rather than heighten the cultural trust between the two, the visit initially serves to exacerbate the distance between them. (142)

The readings of Western culture and literature in terms of their affiliation to colonialism that Said initiated in *Orientalism* and explored further in *Culture and Imperialism* has been followed by a wide range of critics with postcolonial leanings apart from Parry and Suleri. Gayatri Chakravorty Spivak, for instance, can be said to both follow the Said of *Orientalism* and prefigure the Said of *Culture and Imperialism* in her 'Three Women's Texts and A Critique of Imperialism' (1985). In this essay, Spivak foregrounds the racist underpinnings of Charlotte Bronte's *Jane Eyre* which, she thinks, grossly misrepresents the colonised. Taking exception to Western feminism's jubilant celebration of what they see as the victory of the eponymous heroine in the novel, Spivak states that Jane's success is achieved at the cost of Bertha Mason's annihilation – a character who is both woman and colonised. In her words, 'Bertha's function in *Jane Eyre* is to render indeterminate the boundary between human and animal and thereby to weaken her entitlement under the spirit if not the letter of the Law' (Spivak 249).

SHORT TAKES

Camus and Colonialism

An unmitigated support for French colonial rule in Algeria informs the life as well as the works of Albert Camus (1913–60). Frequently seen as one of the major figures of European modernist literature, Camus is also valued as a highly influential philosopher and a political thinker who contributed substantially to our understanding of absurdism, existentialism and nihilism, among others. However, what often went unnoticed was his staunch imperialist stance. This is the point of contention raised by Said in the section 'Camus and the French Imperial Experience' (204–24). Said laments the fact that Camus 'survives today as a "universalist" writer with roots in a now forgotten colonialism' (208). Camus's patterns of hiding the brutalities of French colonial rule in Algeria are essentially the same as Kipling and Forster's misrepresentation of the colonial realities in India. Just as Kipling and Forster either hide or underplay the anticolonial struggles in India, a deeper, contextual reading of Camus reveals his dismissal of Algerian anticolonial struggles. Similarly, in his assumption that Algeria is a rightful possession of the French (and not of Algerian themselves), he resembles Austen, Dickens and Conrad as well. A detailed discussion, therefore, would appear repetitive. A specific tendency of Camus's politics of representation, however, may be pointed out. Said argues that Camus represents the French as highly individualised characters with all necessary details; but, even when at times Camus tends to represent the Arab side of the story, it is very superficial. In Said's words: '[t]his Arab is not named and seems to be without a history, let alone a mother and father' (212).

READING RESISTANCE, WRITING OPPOSITIONS

Titled 'Resistance and Opposition', the third chapter of *Culture and Imperialism* extensively deals with the poetics and politics of resistances to imperialism from almost all over the world. Said attempts to answer a major charge that has been recurrently brought against him since the publication of *Orientalism*: that he does not take cognisance of the resistances to colonialism. In doing so, he accommodates a wide range of anticolonial and humanist thinkers in the book such as Abdul Kader, Aimé Césaire, Leopold Senghor, Frantz Fanon, W. B. Yeats, W. E. B. Du Bois, Wole Soyinka, Chinua Achebe, Hannah Arendt and Ngũgĩ wa Thiong'o. Indian thinkers – anticolonial as well as postcolonial – such as Rabindranath Tagore, Aniket Seal, Partha Chatterjee and Ranajit Guha prominently figure, unlike in any other work by Said. He also makes forays into the problems of decolonised nations, such as nationalism, especially by way of building on the arguments of the thinkers mentioned above.

This is a daunting range and only a reading of the original text can familiarise one with the details of Said's critical engagements with these thinkers and their works. It will be useful here, however, to point out the broader themes and contentions that Said presents in recognition of the struggles of colonised peoples. Given that the book is about cultural politics, his focus is more on the cultural or ideological components of these struggles than chronological accounts of political fights. Said identifies three interrelated topics that he feels have informed the process of decolonisation. The first topic is that of various cultural nationalisms that took shape in protest against imperialism. These could be characterised as revisionist constructions of pre-colonial national pasts that create a sense of pride among colonised peoples and encourages them to counter the feeling of racial inferiority brought in by imperialism. Various kinds of nationalist and proto-nationalist writings in the form of novels, plays, songs, slave narratives, spiritual accounts or autobiographies and prison literature are indispensable parts of this revisionist process. We may add here that Rabindranath Tagore's novels *Gora* and *Ghore Baire* ('The Home and the World'), Raja Rao's novel *Kanthapura*, M. K. Gandhi's famous autobiography *My Experiments with Truth* and Aurobindo Ghosh's spiritual prison diary *Tales of Prison Life* are some of the interesting instances from India in this regard. Said refers to the historical novels of Girgi Zaydan which promoted an anticolonial nationalist consciousness in Egypt. In his unique contrapuntal way, Said also reminds his readers that the narratives of such nationalisms are more imagined than real. In the examples that we have given above, however, Tagore's novels are unique in so far as they simultaneously promote and punctuate the nationalist surges of pre-independent India.

The second topic is about the idea that resistance is not only a reaction to imperialism, but 'an alternative way of conceiving human history' (260). This consciousness leads to a third development where there is 'a noticeable pull away from separatist nationalism towards a more integrative view of human community and human liberation' (261). I would like to add that all these stages of development are reflected in the Indian polymath Rabindranath Tagore's development as a poet and an intellectual. In the beginning of his poetic career, the dominant tone was that of patriotism; singing the praises of his province Bengal in eloquent and melodious phrases. This gradually transformed into a strong sense of Indian nationalism. There is some justification in the commonly held argument that Tagore was the most representative figure of India as a nation before the emergence of Gandhi. However, Tagore became increasingly suspicious of nationalism, particularly European nationalisms, and his lectures on nationalism bear eloquent testimony to the fact that he ultimately saw it as a dehumanising trap whose only merit lay in fencing off other competing nationalisms. Said catches the essence of Tagore's critiques of nationalism with remarkable precision: 'The Nation is for Tagore a tight and unforgiving receptacle of power producing conformity' and India's answer to that should be by providing 'not a competing nationalism, but a creative solution to the divisiveness produced by racial consciousness' (259). It is important to note Tagore's (along with W. E. B. Du Bois's and Said's) repeated warnings that a criticism of colonialism should not translate into an instinctual hatred of Europeans. It is not the Europeans who are responsible for colonialism, Tagore says, but 'the judicious niggardliness of the Nation that has taken upon itself the white man's burden of criticizing the East' (qtd. in *Culture and Imperialism* 259). In other words, Tagore and others like him have also been fierce critics of insular and regressive nationalisms, which is called 'nativism' in contemporary critical parlance.

Frantz Fanon's critical interventions that elaborate on this theme become crucial here. In fact, of all the thinkers and intellectuals that Said chooses to discuss, Fanon seems to receive greater critical engagement than others. Fanon, one of the key anticolonial voices of the twentieth century, finds a place in *Culture and Imperialism* as someone with the double vision of seeing and resisting the atrocities of colonial rule, as well as what he himself called the 'pitfalls of national consciousness' (Fanon n.p.).

SHORT TAKES

W. B. Yeats as a Poet of Decolonisation

One of the two most anthologised sections of Said's *Culture and Imperialism* is the one titled 'Yeats and Decolonization' (the other being 'Jane Austen and the Empire'). Though originally conceived as a part of *Culture and Imperialism*, this highly nuanced critical reading of Yeats was also delivered as a lecture at the Yeats International School at Sligo and the Dia Art Foundation in New York City. Said's point of departure in his re-reading of Yeats comes from his disagreement with what he sees as Yeats's complete assimilation 'into the canon as well as into the discourses of modern English literature and European high modernism' (265). While this canonisation of Yeats is often mindful of his Irish backgrounds and contexts, Yeats's towering significance as a nationalist poet articulating the sufferings and aspirations of the Irish people under a colonial power is often overlooked. Even greater irony lies in the fact that Yeats is often quoted or cited as a poet 'whose poetry warned of nationalist excesses' (283). Lines like 'Things fall apart; the centre cannot hold' or 'The best lack all conviction, while the worst/Are full of passionate intensity' are randomly selected by American liberals to denounce ongoing revolutionary struggles in the non-Western world. As Said phrases it, 'Their use of Yeats is minatory: remain orderly, or you're doomed to a frenzy you cannot control'. However, these thinkers only issue warnings and do not find it worth considering 'as to how, in an inflamed colonial situation, the colonized are supposed to hold the center' (283).

While it is true that at certain points Yeats was discomforted by mindless resistance or violence, what is truer (according to Said) is that Yeats is first and foremost a poet of Irish national resistance to British colonialism. Furthermore, Yeats's dissatisfaction with violence is 'the first important announcement in the context of decolonization of the need to balance violent force with an exigent political and organizational process' (284). Even Fanon's similar assertions come 'almost half a century later' (284). Much like other poets of decolonisation, Yeats's poetic attempts at defining the contours of an ideal community or people are also, in Said's view, symptomatic of a strong and sustained spirit of resistance to colonialism.

Another interesting aspect of Said's piece on Yeats is its broad comparative dimension: he draws parallels between Yeats and a host of anticolonial writers like Wole Soyinka, Pablo Neruda, Aimé Césaire and Mahmoud Darwish. What Said does through these comparisons is that he tries to suggest a common pattern of anticolonial and anti-imperial struggles across the globe.

While all anticolonial struggles are important in achieving freedom from the oppressive power structures of colonialism and imperialism, Said feels the human race must outgrow nativist ideologies which assert that the indigenous cultural identity of one's own place or community is the best and that one must uphold and promote only that. In his words, 'In any case nativism is *not* the only alternative. There is the possibility of a more generous and pluralistic vision of the world' (277).

Indeed, while nationalist ideologies provide an epistemological and moral boost to anticolonial struggles across the globe, they can become orthodoxies in themselves. Every nationalist ideology is mostly built on fixed rules of inclusion and exclusion. While Said does not completely endorse Benedict Anderson's work (he objects to Anderson's 'mistakenly linear periodizations', for instance), he is well aware of the poetics and politics of othering that is often employed by nations and governments, mostly along the lines of imaginary communities, borders and histories (280). One could say that Said and other Palestinians continue to be victims of the nationalist ideology and historiography of Zionism which in turn owes a large part of its origins to the highly destructive and ultimately genocidal constructs of the aggressive nationalism espoused by Nazi Germany.

The need for an incisive critique of aggressive nationalist rhetoric draws Said to Partha Chatterjee and the former models his re-invocation of the corrosive dimensions of nationalist ideologies after Chatterjee. Following Chatterjee, Said talks of how part of the complexities of nationalism also derive from the fact that while anticolonial struggles are generally led by 'poets like Tagore and charismatic presences like Gandhi' (as they can mobilise people to that end to a greater degree), leadership passes to more pragmatic and self-conscious state builders after independence (319). What finally happens, according to Said, is that these newly independent countries sooner or later find themselves co-opted into the system of 'global capitalism, commanded at the top by the handful of leading industrial countries' (320). The struggle for liberation, therefore, must continue well after political independence.

Tagore and Du Bois's critique of nativism or Partha Chatterjee's interrogation of the role of global capitalism in formerly colonised countries, however, are not to be conflated or confused with the view of those who use these and other arguments to suggest that colonialism was a better option. Thinkers like Elie Kedourie, Eric Hobsbawm and Ernest Gellner have, for instance, expressed 'discomfort with non-Western societies acquiring national independence which is "foreign" to their ethos' (261). Such opinions seem to be symptomatic of the persistence of an imperialist ethos among Western intelligentsia which could be called the 'colonial continuum'. Said makes us aware that such an opinion exists among non-Western thinkers and writers, such as V. S. Naipaul, as well. Said has always been critical of Naipaul's representation of the non-Western world, particularly the Islamic world. In *Culture and Imperialism,* however, he finds Naipaul's *A Bend in the River* useful to the extent that it helps illustrate the multifarious problems of newly independent nation states that have often given rise to 'national security states, to dictatorships, oligarchies, one party systems' (320). What he objects to is that Naipaul seems to use such instances to lament the disappearance of imperialism and 'indict the post-colonial states for having succeeded unconditionally in gaining independence' (320).

It can hardly be over-emphasised that European colonisation of the globe has altered the courses of history, geography and economy of colonised nations to such an extent that the world has been split into two unequal halves – a situation which may continue for a very long time. As far as previously colonised nations are concerned, they can neither retreat to a pre-colonial past when they were as autonomous as first world nations, nor can they be at par with first world nations in terms of their share in global capital, metrics of literacy, medical facilities and so on. While the rise of China and Japan may be exceptional, this does not alter the reality of a large population who live in subhuman conditions in most other post-colonial nations. It also seems as if the erstwhile direct colonial exploitation by European countries is being continued in the form of a more intense, albeit indirect, imperial or neocolonial exploitation by the United States of America. The scholarly and cultural misrepresentation of non-Europeans by Anglo-French Orientalists continues to be practised by American media and subject experts and direct colonial exploitation has been replaced by apparently 'universal' humanist phenomena such as globalisation and economic liberalisation. It is on the labour and exploitation of non-European races and peoples that the American empire is being built; a phenomenon reminiscent of how European empires were built.

The fourth chapter of *Culture and Imperialism* is 'Freedom from Dominion in the Future', reminding us that we have to be vigilant lest we once again fall prey to the vicious circles of colonialism even as we are already in the grasp of global capitalism or neocolonialism. His major concern here is 'American ascendancy' – the rise of America as the 'last superpower' after the collapse of Soviet Russia (341). This is yet another recurrent concern in Said's work: *Orientalism*, *The Question of Palestine*, *Covering Islam* and a number of articles all deal with American imperialist and interventionist strategies.[4] It is important, however, to note that Said also places on record the fact that dissenting literature has always existed and survived in the United States. This literature can be seen as acting against 'the overall national and official performance' (347).

Further, Said's critique of American policies or Eurocentrism in general should not understood (as it has often been, unfortunately) as a championing of Arabism or Islamic statehood. He has been sharply critical of the fact that democracy is virtually non-existent in the Middle East, which has only 'privileged oligarchies and privileged ethnic groups' (363) under which the larger body of citizens badly suffers. Similarly, he expresses strongly worded resentment against the rise of religious sentiments in universities located in the Arab world. He alleges that the English language is being trimmed of all its literary affiliations so that it becomes a vehicle for 'Islamic revivalism' (369).

The job of a critic or an intellectual, Said avers, is to resist the dehumanising dimension of imperialism/colonialism; and this resistance becomes effective only when we contest not only the visible forces of oppression (economic and political), but the invisible and more pernicious forces of colonial ideologies which proliferate through literature and culture. Here we can go back to the parallel I drew between Said and Gandhi. The most important axiom of Gandhi's *Hind Swaraj* is that it is not British military power but the Indian's acceptance of British culture which allowed the British a much longer and safer stay in India. Gandhi's observations are also instructive in understanding the concept of 'decolonising the mind' popularised by Ngũgĩ wa Thiong'o. Decolonisation of the mind implies that political independence from colonisers does not make sense as long as the erstwhile colonies remain enmeshed in colonial cultures, languages and other such frames of reference. This is also the spirit of Frantz Fanon's classic work *Black Skin, White Masks* (1952). Said endorses these arguments and re-formulates the difference between political decolonisation and actual freedom as one between 'independence' and 'liberation' (314–40). By independence he means the political fact of colonisers leaving the colonies, which started with the independence of India in 1947. But Said's idea of liberation seems to be more inclusive than Ngũgĩ's 'decolonising the mind' in that it warns against the pitfalls of nativism as well as the continued exploitation of the majority by national elites, even as he harps on the need for greater autonomy from Western cultural influences (something that continues to plague most former colonies).

While Said's contrapuntal readings share common ground with the anticolonial works of Frantz Fanon, Chinua Achebe and Ngũgĩ wa Thiong'o among others, there is a crucial difference between the Saidian approach to Western culture on the one hand, and that of Achebe, Ngũgĩ or Fanon on the other. While the latter seem to favour an almost total rejection of European cultural artefacts and productions, Said professes a deep sense of connection with Western literature and music, notwithstanding his objection to their imperial affiliations. As early as 1972, Ngũgĩ, for instance, called for the establishment of a Department of African Literature and Languages to replace the Department of English in his famous essay 'On the Abolition of the English Department'. In his detailed proposal, Ngũgĩ makes some room for the inclusion of select pieces of Western literature in his proposed literature department, but not for an English department as such. Such enunciations are difficult to find in Said, though he has frequently challenged the Eurocentric pedagogy of Western universities. In spite of his constant disagreement with and resentment at the imperial investments of European literature and culture, Said has a deep appreciation for what he perceives to be their durable artistic and aesthetic merits. His position *vis á vis* the Western canon is therefore something of a middle ground position; more nuanced and balanced than either traditional defenders of the canon (who see it only as an aesthetic corpus) or the schools of oppositional readings of various strands (who see nothing but politics in the canon). This may be because the values of secularism and humanism – themes close to Said's heart – have, by and large, European origins, even though that humanism has been punctuated by racism, colonialism and other prejudices. The idea, therefore, is to realise the full potential of that humanism by delinking it from the aforesaid handicaps and making it truly universal.

However, Said's nuanced critique of Western culture – in part its acceptance and in part rejection – has been objected to by critics like Bernard Lewis and Ibn Warraq. Said's critics and detractors have tried to show him as merely an anti-Western polemicist. But they forget that Said's appreciation of the aesthetic merit of Western cultural texts and traditions is as true as his condemnation of the same on grounds of their racist and colonialist underpinnings. This ambiguity has been best captured by the leading postcolonial thinker R. Radhakrishnan (who also happens to be a former student of Said) when he says that 'Said's sense of belonging to the West is indeed contradictory: he is both Eurocentric and profoundly anti-Eurocentric' (22). I agree with this, but would only replace 'contradictory' with 'contrapuntal'. In other words, both Said's Eurocentrism and anti-Eurocentrism are true and are best read contrapuntally against each other. While his critique of Eurocentrism does not sink into nativism, his conviction about the abiding relevance of humanism makes Said radically different from the anti-humanist epistemological tradition begun by Nietzsche and carried to its extreme by Foucault. Said, in fact, is the liminal intellectual, reading cultures and traditions contrapuntally against each other, without an unthinking affiliation with or abject surrender to any. His critique of Anglo-French colonialism and American imperialism is more visible and prominent only because these have been and are the most powerful and enduring systems of oppression and othering. But that should not be taken to understand that he espouses the causes of Arabism or Islamism as viable alternatives. As I have tried to show, Said's worldliness is situated in the philosophy of an inclusive humanism. The spirit of universal humanism that is always at work behind Said's formulation also manifests itself in his rejection of exclusionist nativist politics like négritude, for instance. We exist with each other, for each other; all histories and all nations are always already connected, even if the connection is not always apparent or pleasant. To borrow Said's own words, territories overlap with each other; histories are intertwined (*Culture and Imperialism* 1). This philosophy is instructive not only to re-locate colonies within the past narratives of colonisers, but also as a way to rise above present as well as future discontent in the relationships between existing countries and peoples.

NOTES

1. For a detailed account of the complex contours of Dickens's racism, please see Grace Moor's *Dickens and Empire*.
2. We must keep in mind that within forty-five years of *Kim*'s publication, the Indian independence movement grew so strong that the British had to leave the crown jewel of their empire.

3. One must remember that the atrocious provisions of Section 377 of the Indian Penal Code which made homosexuality a punishable crime was originally drafted by a colonial law-giver, Lord Macaulay.
4. I have dealt with it in greater detail in the next chapter, especially because Said's critique of American policies largely issue from his disapproval of America's pro-Zionist stance.

REFERENCES

Fanon, Frantz. "Pitfalls of National Consciousness". *The Wretched of the Earth*, Macgibbon and Kee, 1965, *Marxists Internet Archive,* https://www.marxists.org/subject/africa/fanon/pitfalls-national.htm. Accessed 9 December 2022.

Gandhi, Leela. *Postcolonial Theory: A Critical Introduction*. Oxford UP, 1998.

Leavis, F.R. *The Great Tradition.* Chatto & Windus, 1950.

Loomba, Ania. *Colonialism/Postcolonialism*. 2nd ed, Routledge, 2005.

Marx, Karl. "Theses on Feuerbach". *Marx/Engels Selected Works*, vol. 1, Progress Publishers, 1969, pp. 13–15. *Marx Engels Archive*, https://www.marxists.org/archive/marx/works/1845/theses/theses.htm. Accessed 9 December 2022.

Moore-Gilbert, Bart. *Postcolonial Theory: Contexts, Practices, Politics*. Verso, 1997.

Moore, Grace. *Dickens and Empire: Discourses of Class, Race and Colonialism in the Works of Charles Dickens*. Routledge, 2004.

Thiong'o, Ngũgĩ wa. "On the Abolition of the English Department". *The Post-colonial Studies Reader*, edited by Bill Ashcroft et al., Routledge, 1995, pp. 438–42.

Parry, Benita. *Postcolonial Studies: A Materialist Critique*. Routledge, 2004.

Radhakrishnan, R. *History, the Human, and the World Between*. Duke UP, 2008.

Said, Edward. *Culture and Imperialism*. Alfred A. Knopf, 1993.

---. *Orientalism*. Penguin, 2001.

---. *The World, the Text, and the Critic*. Vintage, 1991.

Spivak, Gayatri Chakravorty. 'Three Women's Texts and a Critique of Imperialism". *Race, Writing, and Difference*, special issue of *Critical Inquiry*, vol. 12, no. 1, 1985, pp. 243–61.

Suleri, Sara. *The Rhetoric of English India*. U of Chicago P, 1992.

Chapter Six

Covering Palestine, Representing Islam

ZIONISM AS IMPERIALISM

The dispossession of Palestinians and their struggle for autonomy, self-determination and statehood have been the central motifs of almost all of Said's works, overtly or covertly. While the Palestinian context is implicit in works like *Beginnings* (something that can be gleaned from his later interviews and declarations), it is visibly one of the major concerns in works like *Orientalism* and *Culture and Imperialism*. But there is a whole body of work by Said centred exclusively on the question of Palestine. The most important work in this regard is *The Question of Palestine*, published the year following the publication of *Orientalism*. It sets the tone of his beliefs, assertions and formulations on the question of Palestine, which continues in a series of works including books, articles, public lectures and direct political activities as a member of the Palestinian National Council (PNC), as well as independently. I will examine the core contents of *The Question of Palestine*, which in itself can be seen as an introduction to all his subsequent political works.

However, it is not his first exclusive or explicit work on Palestine. By the time he published *The Question of Palestine,* Said had already published a few articles dealing with the issue, in addition to *Orientalism* which talks about the life of an Arab Palestinian in America as a 'uniquely punishing destiny' (27). Published in 1970 as the opening essay of an edited book,*The Arab-Israeli Confrontation of June 1967: An Arab Perspective*, 'The Arab Portrayed' may well be treated as his 'concept note' for all successive works on Palestine as well as the politics of representation, including *Orientalism*. Said's contestation of the misrepresentation of Arabs by the West began with 'The Arab Portrayed', a theme which never left him.

As we have seen in earlier chapters, the job of a critic and of critique is to make visible what is invisible or less visible. In this chapter therefore, I will also try to foreground the political concerns voiced in Said's books that are not known for being political, even as I engage with his overtly political texts. In other words, Said's representations of the Arab Palestinian world will be explored by way of reading his'academic texts' along with the explicitly political ones. It is the 'political' in Said that constitutes the core of the Saidian oeuvre – this is our hypothesis.

Said has reiterated his commitment to the real world of politics on numerous occasions. As he says in *Reflections on Exile*, 'For myself, I have been unable to live an uncommitted or suspended life: I have not hesitated to declare my affiliation with an extremely unpopular cause. On the other hand, I have always reserved the right to be critical, even when criticism conflicted with solidarity or with what one expected in the name of national loyalty' (565). These remarks make explicit Said's privileging of ethics and praxis over textuality, which is a convenient point from which to examine his stance against Western culture and Western imperialism.

It is important at this point, however, to have a broad overview of the Israel–Palestine conflict for a better understanding of Said's projects.

A BRIEF HISTORICAL BACKGROUND[1]

The Israel–Palestine conflict is an intricate and intensely contested one. This is why the conflict still endures and intensifies with the passing of each day. Only a bare historical, and as far as possible, objective outline is attempted here.

The ownership of Palestine (including the present state of Israel) has been a bone of contention among three major Abrahamic faiths – Judaism, Christianity and Islam. While the Biblical narrative seemingly gives authenticity to a Jewish claim over the land, simply because Judaism is chronologically the oldest of these faiths, the Jewish claim has been challenged by Palestinians (who are mostly, though not exclusively, Muslim by religion) who also derive the authenticity of their claim from the same narratives. In her incisive book *A History of Palestine,* Gudrun Krämer for instance, maintains that the centrality of Palestine to Jewish culture and tradition is an indisputable fact (Krämer 18). However, she rightly reminds us that the foundational narrative in the Bible (The Book of Exodus) indicates that the Israelites were not the original inhabitants of the land and had come from Egypt led by Moses. While the biblical account may not be actual history and more of an imaginary representation, it does indicate that the Jewish people too were initially outsiders to Palestine: 'the Israelites were not indigenous to the land, but had come from outside, and that they had forcibly dispossessed and evicted others: This needed justification, and was justified with the divine promise' (Krämer 19).

As is well known, the two faiths that developed subsequently, Christianity and Islam, also claim to have descended from the Jewish foundational figure Abraham (hence the adjective Abrahamic for all these faiths) and consequently, lay their claims on whatever the Jews held as their own. More interestingly, Islam, while recognising the two other faiths to be Abrahamic, adds that they have moved away from the true path originally shown by God and considers Islam to be the only authentic faith. In other words, Islam's claim to ownership of the Abrahamic tradition overrides all other claims just as 'the revelation sent down to Muhammad renew(ed) and supersede(d) the earlier ones' (31). However, there is a long chronological gap between the emergence of Judaism and founding of Christianity, and an even longer one between the emergence of Judaism and the advent of Islam.

Coming back to the Jewish possession of Palestine, the Jewish people ruled the land from approximately 1300 BCE to 588 BCE. After that, the land was under the possession of Babylonian, Persians, Hellenistic and Roman rulers successively. The Roman occupation continued for almost four hundred years, from 63 BCE to 313 CE. The Roman conquest of Palestine was a disastrous event for the

Jewish people, during which a great number of them were killed and an even greater number exiled and dispersed. This phenomenon is known as the 'Jewish Diaspora' in social science discourses as well as popular culture. The region was under the supervision and control of the Ottoman Empire for about four hundred years (1516–1917) during which an Arab Muslim population grew and consolidated there. By the end of the nineteenth century, it was mostly populated by Arab Muslims (henceforth called Palestinians) along with a Christian and Jewish minority. During this period, the Jewish people were scattered across different parts of Europe. However, given the prominent anti-Semitism of Christian Europe at that time, the plight of the Jewish people was not a happy one. Throughout the seventeenth and eighteenth centuries, a conscious call to return to Israel/Palestine was raised by leading Jewish quasi-religious thinkers called messiahs. By the end of the nineteenth century, this desire of the community found expression in the form of the political philosophy of Zionism. The major document of this philosophy was authored by Austro-Hungarian journalist Theodor Herzl in his 1896 book *Der judenstaat* ('The jewish state'). The Jewish people started returning to their ancestral land and came into contact and conflict with the Palestinian population that had already settled there. It was a predominantly Muslim population, but also included Christians (such as Said's ancestors).

Meanwhile, European colonialism had added a third angle to the dispute. The Palestinians had stood up to Ottoman rule in the region and entered into a treaty with the British. The British government had promised to honour Arab independence if they were successful in freeing the land from the Ottoman Empire. But once the Ottomans were chased away, the British did not honour their promise and in an act of political betrayal (as was common with British imperialism), they not only started ruling Palestine in place of the Ottoman rulers, but also started showing clear signs of support for the founding of a Jewish state in Palestine. In fact, even before the Ottomans were finally defeated in 1918, in a letter written on 2 November 1917, the Foreign Secretary of the UK, Arthur Balfour, declared that the British Government would support the establishment of a Jewish homeland in Palestine. This declaration transformed the previously discussed religious differences into unending political strife between the Jews on the one hand and the Palestinian Muslims and Christians on the other. Known as the Balfour Declaration, it has been regarded as the 'original sin' in the context of the Israel–Palestine conflict. Edward Said's critique of Orientalism in his magnum opus *Orientalism* begins with an exposé of Balfour and the declaration. British rule over Palestine was also subsequently legitimised by a questionable mandate ratified by the League of Nations in June 1922.

However, there was intense opposition to British rule by both the Palestinians and the Jewish people who would come to be known as Israelis. Along with their internal differences, these conflicts manifested as a violent civil war during 1947–48. In the face of these challenges, coupled with the move towards decolonisation all over the world, the British Government referred the problem to the United Nations which, on 29 November 1947, voted for the partition of Palestine. The situation, interestingly, was quite similar to the one that prevailed in pre-Independence India. Just as the British left India after dividing it into two nations, India and Pakistan, a similar offer was tabled before the Israelis and the Palestinians. The land was to be divided into two states; the predominantly Jewish part of the land would constitute the new state of Israel and the rest of the land would be known as Palestine, destined for primarily Arab Muslims (Palestinians). The offer was embraced by the Jewish people who saw it as the fulfilment of their age-old desire for a homeland. The Palestinians staunchly refused to concede to the partition plan on the premise that the entire area of Palestine belonged to them. In fact, till date, hardcore supporters of the Palestinian cause do not recognise the existence of Israel.

By the early part of 1948 the British government had also made it clear that it would leave the region by midnight of 14 May 1948, which was the date on which the mandate ended. Accordingly, on 14 May 1948, British High Commissioner Alan Cunningham left Palestine after lowering the British flag in the port of Haifa. Immediately after that, at midnight on 14 May, the Jewish population of Palestine declared their independence by formally announcing the creation of the independent state of Israel with

David Ben-Gurion as their Prime Minister. The very next day (15 May 1948), there was an attack on Israel by the Arab Muslims of the region supported by the Arab League (a consortium comprising Syria, Transjordan, Iraq and Egypt). The Arab League had opposed the formation of the Jewish state and supported the mandate for a united Palestine. Israel, however, not only withstood the massive invasion that went on for ten months but annexed even greater portions of Palestine. And thus a civil war was transformed into one of the most enduring inter-state wars in human history.

Between 5 and 10 June 1967, there was another war known as the Six Day War (or the June War/Third Arab–Israeli War). The Arabs lost to Israeli forces this time as well, and the latter occupied the Palestinian parts of Gaza and West Bank. This war was a turning point in Said's life and much of his writing about the Palestinian problem are related to the Israeli occupation of the Gaza Strip and the West Bank. In the year 2005, Israel formally withdrew from the Gaza Strip. Israel, however, continued to have certain kinds of indirect control over Gaza even after 2005. Since 2007, the militant Palestinian group Hamas has claimed control over this area. However, there have been conflicting statements issued as to the actual status of the Gaza Strip. In fact, this is more or less the case with what is known as Palestine today. Intermittent conflicts with Israel, internal conflicts between liberal Palestinian forces and Hamas and confusion as to the actual status of the state of Palestine (often referred to as a *de jure* state) all contribute towards making the phenomenon more and more complex every day. There has been renewed tension in recent years, with fierce exchanges of weapons fire and words between the Israelis and Palestinians.

According to the database maintained by The United Nations Office for the Coordination of Humanitarian Affairs (OCHA)[2], between 2008 and February 2023,the Israel–Palestine conflict led to the killing of 6,226 Palestinians, while 1,44,963 were injured. On the Israeli side, there have been 289 deaths and 6,114 injuries during the same period. I have invoked these statistical accounts to show how enduring and pressing the problem is even two decades after Said's death.

Said and Palestine

Although the writings related to Palestine and Islam form the greater part of Said's oeuvre, these political writings are often ignored in academic discussions about Said. While these academic discussions tend to foreground his concerns with textual misrepresentations of cultures and races, the very base from which they stem are often not invoked or are referred to in passing. Bill Ashcroft and Pal Ahluwalia seem to have noticed the paucity of critical attention paid to his writing on Palestine and Islam, issues and sites which offer keys to his critical positions. Commenting on the connections between Said's critical and political texts, they point to the intertextuality that frustrates, and resists, any attempt to separate them: 'To some, Palestine might appear to situate the cranky political scribbling of the cultural theorist, a regular concern for a topical issue that remains peripheral to the most essential concerns of his theory. But this one topic is the key to the prominence of the theme of worldliness in his thinking and writing' (*Edward Said* 117).

This separation of Said's political writings from his supposedly non-political writings, among other things, validates Said's recurrent insistence on 'worldliness'. Such a separation also acts against the grain of Said's own strategies of reading, as is evident in his own self-reflexive subject position. Said's writings on Palestine suggest that his urgency for 'speaking truth to power' (see *Representations of the Intellectual* 63–75) is premised upon his experiences as a victim of Palestinian dispossession. As suggested earlier, the 1967 Arab–Israel war could be seen as the turning point in his life which led him to Palestinian activism even as he remained a professor of English at Columbia University. This can be seen as instrumental in his subsequent constant interrogations of the canonical texts of Western culture as being complicit with power and its structures; with imperialism to be more precise. As we have seen in the foregoing discussions, Said's works – including his autobiography *Out of Place* – reveal that he has always been troubled by and engaged with issues related to power and politics of representation. Said's career, academic or otherwise, is a series of sustained protests against authoritarianism in all its forms, especially power disguised as knowledge, culture, literature. *Orientalism*, a text with a complex blend of ethical and epistemological concerns, makes decisive statements about itself as containing the possibility of being ethically enabling; empowering the marginalised; 'being a reminder of the seductive degradation of knowledge, or any knowledge, anywhere at any time' (*Orientalism* 91).

Said sees the relation between knowledge and politics as operating in two major ways. On the one hand, he seems to be asserting the interconnectedness between the two by indicating that knowledge and politics (or culture and imperialism, in the case of colonisation) are always already related. On the other hand, he pleads for the intellectual's ethical responsibility towards unveiling this connection and to 'speak truth to power'. As Said states unambiguously in *Reflections on Exile,* for instance, 'To enter the public sphere means, therefore, not to be afraid of controversy or of taking positions' (503). Postcolonial criticism notes and has adopted this need to make theory and criticism enabling and liberating.

The Representation of the Arab: Stakes and Contentions

The urgency that Said feels to bring justice to the oppressed is expressed in an explicitly political idiom in his works on Palestine. One has to remember that a major point of contention offered by Said throughout his life and work is that the suppression of Palestinian identity by the West is achieved not only through coercion, but also by the gross misrepresentation of Arabs in European literature and media. Said's attempts at privileging the marginal in his reading of the major signposts of European literature and culture can be seen as largely motivated by his objection to the misrepresentation of the Arabs and the non-West in Western culture and the Western canon. While there is clear reflection of the Gramscian concept of 'hegemony' (which means 'rule by consent') in this view, the major influence seems to be Said's personal experiences of exile, othering and dispossession which were always part of his existence. This idea was the moving spirit behind *Orientalism* and its sequel *Culture and Imperialism*. His works on the Palestinian cause, seen in this light, are best seen as allied to his critical texts and vice versa.

As mentioned earlier, Said's rebuttal of the misrepresentation of Arabs, Islam, and particularly the Palestinians, has its official beginning in 'The Arab Portrayed' which is the opening essay of Ibrahim Abu-Lughod's 1970 collection *The Arab-Israeli Confrontation of June 1967: An Arab Perspective.* As the subtitle makes clear, the book was designed to bring to the fore the Arab point of view in the context of the Israel–Palestine or Israel–Arab conflicts. As Malcolm H. Kerr says in his 'Foreword' to the book, 'Israel is seen as a "Western" state populated by technologically minded, energetic, democratic, pioneering frontiersmen who are transforming a wilderness and providing a home for the persecuted; the Arabs are seen as exasperatingly inscrutable, unreliable, inept, backward, authoritarian, and emotional. Israel is our staunch friend; the Arabs throw stones at American embassies' (i). In these two lines, Kerr has summed up the main contention of not only this essay by Said, but all his books on the Palestinian issue (including *Orientalism*) as far as the issue of Arab misrepresentation is concerned. Kerr states further that the essays of the book 'written by Arab scholars living in the United States and Britain, provide a badly needed antidote to the one-sided and selective attention given in this country to the Middle East conflict' (ii).

Borrowing Kerr's trope, it can be said that Said's writings are therapeutic, intended as antidotes to the prejudiced but predominant Western narratives about Palestinians. In the beginning of 'The Arab Portrayed', Said shows how an Arab is generally represented in American films: 'He comes on as an over-sexed degenerate capable—it is true—of cleverly devious intrigues, but essentially sadistic, treacherous, and low. For example, the Arab leader is often seen snarling at the captured American hero and a blonde girl, "My men are going to kill you, but—they like to amuse themselves beforehand". He leers suggestively as he speaks' (1).

Indians reading this would be reminded of the popular Bollywood classic *Sholay* in which a very similar situation is shown (with Amjad Khan as the leering villain Gabbar Singh); only here, the villains are not Arabs. The American media presents and promotes a distorted, stereotypical image of Arabs which justifies and reinforces the discrimination against Arabs, Palestinians or otherwise, via popular imagination. Ironically, such negative representation and consequent persecution was meted out to the Jewish people themselves till

World War II. A student of English literature may recall here the portrayal of Jewish characters in Christopher Marlowe's *The Jew of Malta* and William Shakespeare's *The Merchant of Venice*, to cite only two prominent examples.

By strange turns of history and politics, the Jewish people, who were persecuted by the Christian West for a very long time culminating with the Holocaust, have turned into persecutors themselves. Said, however, maintains that the fact that you have been discriminated against in the past, however badly, does not give you the legitimacy or entitlement to persecute others subsequently. That is what the Israelis, according to Said, have been doing.

THE QUESTION OF PALESTINE REVISITED

Edward Said's *The Question of Palestine* (1979) is a more than a personal narrative of the causes behind and the losses incurred in the process of the dispossession of the Palestinians from their homeland. It can be said that though the book is primarily dedicated to the Palestinian cause and involves Said's personal life, it also strongly bears out Said's humanist convictions and concerns. Said does not argue for the rights of the Palestinians from the standpoint of the superiority or uniqueness of the Palestinian identity; he does it from a humanist's point of view. This is a key point in Said's fight for the Palestinian rights that is often misunderstood by people. This is how Said foregrounds the concept of universal human rights, premised on which he subsequently continues his intense argument for the rights of the Palestinians: 'no human being should be threatened with "transfer" out of his or her home or land; no human being should be discriminated against because he or she is not of an X or a Y religion; no human being should be stripped of his or her land, national identity or culture, no matter the cause' (*The Question of Palestine* xlii).

This assertion confronts the discriminatory practices against the Palestinians by the West, primarily the Anglo-American West, and the international communities backed by them. While Said does not deny the history of injustice meted out to the Jewish people by Europeans in the past, he argues that historical injustice to the

Jewish people should not be used to justify the dispossession of the Palestinians from their homeland. It can be said that the binary that Orientalism as a discursive field has built up between the Orient and the Occident plays a vital role in this discrimination. Palestinians are uncritically clubbed together with other Arab groups as representing a ferocious terrorist Islamic force, a threat to Western hegemony. As part of what is clearly politics of representation, the Jewish people are seen as people of culture and as friends to Western cultures and countries. Said feels that the purpose behind this gross misrepresentation is to keep the Middle East under civil and political pressure which, in turn, would ensure the permanence of Western hegemony.

Said's analysis of the history of Arab–Israeli conflict foregrounds the role of representation as a determining factor behind the ascendancy of Israel. The atrocities of the Holocaust notwithstanding, since its inception in 1948 'Israel has enjoyed an astonishing dominance in matters of scholarship, political discourse, international presence, and valorisation' (xiv). This helped forge a positive image of Israel which was thought to 'represent the best in the Western and Biblical traditions' (xiv) and which helped it affiliate its ideology to those espoused by the West. It was also repeatedly stressed that the hard work, talent and sincerity of the Israeli Jewish people transformed the arid and empty land of Palestine to one of the most fertile and resourceful places of the world – a representation that does not take note of the pre-1948 Arab presence in the area. Arabs, to the contrary, were associated with villainous, criminal and other such negative traits (xiv). Throughout his political and academic career, Said has also repeatedly pointed to the fact that it is the United States of America which is the strategic ally and chief patron of Israel and 'unlike Europe, the only outside force willing to play a direct role in the Middle East' (xxiii). This is also the major point made by Noam Chomsky who has provided greater details of America's imperial interventions against the Palestinian cause in his *Fateful Triangle: The United States, Israel, and the Palestinians* (1999); the book, interestingly, has a 'Foreword' by none other than Said himself.

In addition to his critiques of the relationship between Israel and Palestine, Said also exposes the internal problems of Palestinians and Arabs. He is, in this regard, quite similar to Indian reformers and intellectuals of the nineteenth and twentieth centuries like Vivekananda, Tagore and Gandhi who had to take stands against imperial as well as internal vices. In this connection, Yasser Arafat is one of the focal points of discussion for Said. Arafat and Said are roughly contemporaries, and had been close friends in addition to being close political allies for quite some time before they lost trust in each other's abilities or aspirations. Said's dissatisfaction with Arafat's tactics and praxis was clearly visible after the Oslo Accords (1993), and Said was one of the very first persons to see the incongruities and limitations of the Accords. However, signs of Said's dissatisfaction with Arafat are already prominent in the 'Preface' to the 1992 edition of *The Question of Palestine.* With a 33-page detailed historical engagement with all that had happened in the arena of Palestinian politics since the book was first published (1979), this 'Preface' can be justifiably considered a chapter in its own right. While he takes note of all of Arafat's major contributions, Said also expresses his unhappiness with the former's leadership. Arafat, for example, is said to have 'presided over Palestinian losses of major proportions', which includes the continuous loss of territory to Israeli settlers on the West Bank, Gaza and East Jerusalem; the 1982 Israeli invasion of Lebanon; and the Gulf crisis of 1990–91. Said's opposition to Arafat is in keeping with his idea of the oppositional critic, the intellectual who does not take sides with any power group. Said holds that Palestinian liberation should finally lead to a postnational site rather than to insular local identities and speaks against the concept of a nativist Palestinian nationalism. This is an instance of Said's practical application of his theory of non-nativist, non-violent rewritings of human history which stands firmly against 'systems of thought like Orientalism, discourses of power, ideological fictions—mind forg'd manacles' (*Orientalism* 328)

What I suggest is that Said was fighting for the Palestinian homeland and Palestinian rights on the principles of human rights, and not along any Islamic or Arab ideology as such. This is different from fighting for a nationality or homeland on the grounds of racial supremacy, exceptionalism, and so on. The ideology of the pro-

Islamic groups fighting for Palestine exemplifies such premises, while Said's arguments are gathered around human rights and secularism. His strong criticism of the Islamist forces in the Arab world which we discuss later in this chapter bears testimony to this.

For Said, liberation suggests freedom from all kinds of oppression for everyone and not just political independence as a nation state. Without the spirit of liberation, independent nations too can become oppressive power structures by replicating the mechanisms of colonial rule. According to him, that is what has happened in the Middle East. In *Culture and Imperialism,* he points out how democracy is being suppressed in Arab countries by autocratic nationalisms: 'there are either privileged oligarchies or privileged ethnic groups' (363). However, for Said, the internal problems of the Arab nations seem to be a lesser evil in comparison with the continued cultural imperialism of the West which manifests its ugly designs through frequent interventions in the Arab world on the one hand (the Gulf Wars, for instance) and keeps the growth of Palestinian self-determination in check through its support for Israel on the other.

Though almost ten years had passed between the writing of 'The Arab Portrayed' and *The Question of Palestine*, there seemed to be no change in the perception of Western media and scholarship about the nature of Arabs, Palestinians and Islam. Orientalist parameters had infiltrated 'the structure of signs and plays' of contemporary human and social science. European cultural and scholarly texts continued representing the Orient, Arabs and Islam as unchanging. There also seemed to be an ever increasing body of scholars and experts who reinforced such prejudices in the garb of specialists and experts and 'tended to monopolize discussion, principally by using social science jargon and ideological clichés masked as knowledge' (*The Question of Palestine* xl).

Said goes to the extent of suggesting that Zionism itself draws much of its strength in persecuting the Palestinians not from Zionism per se, but from Orientalist structures and stereotypes of Western scholarship that are inevitably based on an 'entrenched cultural attitude towards Palestinians deriving from age-old western prejudices about Islam, the Arabs, and the orient' (xl). Zionism and Orientalism are discourses that sustain each other in a symbiotic relationship, and this view seems to help judge Zionism against a larger network of culture and politics. It will be useful to look at further details of this connection as provided by Said.

Zionism as Neo-Orientalism and Its Victims

The awareness that the assertion of the social sciences being related to Orientalism could be seen as 'too sweeping a statement' (*The Question of Palestine* xl) leads Said to re-assert the claim (xl). Said is critical of the manner in which American history and historiography make forays into Palestinian and Arab issues: 'No foreign affairs symposium, scholarly book, or moral attitude taken is complete without some reference to Palestinian (sometimes also known as "Arab") terrorism' (6). Arab terrorism or backwardness is a favourite theme with popular movies like *Black Sunday* or *Sorcerer* where 'the Palestinians have *canonically* been associated with all the characteristics of refugees who—depending on the occasion—fester in camps, are a political "football" being used by the Arab states, are a breeding ground for communism, tend to procreate like rabbits, and so forth' (6; emphasis added). Said underscores how, at times, Palestinians are also grossly misrepresented as a more accomplished community of Arabs, constituting an elite group in the Arab world (6). Both these are, needless to say, representational extremes, and far from reality.

Further, Said finds the lack of concern shown by the intellectuals of Europe in general to the exclusion of the Palestinians from their land as surprising, especially given their overwhelming sympathy for the apartheid victims of South Africa. Instead of being an innocent search for nationhood, Zionism, according to Said, has become a violent operational strategy adopted by the Israelis against the Palestinians. Orientalist stereotypes, such as the ones discussed in the previous paragraph, provide the ideological basis of Zionism, and in his Palestine related works Said actually develops an implicit but sustained parallel between Palestine and the Orient on the one hand, and Israel and the Occident on the other. Said argues that, like Orientalism, Zionism goes hand in hand with European colonialism despite the prevalence of Western anti-Semitism. In other words, while Zionism is primarily seen as a response to the intense anti-Semitism of Europe, particularly Germany, its rise 'also coincided with the period of unparalleled European territorial occupation in Africa and Asia, and it was as part of this general movement of acquisition that Zionism was launched initially by Theodor Herzl' (*The Question of Palestine* 69). According to Said, even as a political philosophy, Zionism never spoke of itself only as a liberation movement for the Jews, 'but rather as a Jewish movement for colonial settlement in the Orient' (69). While Said's attempt to situate Zionism against the backdrop of Western imperialism is consciously political and may appear to be a polemic of sorts, he squarely bases his argument on evidence drawn from a wide range of sources which include travel narratives, history books, memoirs, novels as well as writers of political economy and political philosophy from nineteenth century Europe. There is still a remarkable openness with which Said rewrites the Palestinian history especially for the Western reader: 'I have called my book a political essay because it tries to put our matter before the Western reader, not as something watertight and finished, but as something to be thought through, tried out, engaged with—in short, as a subject to be dealt with politically' (xli).

In what appears to be a repetition of his arguments in *Orientalism,* Said reiterates in *The Question of Palestine* his postulations on the construction of the imaginary Orient by European scholarship. This imaginative geography which had ensured that 'everything to the east of an imaginary line drawn somewhere between Greece and Turkey was called the Orient' provided the West with the rationale for engaging in colonialism as a civilising mission premised on fallacious notions about 'the Oriental despot, Oriental sensuality, splendour, inscrutability' (3). Evidently, the European imagination about Oriental romance, mysticism and exoticism did not remaina textual or imaginative affair, but led to possibly the most dehumanising event in human history: colonialism. More importantly, along with constructing a definitive image of the Orient as a particular space, such representations also constructed the Oriental as a permanently inferior race, and consequently (as Said sees it), by 1918 about 85 per cent of the world were occupied by European colonial powers (3).

In explaining how European literature contributes to this twin process of exoticising and othering, Said focuses on travel writing. The travellers in their description of non-Western places often give effect to an always already bias against the place by showing it as inhabited by 'uncivilized' people, or even as empty space. While in *Orientalism* Said has taken a broad overview of the travel narratives about the Orient in general (see Chapter 3), *The Question of Palestine* focuses on travel accounts directly related to Palestine. According to Said, it is the depiction of the Palestinians as 'uninteresting and undeveloped' by writers like Mark Twain that helped intensify the colonial attitude of the West towards Palestine. These writers busied themselves in imagining and identifying the land as a fertile ground for European colonial expansion: Palestine was seen as a place to be possessed *anew* and reconstructed (9).

The link between travelogues and imperialism has been developed and discussed at length in *Orientalism*, and these discussions have led to a non-canonical interpretation of canonical travelogues as being complicit with the imperial ideology. Further, as previously suggested, the thesis about the travel–colonialism nexus has been a fertile field of enquiry within and outside postcolonial theory. Critics have further dealt with the rise of travel and travelogues along with the trajectories of colonialism, some notable works being Stephen Greenblatt's *Marvellous Possessions* and Mary Louise Pratt's *Imperial Eyes*.

On the issue of the representation of Palestine in travelogues, especially in Lamartine's writings, Said contends that Palestine has been misrepresented as empty and unoccupied. In *Orientalism*, Said offers the term 'topos' to explain the process of turning the Oriental space into an Orientalised space by means of 'a set of references, a congeries of characteristics, that seems to have its origin in a quotation, or a fragment of text, or a citation from someone's work on the Orient, or some bit of previous imagining, or an amalgam of all these' (*Orientalism* 177). Said speaks of Lamartine's tour of the Orient in 1833 as filled with biases, predispositions and sympathies such as his hatred for the Romans and Carthage, love for Jews, Egyptians and Hindus, and so on. All his initial encounters confirm his preconceptions regarding the Orient and the Orientals, but as soon as he reaches Palestine, 'he becomes the incorrigible maker of an imaginary Orient' (177). Said's observation on Lamartine's travel and work offers a deeper understanding of the cultural politics of imperial/Orientalist travel writings. It was, for instance, Lamartine, who observed in his *Voyage en Orient* that Orientals (by which he mostly implied the Islamic world) are lazy, their politics capricious, passionate and futureless. Most ironically, one also witnesses how he comments elaborately on the quality of Arabic poetry while being completely ignorant of the language. In denigrating Prophet Muhammed, he is caught in the same fallacy. He comments that the Arab land is wonderful because every credulous or fanatical man could become a prophet there. Said asserts rather pointedly that Lamartine has himself become a prophet merely by residing in the Orient (178).

Said's reading of the misrepresentation of Palestine by Lamartine is of course a part of his project of unmasking the political implications of apparently innocent texts, restoring the 'worldliness' of texts oppressed under the burden of literary–aesthetic readings on the one hand, and high theoretical 'textual' readings on the other. Indeed, Said's reading of Lamartine and relating it to the Zionist occupation of Palestine is one of the best examples of the interconnectedness of the text and the world that Said argued for in texts like *Orientalism, The World, the Text, and the Critic* and *Culture and Imperialism*. The scholarly and cultural texts of imperialism exist in a deeply symbiotic relationship with the actual process of colonisation (as has been discussed in previous chapters); they constantly invoke and reinforce each other, and hence are best understood as 'working contrapuntally together' (*Culture and Imperialism* 234). The concern with the relationship between politics and culture, between theory and praxis, turns Said's works into informed interrogations of texts and authors in relation to their sociopolitical reality. It establishes, among other things, the imperative of political readings of cultural artefacts, thereby instantiating the intertwined territories of ethics and epistemology.

Lamartine's less-than-desirable influence on the history and identity of the Palestinians has been succinctly recorded in *The*

Question of Palestine. While its critique of Lamartine's travel writings is one of the earliest models of reading travel narratives against the grain, *The Question of Palestine* also prefigures Said's strategy of contrapuntal readings of literary texts in his detailed reading of George Eliot's last novel *Daniel Deronda* (1876) as a 'Zionist' text, written even before the term Zionism was officially created and used. In Said's words, 'The unusual thing about the book is that its main subject is Zionism' (60). The representation of the 'East' and Palestine by the likes of Lamartine served the purpose of preparing Palestine as a Jewish land in the days to come. They reduced the living reality of a huge Arab population into either myth or an 'inferior' existence which had to be usurped and developed by European powers. Lamartine himself had said in his infamous *Resume* that the land was a fit place for a French colonial project (*The Question of Palestine* 9).

Racism, Karl Marx and J. S. Mill

In *The Question of Palestine*, the interrogation of the pro-Jewish tendencies in George Eliot's *Daniel Deronda* is immediately followed by an allegation of racism against Karl Marx, along with John Stuart Mill. While Mill's imperialist biases are more or less accepted, Said's indictment of Marx as a racist in this book (as well as *Orientalism*) is problematic given that Marx's philosophy has been regarded as the primary motivation behind a wide variety of liberation movements in the twentieth century. Marx is generally regarded as the precursor of postnationalism as well, based on the fact that his call for international unity among the working classes can be seen as laying the foundations of a postnational communist solidarity. However, in Marx's scheme of things, the British colonisation of India is justified as it liberated India from what he thought was medieval autocracy, despotism and superstition. According to Said, what escaped Marx's sight was that in doing so, he was not only legitimising the inhuman exploitations of imperialism, but also suggesting that white races were better equipped or better qualified to 'improve' Oriental society: 'What . . . Marx did not see a hundred years earlier when he wrote about the British in India—is that there was a national right being violated even by a "technical and dynamic civilization" when it made colonial incursions upon "the miserable masses."' (*The Question of Palestine* 32–33). Said, thus, tries to argue that all the humanists and other representatives of nineteenth century Europe were primarily 'racist(s) with a greater or lesser degree of virulence depending on the individual' (66). While Ernest Renan was, for instance, an outright anti-Semite, George Eliot did not think it worth her time to bother about races that could not assimilate with European ideas (66). Similarly, though both Karl Marx and John Stuart Mill are widely known, read and celebrated for their long standing opposition to injustice and oppression, they 'believed that such ideas as liberty, representative government, and individual happiness must not be applied in the Orient for reasons that today we would call racist' (65). While labelling Marx a racist is deeply problematic (see Chapter 3), it is not difficult to see that he too operated within a frame of references that was Eurocentric.

What stands out in Said's assessment of Marx and Mill is that Said is always acutely aware of the other side/s of any given person, event or phenomenon. This contrapuntal awareness – to use a term developed by Said himself – is at work in the entire Saidian oeuvre. For instance, the English novel for Said is not only about English society and culture; it is also about England's colonies, imperial exploitations, inhumane rhetoric and practice of exercising control over other societies, territories and cultures. The same is the case with Zionism. While the Jewish people and the greater part of the world see Zionism as the gain of selfhood and political autonomy for the Jewish people, Zionism – either in its ideological imaginations or practical applications – is not only about the Jewish people; it is also about those countless Arab Palestinians whom Zionism has annihilated, displaced or suppressed as secondary citizens within the state of Israel. Zionism needs to be seen not only from the standpoint of its beneficiaries, but also from the perspective of its victims. This is the humanism of Edward Said: a strong and worldly humanist vision rooted in actual politics with a keen awareness of other realities. I would like to call this 'contrapuntal humanism', of course with the contrapuntal awareness on my part that words, jargon or neologisms did not matter much to Said. What was more important for him is a greater degree of freedom and liberty for all human beings than they currently have.

SHORT TAKES

After the Last Sky

Published in 1986, Said's *After the Last Sky* is a collaborative work with photographer Jean Mohr. It carries forward the issues raised in Said's previous works on Palestine, most notably *The Question of Palestine*, by displaying a series of photographs (taken by Mohr) highlighting the plight of the Palestinians. As Said says in the 'Introduction', the purpose of the book is to counter the 'harmful representations of Palestinians, and replace them with something more capable of capturing the complex reality of their experience' (6). The major features of the Palestinian existence are 'dispossession', 'dispersion' and 'stateless exile' which rendered them a 'dispersed national community' (6). Said's reservation about objectivity in scholarship that he made famously available in *Orientalism* is also re-invoked in *After the Last Sky*. He unambiguously declares that 'this is not an objective book'; the idea at play behind the book is to show Palestinian realities through Palestinian eyes (6).

Another important point here is its critique of the moves of not only the 'Israeli enemies' of Palestine, but its 'Arab friends' as well. Commenting on this strange predicament, Said says that, at times, it is not easy to decide 'where and by whom the treatment is worse' (5). This predicament has an immediate context which is directly connected to the genesis of the book itself. In 1983, while working as a consultant to the United Nations for a conference on Palestine, Said suggested that there should be a photographic essay on Palestinians in the conference. The idea was vehemently opposed, surprisingly enough, by a few major Arab states (and not by the US or Israel, as they had already refused to be part of the conference itself). Finally, there was a compromise and the photos were allowed, but without the attached comments: a move that damaged the entire idea of the photo essay suggested by Said (Bayoumi and Rubin 268). The idea was retrieved by Said in the form of *After the Last Sky*.

Further, as Said was barred from entering Israel at that point of time, he could only gain access to photos of dispossessed Palestinians through a European photographer, which is what Jean Mohr did. While the thematic preoccupations of the book can be found in Said's other works on Palestine as well, what makes *After the Last Sky* particularly interesting is its style of a photographic representation of reality (coupled with narrative comments). This is something unique in the entire Said canon: while photographs are present in his memoir as well, it is not exactly a work that is a photographic representation of realities.

SAID, ISLAM AND WESTERN MEDIA

Along with *Orientalism* and *The Question of Palestine,* Edward Said's *Covering Islam* (1981) constitute a trilogy that seeks to counter Western representations of the peoples and cultures of the East, especially Arab peoples and Islamic cultures of the Middle Eastern countries. Said's basic premises in this regard are to be found in *Orientalism*, a detailed analysis of which has been made available in Chapter 3 of this book. It is sufficient to recapitulate here that in *Orientalism*, Said has argued with substantial evidence from a wide range of subjects that the image of the Orient (particularly the Islamic Orient) created by Western scholarship is both a misrepresentation and driven by the desire to control the East. In *Covering Islam*, the same point is established by more or less the same methodology. To use an expression from research in the humanities (which both these books primarily are), the difference between *Covering Islam* and *Orientalism* lies neither in hypothesis nor in conclusion, but rather in scope and materials used. While the scope of the former book is the overall representation of Orient (more specifically, the Middle East), the latter chooses to focus on the representation of one of the major religions of the Orient, Islam. And while the materials used for the former book have been drawn from literary writings, travel narratives, histories, linguistic studies and other cultural archives of the West, *Covering Islam* focuses particularly on the Western media. Said's research leads him to conclude that contemporary Western media is as guilty of producing and distributing inaccurate and infelicitous images of Islam (and hence, the Orient) as was the Orientalist cultural and scholarly texts: 'It is only a slight overstatement to say that Muslims and Arabs are essentially covered, discussed, apprehended, either as oil suppliers or as potential terrorists. Very little of the detail, the human density, the passion of Arab-Muslim life has entered the awareness of even those people whose profession it is to report the Islamic world' (*Covering Islam* 28).

According to Said, all such activities on the part of Western media and scholarship are indicative of Western civilisation's fear of Islam as a threat to the former's imperial mission (lii). Additionally, America and other Western countries want as much control over the oil reserves of the Middle East as possible for material reasons. The perpetual creation and reinforcement of negative images about Islam underpins and provides a logic for American interventionism in the Arab world in much the same way as the hoax of a 'civilising mission' provided the Anglo-French empire moral legitimacy to carry out the project of colonialism in the East.

It needs to be reiterated at this point that Said was not a defender of Islam as such. In fact, he has lamented being misunderstood as a new prophet of Islam or Arab Exceptionalism, which was far from his real purpose. To the extent that Arabs, Islam or the Orient for that matter are misrepresented by the West (catering to the ulterior motives of colonialism or economic imperialism), Said felt it was his duty as a humanist and a secular intellectual to resist these misrepresentations by exposing the falsehood behind them. He derives his intellectual and emotional strength neither from the religious doctrines of Islam nor from Christianity (the religion he was born into), but from a strong secular belief in human life and human history as human constructs. This view of Said, while evidently informed by the constructivist emphasis of poststructuralism, is more in sync with the eighteenth century Italian thinker Giambattista Vico, to whom Said returns *ad infinitum*.

THE POLITICS OF DISPOSSESSION: A CONSOLIDATED VISION

Subtitled 'The Struggle for Palestinian Self-Determination 1969–1994', Said's 1995 book *The Politics of Dispossession* is a collection of thirty-eight essays on Palestinian politics written over a period of twenty-six years. Put together, they provide a useful roadmap to help us understand the course of the Palestinian struggle for independence over those two decades. Additionally, these essays provide a much larger exposure to Said's personal involvement in terms of his wide-ranging, daring political activities devoted to the Palestinian cause. It is therefore an indispensable volume for those who want a comprehensive understanding of the 'political' Said (though my argument is that he has never been apolitical) as well as for those who want to be privy to an active insider's view of the Palestine issue.

The key message of the book seems to be that while the increasing momentum of the Palestinian struggle and their attempts at self-representation has brought about some change to how Palestinians are viewed by the West, the changes have been visible only in a certain section of the public. In other words, what is lamentable is that, by and large, there has not been much change in US government policy in terms of being a patron to the state of Israel. This is as true today as it was in 1995, the year *The Politics of Dispossession* was published. However, it would perhaps not be fallacious to argue that with a greater amount of public support for the Palestinian cause, at some point the US would take a politically neutral stance regarding the Israel–Palestine issue. This expectation, among other things, is also based on Said's observation in *The Politics of Dispossession* that 'by the third year of the *intifada,* according to some Gallup polls, 45 percent of the American population was in favour of the Palestinian self-determination as opposed to the 24 percent who were not' (xxvii).

The Politics of Dispossession, interestingly, also contains pieces which record Said's voice on political issues other than the Palestinian crisis, albeit with indirect links to it. There are, for instance, clear statements condemning American involvement in the Gulf War of 1991. Under the leadership of Saddam Hussein, Iraq had invaded and annexed Kuwait, a country abounding in oil reserves. The United Nations had asked Iraq to withdraw, which was not honoured by Saddam Hussein and his troops. Subsequently, the US, along with the UK, started a joint army operation against Saddam which eventually turned into one of the biggest military alliances since World War II. A tragic event which all important powers of the world became party to, the Gulf War caused thousands of deaths (as per *Encyclopaedia Brittanica* Iraqi military deaths alone numbered up to 100,000, for instance) and other devastations that had a cumulative effect on the world in terms of economy as well as ecology.

While Said does not support Saddam Hussein's regime and decisions, he undertakes several critical and political inquiries to point towards how things may have come to such a pass. 'Behind the Moves of Saddam Hussain' is an insightful essay which offers a critique of both America's interventionist policies and Saddam Hussein's dictatorial leadership as inhumane and undemocratic. While Saddam had, Said asserts, turned Iraq 'into a graveyard for democracy', what the American campaigns designed to demonise Saddam left out is that Saddam's moves 'have been shaped to a considerable degree by U.S. Middle East Policies' (278). Above all, the military invasion by US and its allies showed no humane concern for the possible casualties of the war and had 'little concern for the unfortunate residents of Kuwait itself' (278). While Saddam Hussein definitely needed to be countered on several legitimate grounds, it 'could have been dealt with by something less than a war of a million combatants' (283). Further, while America felt its moral duty was to end Saddam's oppression of other countries at all costs, it has never shown any intent to take steps against the similar oppression of Palestinians by Israel. Said argues that '[E]very Arab is agonisingly aware that because of an American green light, the Israeli army in 1982 invaded Lebanon, killed 20,000 people, attempted to destroy the PLO, set up a basically puppet government, not to mention their earlier violation of Syrian, Jordanian and Saudi air-space, and bombing of Iraq and Tunis' (279). This powerful exposure of American hypocrisy is preceded and followed by what Said feels are the actual causes behind America's double standards. The immediate motivation behind American interventions in the Middle East seems to be a strong desire for control over petroleum production in Gulf countries. The more persistent reason seems to be the Western prejudice against Arabs and other peoples of the Orient, as Said has argued in most of his critical and political works.

The major difference between his later works and *Orientalism* lies, in my view, in the fact that Said becomes increasingly critical of the Arab world as well, which could be said to add to his credibility as an impartial intellectual. According to Said, much of the suffering that the Arab people are undergoing have also resulted from their unwillingness or inability to come up with effective counter-discourses against the representational practices of America and Israel. He therefore calls for the creation of a 'combination discourse' which would simultaneously oppose the internal oppressive authorities of the Arab world while at the same time focus on humanist values like 'affection, sympathy, association (rather than antagonism, resentment, harsh religious fundamentalism, vindictiveness)' (292). This trend of self-criticism has led Said to see the widely celebrated Oslo Accords of 1993 as a historic blunder on Arafat's part, whom he had canonised almost unquestionably in earlier pieces like 'Solidly behind Arafat' (*The Politics of Dispossession* 101–03). While Arafat's followers and the pro-Israel–US camps saw the Oslo Accords as a 'historic breakthrough' Said read it in 1995 as 'an instrument of Palestinian surrender, a Palestinian Versailles' (xxxiv).

Negotiating the intricate politics of the Accords is beyond the scope of an introductory work like this, but what I want to emphasise is Said's ability to be self-critical even as he critiques his political others. His resentment against the Accords makes it very clear that he is not faulting Israel or the US for this blunder, but the Palestinians themselves; the Palestinian leadership, to be more accurate. This, among other things, vindicates Said's own conviction regarding the double vision of the exile. As a Palestinian who was also an American, Said could see things that an exclusively Palestinian or American identity would not allow.

Further Perspectives on the Palestine-Israel Conflict

As previously suggested, due to its uniquely complicated geopolitical location and history which is connected to all three major Abrahamic faiths, the Palestine area (Israel–Palestine area, to be technically correct) is sacred to all three Abrahamic faiths: Judaism, Christianity and Islam. As per the claims of the oldest of this group, that is the Jewish people, the land is part of the 'the Promised land' that the Old Testament God had bequeathed to them. In the Book of Genesis, the very first book of the Old Testament, God promises Abraham, 'To your descendants I give this land, from the Wadi of Egypt to the great river, the Euphrates— the land of the Kenites, Kenizzites, Kadmonites, Hittites, Perizzites, Rephaites, Amorites, Canaanites, Girgashites and Jebusites' (Genesis 15:18–21 New International Version). In Genesis itself, the promise was repeated to Abraham's son Isaac and Isaac's son Jacob. King David and his son King Solomon are supposed to have consolidated the Jewish kingdom in the area by taking Jerusalem – which David had wrested from the Jebusites – as their capital.

Though Said and other pro-Palestinian thinkers do not want to emphasise this claim (whether historically accurate or not), Jewish intellectuals and politicians highlight the divine gift theory to justify their claim. Indeed, there seems to have been a Jewish presence in the area before the Islamic Arab presence. While the Genesis stories sound mythical, these seem to contain the relics of a history much like other myths across cultures. Further, excavations and archaeological research has confirmed the presence of a Jewish settlement in the disputed land. One could argue that the most famous Jewish person to have lived in those areas was Jesus Christ. The places connected to him became sacred to Christians later, making Jerusalem – the place of his crucifixion – a highly contested site divided between Jewish and Christian claims of ascendancy.

After the emergence of Islam however, the Arabs captured Jerusalem and other parts of the land in the seventh century CE. As discussed earlier, Islam tried to use foundational parts of the Jewish or Abrahamic tradition as its own, and consequently laid its claim on things and areas belonging to the Jews as well as Christians. As part of the historical phenomena called 'the Muslim conquest of the Levant', the kingdom of Jund Filastin – the direct predecessor of today's Palestine – was established in the 630s. Islam, it may be noted here, also claims the figures of Adam, Noah and Abraham glorified in the Old Testament for itself, recognising them as well as Jesus Christ as important prophets in its religious tradition. Islam also stakes the claim that the founder of Islam, Prophet Mohammad, is the final prophet in the Abrahamic/Judeo-Christian tradition. This is accepted neither by the Jews nor by the Christians. None the less, Jerusalem, containing the holiest shrines of the Jews and the Christians, is also considered sacred by Sunni Muslims as the place from where the Prophet ascended to heaven for a direct vision of God (Allah) and hence, second only Mecca and Medina. Thus, all these three faiths claim the Old Testament patriarchs as their originators and hold the same land as central to their religious and cultural traditions.

These contestations have given rise to two of the most enduring conflicts of human history. First, the Israel–Palestine issue, which is our chief concern here. This section is an attempt to provide a larger historical background to the issue, which is unfortunately either absent or very vaguely hinted at by Said. The second conflict was the almost two-hundred-year-long history of the Crusade: intermittent wars engaged in by Christian Europe during 1095 to 1291 CE as part of their pledge to free the 'holy land' Jerusalem from Muslim occupation. This, too, is seriously played down in Said's oeuvre if not omitted altogether, making the strife between the West and the Islamic world appear to be mostly grounded in nineteenth and twentieth century Orientalist misrepresentations and European imperialism only. These absences or silences in Said could be due to the fact that his disciplinary training was not in History or Political Science, but English and Comparative literature.[3]

This, however, does not take away anything from the unspeakable suffering the Palestinians have undergone, especially since 1948. Irrespective of the degrees of legitimacy in terms of being the 'original inhabitants' of a land, all human beings must have access to all human rights regardless of their histories, races, castes, creeds or locations. This is the motto of Saidian humanism, and he often relates it to famously available documents like the 'Universal Declaration of Human Rights'. It is also important to note at the end that, in spite of his lifelong opposition to Zionism and the dispossession of the Palestinians, Said has also been an advocate of a bi-national state where Palestinian and Jewish histories and present realities would not contradict but complement and corroborate each other. In other words, Said's antidote to Zionism is not a competing Arabism but an inclusive humanism, which has larger implications for all such contested domains. This is also the message of his last detailed discussion on the issue, which he enters into by taking Sigmund Freud's last work as a point of departure; a message and work that will be discussed in the next chapter.

NOTES

1. Most of the data that I have presented here has been collected from Said's works like *The Question of Palestine* and *The Politics of Dispossession.* Additionally, Chomsky's *Fateful Triangle* has been of immense help for further understanding of the background to the current imbroglio over the contested region. An extremely useful historical detailing of the Israel–Palestine conflict can be found under theUnited Nation's entry 'The Question of Palestine' (https://www.un.org/unispal/history2/origins-and-evolution-of-the-palestine-problem/part-i-1917-1947/). I have also taken the liberty of cross-checking some dates and years against the Britannica entries on the history of Palestine (https://www.britannica.com/topic/history-of-Palestine). I must acknowledge my gratitude to all the authors concerned, of the books as well as the online entries.
2. https://www.ochaopt.org/data/casualties#
3. His fervent appeals for reading literary texts historically and politically stem from his understanding of the limitations of a purely literary or aesthetic training. Driven by the same limitations of having a purely literary/aesthetic training himself, he would often speak for the amateur rather than the professional, of the greater importance of Gramsci's hegemony and counter-hegemony than Lukács's historical consciousness.

REFERENCES

Abu-Lughod, Ibrahim, editor. *The Arab-Israeli Confrontation of June 1967: An Arab Perspective.* Northwestern UP, 1970.

Ashcroft, Bill and Pal Ahluwalia. *Edward Said.* Routledge, 1999.

Bayoumi, Moustafa and Andrew Rubin, editors. *The Selected Works of Edward Said.* Bloomsbury, 2021.

Britannica, The Editors of Encyclopaedia. "Persian Gulf War summary". *Encyclopedia Britannica*, 1 March 2007, https://www.britannica.com/summary/Persian-Gulf-War. Accessed 4 January 2023.

Chomsky, Noam. *Fateful Triangle: The United States, Israel, and the Palestinians*. Pluto, 1999.

Krämer, Gudrun. *A History of Palestine*. Translated by Graham Harman and Gudrun Krämer, Princeton UP, 2008.

Said, Edward. *After the Last Sky: Palestinian Lives*. 1986. Columbia UP, 1999.

---. "The Arab Portrayed". *The Arab-Israeli Confrontation of June 1967: An Arab Perspective*, edited by Ibrahim A. Abu-Lughod, Northwestern UP, 1970, pp. 1–9.

---. *Covering Islam.* 1981. Vintage,1997.

---. *Culture and Imperialism.* Alfred A. Knopf, 1993.

---. *Orientalism.* 1978. Penguin, 2001.

---. *The Politics of Dispossession: The Struggle for Palestinian Self-Determination, 1969-1994.* Pantheon Books, 1994.

---. *The Question of Palestine.* Routledge & Kegan Paul., 1979.

---. *Reflections on Exile and Other Essays.* Penguin, 2001.

---. *Representations of the Intellectual: The 1993 Reith Lectures*. Pantheon Books, 1994.

The Bible (New International Version). "Genesis 15:18-21". *Bible.com*, https://www.bible.com/bible/111/GEN.15.18-21.NIV. Accessed 11 November 2022.

Chapter Seven

Humanism after Posthumanism

INTELLECTUALS FOR A LIVEABLE FUTURE

Published posthumously in 2004, *Humanism and Democratic Criticism* includes critical essays written during the last few years of Said's life, from 2000 to 2003. The book therefore may be reasonably seen as his final words to humanity. Written at what happened to be the culminating point of Said's career, they also represent his 'late style', a term he introduced into the English critical tradition in some of the lectures he delivered on the topic during the same period. Another important work in this last phase of Said's life is a monograph on Freud, written in 2001 and first published in 2003. Before discussing the contents and concerns of Said's book on humanism, we will have a close look at his works on late style and Freud.

LATE STYLE IN MUSIC AND LITERATURE

'Edward was in the process of writing this book when he passed away on Thursday morning, September 2003', Said's wife Mariam lets us know in the 'Foreword' to his posthumously published work *On Late Style: Music and Literature against the Grain*. The volume was actually prepared based on Said's working notes by Michael Wood, who assures in the 'Introduction' that the words are all Said's own. A hesitation and unwillingness to accept it on par with Said's other published works, however, may persist with those who are familiar with Said's habit of meticulously editing his manuscripts before and during the process of publication. Nonetheless, the notes have their own importance and they too are Said's works, in the final analysis. Along with *Humanism and Democratic Criticism*, *On Late Style* is the culmination of a profound life that started with *Joseph Conrad and the Fiction of Autobiography*.

The central figures of *On Late Style* are Theodor Adorno and Said himself. The frustration caused by the Oslo Accords drew Said closer to music than ever before, minimising, if not causing him to leave altogether, his political investments. While *Humanism and Democratic Criticism* and *Freud and the Non-European* still display some of his political verve, it is almost totally absent in *On Late Style*. In addition to the frustrations caused by the Oslo Accords, there was also a sense of impending death looming large in his mind since he had been diagnosed with leukaemia in 1991. Both these led him to think increasingly about the late style in music and literature in the last decade or so of his life, especially in connection with Adorno. In fact, the phrase 'late style' was originally coined by Adorno. During the final years of his life, Said also gave a series of lectures at Columbia University and other places on the topic.

The key issue that Said explores in the book on 'late style' is the relation between 'bodily condition' and 'aesthetic style' (*On Late Style* 1). In other words, what are the changes that are brought about in the works of writers and musicians when there are acutely aware about their impending death, beset by factors like 'the decay of the body, the onset of ill health' (6)? He goes on to relate it with two of his favourite motifs, the condition of exile and Vico's idea of human history. While the distinction between bodily condition and writing replicates the broader distinction between nature and human history (in the Vichian sense), lateness in style is also 'a kind of self-imposed exile from what is generally acceptable, coming after it, and surviving beyond it' (16).

Said's study of select great artists in the book reveals that there can be two types of late styles, thematically speaking. One is that of harmony, acceptance and compassion – of greater wisdom – which becomes visible as the author or the artist reaches the end of his or her life. Said cites the well-known examples of Shakespeare's *Winter's Tale* and *The Tempest,* and Sophocles's *Oedipus at Colonus* as representative of this type of late style. In fact, there are plentiful examples of this type of lateness. There is, however, another kind of late style: where everything is left in disarray, there is no attempt at all towards the wisdom, harmony or maturity that is commonly associated with ageing. 'But what of artistic lateness not as harmony and resolution but as intransigence, difficulty, and unresolved contradiction? What if age and ill health don't produce the serenity of "ripeness is all"?' (7).

It is with this kind of lateness that Said is concerned in this book. While Adorno, Beethoven and Jean Genet (French novelist) are some of the key examples that we encounter in this book, we shall also look at Said's own work on Freud as an example of the second kind of late style in the following discussion.

Contrapuntal Vision as Late Style in *Freud and the Non-European*

Said's *Freud and the Non-European* is an outstanding example of his contrapuntal reading at work, as well the kind of late style he preferred – choosing contradiction and disarray over harmony and unity. In this short but incisive analysis of Freud's *Moses and Monotheism*, Said reads the formidable patriarch of psychoanalysis not so much as a psychoanalyst, but as one who had a strong interest in the cultural politics of race and religion. Written and published in the year Freud died (1939), *Moses and Monotheism* displays Freud's 'late style', and Said claims that the book is a classic example of the idea (*Freud and the Non-European* 503). Said's analysis of the Freud text in the last phase of his life, by the same token, reflects something of Said's own late style. The original text of *Freud and the Non-European* was prepared as a lecture to be delivered before the Freud Society of Vienna, which had invited Said in 2001. The society surprisingly withdrew the invitation later on the grounds that Said's presence and speech there may influence upcoming election results in favour of a certain anti-Semitic candidate. It was a sorry state of affairs, especially given the fact that Said was fighting the last stage of his protracted and intensely painful battle with leukaemia and would pass away the very next year. However, there was some respite: the Freud Museum of London almost immediately requested Said to deliver the same talk there.[1]

There are quite a few interesting parallels between Said and Freud, in terms of both life experience as well as their methodology. Freud's exilic stay outside his own land, for instance, has a direct parallel in Said's loss of his homeland. This, however, is not the only similarity between the two, nor the only reason as to why Said chooses to speak on Freud with so much passion. What Said finds more interesting about Freud is the fact that, much like Said himself, Freud was always suspicious of any given idea, belief or philosophy. Freud, in fact, was highly sceptical of his own religious, cultural and social antecedents, much like Said's reservations against Arab authoritarianism and reactionary moves even as he critiqued Western imperialism throughout his life. Further, Freud tried to look for what prevailing social and cultural systems suppressed, both in the individual psyche as all as in collective behaviour. This is close to Said's reading of literary, cultural and philosophical discourses for what lies beneath their surface of aesthetic, epistemological pretensions. Freud's forays into the unconscious, insistence on the existence of erotic experience in childhood and recurrent emphasis on the repressed as well as the return of the repressed are, much like Said's works, important instances of reading for silences, absences and exclusions. As Said notes, 'Freud is a remarkable instance of a thinker for whom scientific work was, as he often said, a kind of archaeological excavation of the buried, forgotten, repressed and denied past' (502). In hindsight, Freud can be said to have applied the strategy of contrapuntal reading to whatever he brought under his scrutiny.

Moses and Monotheism is no exception to this general trend. The book shocked the contemporary world by claiming that Moses, the religious and cultural forebear of the Jewish people (and other Abrahamic faiths) was not a Jew himself, but an Egyptian: 'Moses is an Egyptian—probably of noble origin whom the myth undertakes to transform into a Jew' (*Moses and Monotheism* 22). Freud has considered the risks and troubles that such an assertion would invite, but as he says in the very beginning of the book, 'No consideration, however, will move me to set aside truth in favour of supposed national interests' (1). Both these statements reflect, as argued earlier, Freud's dedication to and the tremendous capacity for reading against the grain, for speaking truth to power. It is these attributes of Freud's personality that makes Said take him very seriously. Said had already explored the poetics of Freud in *Beginnings,* now he sought to engage further with Freud's politics.

Freud's identification of Moses as an Egyptian, as I have argued, is a contrapuntal reading of Biblical and Abrahamic originary myths. Contrapuntal reading, however, is a never-ending process, and Said carries the job further by applying the method on Freud himself: looking for gaps, silences and misrepresentations in the Freudian oeuvre. One of the major lacks that Said identifies in Freud is his near dismissal of the non-European world, barring a few passing references to places like India or China. Though Freud cannot be said to have served the cause of imperialism the way Orientalists like Renan or Sacy did, the fact remains that Freud too was Eurocentric (*Freud and the Non-European* 497).

Coming back to the issue of Said's late style, it must be remembered that by the time he wrote this critique of Freud, the combative tone of the Said who wrote *Orientalism* had mellowed significantly. This is not to say that he dispensed with the issues raised in *Orientalism* and other texts; the issues continue, and the very title *Freud and the Non-European* is indicative of a continuation of his earlier contentions. But Said seems to be more accommodating, more forgiving. At least, it seems as if he is trying to look for the reasons why Freud did what he did from a sympathetic standpoint. The words which immediately follow his assertion that Freud was Eurocentric puts this sympathetic tone on display:

> . . . and why should it not be? His world had not yet been touched by the globalization, or rapid travel, or decolonization, that were to make many formerly unknown or repressed cultures available to metropolitan Europe. He lived just before the massive population shifts that were to bring Indians, Africans, West Indians, Turks and Kurds into the heart of Europe as guest-workers and often unwelcome immigrants. (497)

The acceptance and contextualisation of Freud's ignorance about the Orient, however, is not the result of Said's late style only. Freud was an early critic of Zionism and expressed his strongly worded resentment against the plan of a massive Jewish immigration to Palestine to create Israel, which would amount to dispossessing the natives there. In a letter written in 1930, Freud saw the project as the transformation 'of a piece of Herodian wall into a national relic, thus offending the spirit of the natives' (qtd. in *Freud and the Non-European* 507). Five years later, he would change his position and appreciate the attempt to reclaim Israel for the Jewish people. These vacillations, Said seems to suggest, are the typical symptoms of an exilic as well as oppositional intellectual who kept thinking of and rethinking their critical positions.

As already foregrounded, the most interesting thing about Freud is that he has always undercut assumptions about rigid identities and cultures, including his own. His endorsement of the Jewish cause after his initial denial is again substantially balanced by his last work *Moses and Monotheism* where he insists that the foundational figure of Judaism (and hence, of Zionism too) was himself a non-Jew. The empirical or historical veracity of the statement may be subject to scrutiny, but what is more important and in fact instructive for us, as Said argues, is the sheer courage and ability of the likes of Freud to go against their own cultures, even against themselves. Further, in his 'deconstruction' of the Jewish identity, Freud underscored the fact that 'identity cannot be thought or worked through itself alone; it cannot constitute or even imagine itself without that originary break or flaw which will not be repressed' (*Freud and the Non-European* 517). The solution to the Israel–Palestine crisis, Said suggests, lies in understanding this constructedness of identity on the part of both sides so that a bi-national state is created where 'Israel and Palestine are parts, rather than antagonists of each other's history and underlying reality' (517).

HUMANISM AND DEMOCRATIC CRITICISM FOR A DEMOCRATIC FUTURE

If there is anything that could be called Edward Said's 'will' in academic, cultural and political terms, it would be *Humanism and Democratic Criticism*. The essays included in the book are best seen as Said's final words on the world and humanity at large, his last will and testament of his legacy. In this, he makes it very clear that an untiring struggle towards an inclusive humanism based on democratic principles is his most cherished ideal and best loved legacy; and it is the duty of intellectuals and scholars to continue this struggle in spite of, or probably because of, the impossible odds against it. Humanity as well as the humanities will have to play a central role for the realisation of a humanist future for a world that would be, above all, inclusive and democratic.

In envisioning such a pivotal role for humanities departments in universities and for their inmates, Said comes close to figures like Mathew Arnold and F. R. Leavis. Arnold's *Culture and Anarchy* and Leavis's *English Literature in our Time and the University* can be seen as the key forebears of Said's unstinted promotion of the humanities. However, there are a few marked differences. First, Arnold and Leavis's vantage point is that of European and English literatures, while for Said, the humanities as a whole, including non-Western literatures and subjects other than literature, are equally important. In other words, culture, for Said, is not only literary but a whole way of life. Second, unlike Arnold and Leavis, he is acutely aware of the ideological pitfalls of the Western canon, of its literatures and humanities. Third and most importantly, being acutely aware of the ideological pitfalls of the European humanities – especially in their complicity with the politics of class, race and colonialism – Said believes in an inclusive approach towards teaching and practising the humanities which will not be restricted either to a handful of select classics, or to equally few students from elite and privileged backgrounds. The humanities are most unlike its selves when it slams its doors in the faces of all those texts, authors and peoples it does not want to include.

The essays of the book, from the viewpoint of style, are more in the nature of 'reflections' than scholarly or academic articles. Their value is, however, not diminished but rather magnified as the looser structure of the personal essay gives the author a flexibility and freedom to a certain degree denied by the constraints of academic and scholarly writings. However, Said was always something of a Trojan horse so far as the disciplinary rigours and jargon idiosyncracies of academics are concerned. He never believed in the dictum of 'art for art's sake' (read 'art' as scholarship, academics, erudition and so on) and consistently made a strong case in favour of 'art for humanity's sake'. *Humanism and Democratic Criticism* is not an exception to this abiding concern for humanism and humanity. Perhaps it is the most powerful example of his motto.

The starting point of the book is Said's exilic and bicultural status, an issue which is of such paramount significance to him that there has hardly been a book by him where it is absent. While he lived and taught in the US for four decades 'as a practising humanist, teacher, critic and scholar' and that was the world he knew best, the legacy of his birth and initial upbringing in a non-Western culture looms large which leads him to reiterate his 'amphibious or bicultural' status and assert that he is especially aware of 'perspectives and traditions other than those commonly thought of as uniquely American or "Western"' (*Humanism and Democratic Criticism* 1). Admittedly, he therefore views American culture both as an insider as well as an outsider, and with this 'slightly peculiar angle' (2) of vision, Said takes note of the erosion and decadence that have entered humanist practices in particular and academia in general. But – and this is very important – unlike his more conservative Western contemporaries and predecessors, he also sees a lot of positive changes which must be defended, celebrated and intensified. The positive change, so far as Said is concerned, is primarily the inclusion of the non-West, his much beloved and erstwhile colonised 'Orient', into American academia in at least three levels: first, the inclusion of non-Western texts in the curriculum; second, the appointment or induction of faculty members from the non-West in bigger numbers (when he had joined an American university at the beginning of his career, such a hire was unthinkable and we know now, that for a long time Said was thought to be a Jew and not a Palestinian); and third, an equal or much greater number of students from non-Western cultures and regions making it into American (and, we may add, all Western) universities. These, according to Said, are the reasons behind the conservative critics' decrying of current humanist practices.

The lack or failure of the university and the humanities, however, comes from their ever-increasing withdrawal from the world and entering into cocoons and fiefdoms of specialisations, jargon and textualities. This, as I have tried to show throughout the book, is another recurrent theme of the Saidian oeuvre with a definite beginning in his *The World, the Text, and the Critic*, if not before. For him, a scholar or an academician is nothing if not worldly. For a more comprehensive understanding of his arguments against conservative yet widely influential thinkers like Harold Bloom and Allan Bloom's resentment against the humanities and the university system, we would need to look into certain details as explained in *Humanism and Democratic Criticism*.

Closure between the Blooms

The state of affairs in European and American university systems has been seen as highly deplorable and lamentable by many of Said's contemporaries and predecessors. He engages with a host of them, often disparagingly and dismissively, as passing references. These include F. R. Leavis, T. S. Eliot, John Dewey, Lionel Trilling and James Clifford. The two thinkers Said chooses to counter in greater detail are Allan Bloom and Harold Bloom, both upholders of a traditional and inalterable Western canon. While Said is keener on rereading the Western canon than abolishing, annihilating or dismantling it and replacing it with some other canon – say, Asian or Arabic – a sacrosanct literary or cultural canon is a concept against which Said has been offering his tropes of anti-dynastic, secular, contrapuntal and democratic criticism all through (see Chapter 5 for a detailed discussion). But in their recurrent insistence on an imaginary set of great texts which are to be venerated as the permanent storehouses of human culture (actually Western culture), the Blooms join in perpetuating the cultural politics of marginalising, oppressing and annihilating the cultural others of the white, male, European and capitalist 'Great Tradition'.

While critical readings of diverse political/sociological strands and hues have objected to the ideological underpinnings of the so-called great books of the Western canon, especially in terms of their complicities with the politics of race, class, gender, colonialism and so on, apologists for the canon, like Harold Bloom, seek to hold on to the same books on the grounds of aesthetic excellence and universality (the same reasons that have been discredited by most kinds of political readings). As has been discussed earlier in the book, 1993 saw the publication of Said's *Culture and Imperialism* which is primarily an unmasking of the colonialist and imperialist ideologies of the English novel throughout the course of its existence. The very next year, Harold Bloom's *The Western Canon: Books and Schools of the Ages* was published, which challenged the core arguments of Saidian and other political readings with an 'official' attempt to declare 'the Western canon'. While the choice of texts is definitely based on Bloom's personal preferences, he does not hesitate to call it '*the* western canon' instead of 'a western canon'. This, among other things, is highly reminiscent of Leavis's titling his four chosen authors as 'the great tradition'. One would like to believe that a rational mind, including those who are insiders to the European or Western tradition, will see such titles as highly arrogant, if not idiosyncratic. But Bloom became all the more powerful and sought after as a critical voice after this book. This shows the continued presence of the undercurrents of racism, patriarchy and Eurocentrism in Western academia, regardless of the resistance to these offered by Said and others. In fact, Bloom vehemently opposed all new writings generated by feminist, African American or postcolonial consciousnesses as lacking in aesthetic merit, and repeatedly warned against reading those texts.

Harold Bloom does not appear to be an ally of revisionist readings of any kind at all, despite his 'deconstructive' beginnings, and he makes a rather arbitrary difference between what he sees as 'literary criticism' and 'cultural criticism'. Cultural criticism is Bloom's umbrella term for all political and ideological readings and writings and he brushes them aside under the rubric of a 'school of resentment'. Bloom's recourse to a rhetoric of blame, if I can call it that, also seems to be indicative of the fact that his canon and its practitioners (including himself) are being interrogated intensely by these alternative readings (compare the situation to that of the crisis in Orientalism discussed in Chapter 3). This anxiety over the loss of an authentic and authoritative Western canon which has worked hand in hand with Western imperialism (among other things) leads Bloom to close his canon to any possibilities of alternative, mainly non-Western, traditions of reading and writing. He sees these as 'unhealthy' responses to the Western canon. By his repeated assertions ('iterations'to use a Derridean term) about the secondary, derivative nature of non-Western literatures and traditions, what Bloom is arguing for is an intensified, unapologetic continuation of Western literature as both a cultural and a curricular category.

The selection of twenty-six authors, out of which as many as twenty-two are male, shows how Bloom seeks to restore authors and texts that have been identified by contemporary critical thought as upholding the traditions and values of a male, white, European Christian (and mostly heterosexual/heteropatriarchal) society, and not universal humanist values. The prominent presence of authors like Chaucer, Cervantes, Montaigne, John Milton, Samuel Johnson, Wordsworth, Jane Austen, Walt Whitman and Proust in Bloom's list does not admit the presence of a Tagore, Rushdie or Naipaul, even though they are highly valued among Western readers themselves. While Bloom indicates that he has chosen the authors for their aesthetic merit, aestheticism is not something that can be defined as per his own assertion: 'Pragmatically, aesthetic value can be recognized or experienced, but it cannot be conveyed to those who are incapable of grasping its sensation and perception' (Bloom 17). Paradoxical as the statement is, it also exposes the central irony of the notion of canonicity itself. To define something is to demystify it, make it vulnerable to counter-definitions and scrutiny. Canons and traditions which are primarily put in place for ideological control of societies and peoples cannot consciously risk doing that.

Contrary to the assertions and beliefs of Harold Bloom and others like him, Said does not find the idea of aestheticism as an independent category credible. Two key terms for Said are 'secular' and 'worldly', which he had clearly defined as early as 1984 in *The World, the Text, and the Critic.* In that book, as we have already discussed in Chapter 4, Said had vociferously challenged the idea of an apolitical canonicity, just as he had exposed the political investments of knowledge and scholarship in *Orientalism* before that. Ever since, Said has been opposing the idea that literature, culture or knowledge work independently of politics. Further, in so far as European or Western literature is concerned, the main political fact that they legitimise or normalise is that of imperialism.

Bloom's attempts at upholding those literary traditions without due acknowledgement of this tendency are a promotion of exploitation and oppression in the name of promoting the humanities. As Said says in the *World, the Text, and the Critic,* he is challenging two axioms of Western humanities, critical schools and academia: their Eurocentric orientation and suppression of the political in literature and culture (22–23).

In other words, canons, literary or otherwise, are not to be seen as repositories of universal and eternal values to which one frequently (or infrequently) returns to be 'cultured', 'educated' or 'enlightened'. Rather literary texts, like all other human artefacts, are grounded in the sordid realities of human existence. Let alone canons or cultures, anything man-made can be and should be subjected to human scrutiny and oppositional criticism again and again; this endless interrogation of given sets of beliefs, norms, values and traditions constitute the essence of humanism. This is the real spirit behind the mode of humanism or criticism that Said espouses.

This practice also constitutes the core of his arguments about the representations of the intellectual, which is about representing truth before power, truth in spite of power. In many ways, the first two chapters of *Humanism and Democratic Criticism* constitute a reassertion of the ideas and ideals of secular criticism and the worldliness of texts as formulated in *The World, the Text, and the Critic*; ideals that have become recurrent tropes in the Saidian oeuvre after 1984. It is in this twin spirit of secular criticism and a faith in worldliness of texts that Said rejects Bloom's vision of the Western canon as 'the most extreme kind of dismissive aestheticism calling itself canonical humanism' (*Humanism and Democratic Criticism* 27). Said seeks to expose Bloom as a European heteropatriarchal imperialist by pointing out that Bloom's 'school of resentment' does not 'include everything said or written by the non-European, non-male, non-Anglo educated upstarts who don't happen to agree with his tiresome vatic trumpeting' (27). Said goes to the extent of commenting that Bloom's *The Western Canon* showcases the latter's 'absence rather than an invigorating presence of mind' (27).

Bloom and other gatekeepers of the Western canon (of any canon for that matter) also seem to forget the crucial fact that many of the figures of today's canon were yesterday's rebels, insurgents and anti-heroes (28). For instance, the character most central to Western culture, Jesus, was considered a heretic and rebel by his own community till the advent of Christianity. The same applies to Martin Luther till the advent of Protestantism, or Mohammad till Islam became a force to reckon with. Coming to literature, the most canonical figure of English literature (with all due respect to theories against the canon), William Shakespeare, was perceived as lacking in education and classical exposure by the established playwrights of his day, the University Wits, as well as Ben Jonson. John Donne, the leading Metaphysical poet, was seen in a very poor light for at least three centuries till Eliot's 'The Metaphysical Poets' made him a central figure.

Interestingly, the blooming of Bloom's Western canon has a direct forebear and predecessor in yet another Bloom: Allan Bloom's *The Closing of the American Mind: How Higher Education Has Failed Democracy and Impoverished the Souls of Today's Students* (1987). The subtitle aptly indicates the main argument of the book, which is that the acceptance of moral and epistemological relativism by universities have paradoxically led to the closing of the American mind. Allan Bloom's remedy is much the same as that of Harold Bloom: a return to the 'great books'. The only difference is that the latter's great books are primarily literary, while Allan Bloom's choices include more philosophical works. This does not seem to make a difference as finally both the Blooms call for a closure of the Western canons, literary and philosophical. The sanctity of the Western canons, the Blooms argue, has to be protected by guarding them against any possible change; by which they mostly mean, explicitly or implicitly, inroads and influences from the non-West. In Said's eloquent phrasing, 'This was another way of saying that too many undesirable non-Europeans had suddenly appeared at "our" gates' (*Humanism and Democratic Criticism* 18). Just as he sees Harold Bloom's *The Western Canon* as an exhibition of the author's absence of mind, Allan Bloom's book represents the nadir of 'anti-intellectualism in American life' for Said (18). Said reiterates his strong support for both the inclusion of non-Western content into the Western canon and political activism geared towards the liberation and emancipation of humanity. For him, education, humanist or otherwise, is not something that repeatedly venerates select authors from the past amongst a handful of elites behind closed doors; it is about 'investigation, criticism and humanistic enlargement of consciousness' (18).

As Said repeatedly asserts, 'For my purposes here, the core of humanism is the secular notion that the historical world is made by men and women, and not by God, and that it can be understood rationally ' (11). His long standing ideal in this context is Giambattista Vico. This eighteenth century professor of rhetoric from Naples has remained a figure of unending significance for Said. However, citing a thinker who is widely known for his anti-Enlightenment philosophy to bolster one's case for a 'rational' understanding of human history is not without its problems as a rationalist interpretation of human history or the universe is a legacy of the Enlightenment. But, as I have argued earlier in the context of his selective use of Foucault and Gramsci, Said is not always known for his accuracy in quoting and using authors and thinkers, especially when he uses them as theoretical models. He more often takes them to mean what he thinks they mean. And in *Humanism and Democratic Criticism* he has explicitly stated this: 'I shall be making highly selective use of what others have said' (5). His use of Vico certainly seems to prove his point. Also, this support for the modification of theories and theorists, to remind ourselves, is something Said theorised elaborately on in his famous essay 'Travelling Theory' (see Chapter 4).

Contrapuntal Humanism

Returning to Said's position on the contours and contents of the humanities, it can be said that the very things conservatives like Harold Bloom and Allan Bloom find lamentable – namely, pluralism and politicisation – are for Said liberating and laudable. Leavis's much contested phrase in *The Great Tradition* about his selected great authors exhibiting a 'reverent openness before life' (9) becomes crucial here; although Leavis's actual position or praxis was the very opposite of 'openness'. It is not Leavis but Said with his ideas of the humanities, humanism and the so-called 'great tradition' who exhibits this 'reverent openness before life'. In Said's work this should be understood as his equal valuation of all cultures and traditions. At the same time, he reserves the right to interrogate those cultures and traditions as well.

Borrowing a trope from his *Culture and Imperialism* (Said in his turn borrowed it from Western music), I would like to call Saidian humanism 'contrapuntal humanism'. I do not claim any originality in this; the concept is Saidian and the trope too, is his. I have just reworded and rephrased it for both difference and, more importantly, clarity. Contrapuntal humanism is acutely aware of the pitfalls of traditional humanism which, having its origins in the European Renaissance, has a hugely Eurocentric bias as seen in its two avatars of Christian humanism and secular humanism. One may use the term 'secular humanism' to mean what I call 'contrapuntal humanism'. But secular humanism is a term which has been in existence long since, and while it is mindful of the limitations of religiosity in its rejection of the tag 'Christian', its Eurocentric or Western biases still remain. Contrapuntal humanism, essentially being suggestive of counterpoints, continues to critique the othering and marginalisation that humanism has given rise to and perpetuated, so that these are not repeated/replicated.

Another 'intention' behind arguing for this method is to ensure that the humanities and humanism are more involved in addressing ecological concerns, which are the most pressing issues demanding our attention in the present world for the collective survival of humanity. The term 'humanism' itself invokes an anthropocentric world view which is not only anachronistic today, but adds to the threat of our collective demise. I personally feel that more than the absence of gender or class concerns in Said's works – that feminist and Marxist critics have pointed out – it is the absence of ecological concerns and consciousness that limits Said. While there are occasional, marginal references to ecological issues in texts like *Culture and Imperialism* and *The Politics of Dispossession,* these are, to use a cliché, 'too little, too late'. None the less, one can correlate the influence of his monumental studies and research on imperialism, coupled with the rise of ecocriticism, to the production of such significant documents like Alfred Crosby's *Ecological Imperialism* (1986) which show how ecology and nature have been the worst victims of Euro-American industrialism and imperialism, while the pernicious web of colonial mimicry has pathetically disabled the colonised world from taking effective steps against this vast loss.

INTELLECTUALS, SCHOLARS AND CRITICS FOR A HUMANE FUTURE

The central phenomenon that this final critical book by Said wants to stress again and again is humanism. However, it is not a chronological survey or history of humanism, nor is it an analysis of all underlying assumptions, epistemology or philosophy of humanism. It is focused on the issue of 'humanism and critical practice' (2); what should practitioners of humanism do for the world as well as the text and how should they go about their work 'in today's turbulent world' (2), constitute Said's chief concern here. This, as already suggested above, is not a new thing for Said. However, the repetition of the point is significant, as it is the most emphatic and recurrent wave in Said's oeuvre. As I have discussed in the course of this book, ever since the Arab–Israel war of 1967, Said's critical and actual energies have been directed towards encouraging scholars, intellectuals, writers and teachers to come out of their texts into the 'real' world. While theoretical formulations on the contours and contents of this role are to be found, along with the book under discussion, in *Beginnings* (anti-dynastic criticism), *The World, the Text, and the Critic* ('worldliness' and 'secular criticism') and *Representations of the Intellectual*, books like *Orientalism*, *The Question of Palestine*, *After the Last Sky*, *Culture and Imperialism* and *The Politics of Dispossession* can be seen as practical examples of how this role is performed by Said himself.

The most crucial constituent of the intellectual's role for Said is 'speaking truth to power'. While this includes truths of all hues and shades, the most important truth for Said is that imperialism and colonialism were utterly dehumanising projects that continue in various forms despite geographical decolonisation. While French and British imperialism attempted to suppress the ugly truths of colonial exploitation by invoking the moral rhetoric of a 'civilising mission', the US continues its imperial interventions in every corner of the world in the name of protecting humanity and democracy (50). No resentment or protest from regions affected by American neo-imperialist policies (such as Iraq or Palestine for that matter) can contain or mitigate the continued onslaught of America's organised state power. It must be noted again that Said has also been an incisive critic of the oppressive structures of different Arab regimes as well, and has called out Saddam Hussein as a tyrant and a despot even while he critiqued America's role in the first Gulf War.

In Said's view, it is the job of the humanist intellectual, Eastern or Western, to join the struggle against imperial interventionism, be it American or of any other country. To draw an interesting analogy, just as for Foucault 'Anthropologization is the great internal threat to knowledge in our day' (*Order of Things* 238), for Said the greatest dangers are 'Eurocentrism' and 'American Exceptionalism'. And these two dangers are, needless to say, not mutually exclusive. Scholar, critics, humanists and intellectuals should endlessly interrogate the very premises of such corrosive power structures for a truly humanist and democratic future. Edward Said himself, I would like to believe, provides us with the best example of this role and perhaps the only figure who is comparable to him is that of his friend and kindred spirit Noam Chomsky. Few intellectuals or scholar-writers have gone to the extent that these two have, in not only critiquing but opposing tooth and nail the oppressive ideologies of the government of the country they live in. In Said's case, added to this is also his fierce opposition to everything British and French imperialism have stood for. In Said, therefore, there is no gap between his epistemological formation and ontological action: between theory and practice, scholarship and ethics. It is precisely due to this that he has become a humane force to reckon with, a force to whom we shall keep returning for years to come. This, therefore, is no conclusion but only a beginning.

NOTE

1. I have followed the account given in Bayoumi and Rubin, pp. 494–95.

REFERENCES

Bayoumi, Moustafa and Andrew Rubin, editors. *The Selected Works of Edward Said: 1966-2006.* Bloomsbury, 2021.

Bloom, Harold. *The Western Canon: The Books and School of the Ages.* 1994. Papermac, 1996.

Foucault, Michel. *The Order of Things.* 1966. Vintage, 1994.

Freud, Sigmund. *Moses and Monotheism.* Hogarth Press, 1939.

Leavis, F.R. *The Great Tradition.* Chatto & Windus, 1950.

Said, Edward. "Freud and the Non-European". *The Selected Works of Edward Said: 1966-2006*, edited by Moustafa Bayoumi and Andrew Rubin, Bloomsbury, 2021, pp. 494–517.

---. *Humanism and Democratic Criticism.* Columbia UP, 2004.

---. *On Late Style: Music and Literature against the Grain.* Pantheon, 2006.

Glossary of Select Terms

Agency: in critical theory, the term is used to imply an individual's ability to act on their own, to choose their own course of action independent of external forces. Oppressed individuals or groups within any given power structure are generally marked by a lack of agency; for example, the colonised under colonialism or queer individuals in patriarchal societies.

Antidynastic criticism: a critical term coined by Said in *Beginnings* to describe Foucault's critical methodology. While scholars working in traditional ways share a dynastic relation with their field in so far as they carry forward the works of their predecessors, Foucault's methodology is exactly the opposite of this. Foucault would look for gaps, ruptures, inconsistencies and the like in the works of his predecessors. The term can also be used to describe poststructuralist criticism as well as theories of political readings in general, as both are interested in reading against the grain. The concept of 'antidynastic criticism' is actually central to Said's own critical formulations, and it recurs in his subsequent works with newer names like secular criticism, contrapuntal reading and democratic criticism. All these imply oppositional reading and criticism.

Canon: in literary and cultural studies, the word 'canon' refers to a set of texts generally regarded to be of the highest aesthetic calibre or merit in any given literary tradition. Originally an ecclesiastical term, 'canon' has almost completely replaced the word 'classic' in critical discourses. It is the general contention of various theoretical schools that the English (and Western) canon includes texts which generally uphold patriarchal, heterosexual, capitalist, Eurocentric and, for our purpose here, colonial ideologies. Consequently, there is an increasing move to do away with the English/Western canon by replacing it with texts that it excludes. Said, as has been my argument in this book, is more in favour of re-reading the canon than replacing it. See Chapters 5 and 7 for further discussion.

Contrapuntal reading: reading a text for what is hidden in it rather than given; see *antidynastic criticism* and *canon* above. Also see Chapter 5 for a more detailed discussion.

Democratic criticism: the term Said uses in *Humanism and Democratic Criticism* to define criticism as an open ended enquiry into life and literature, society and culture. For all practical purposes, it is a renaming of what he calls 'antidynastic criticism' in *Beginnings*, 'secular criticism' in *The World, the Text, and the Critic* and 'contrapuntal reading' in *Culture and Imperialism*. See Chapter 7 for further discussion.

Filiation and **Affiliation:** by 'filiation', Said refers to the human connections built on the basis of natural or biological relations, like the family or the clan. In contrast, 'affiliation' attempts to create groups of human beings based on professional or ideological connections. See Chapter 4 for further discussion.

Humanism: an epistemological and philosophical position that gives priority to the freedom, development and progress of all human beings, irrespective of race, caste, geographical location and so on. The roots of humanism are often traced to the worldview of the ancient Greeks and Romans which was revived during the Renaissance and reinforced by sociocultural phenomena like the Enlightenment. Poststructuralist thinkers like Foucault, however, have pointed out several drawbacks of humanism and argued for an anti-humanist or posthumanist position. Said, although acutely aware of the Eurocentric contours of humanism, believes that its core egalitarian principles are of enduring relevance to humanity.

Imaginative geography: a term used by Said to refer to Orientalist constructions of the Orient which were more a product of the assumptions and norms that underlie Orientalism than the actual geographical and historical realities of the Orient.

Intifada: *Intifada* or *intifadah* is an Arabic word which literally means 'shaking off', and by extension, has also come to mean revolution, rebellion, or uprising. In the Palestinian context, it is specifically used to refer to the two Palestinian insurrections against Israeli occupations of the West Bank and Gaza Strip that took place during 1987–93 and 2000–05.

Levant: is roughly synonymous with the Middle East, referring especially to the region which comprises countries such as Iraq, Syria, Israel, Lebanon, Egypt, Jordan and the Palestinian territories. Having its origins in the Italian *levante*, its etymological meaning is 'oriental'.

Philology: etymologically implies love of language, and in practice refers to the field that studies the historical development of languages across ages. In *Orientalism*, Said shows how the European mode of philology also helped the growth and consolidation of the Orientalist mindset, and hence, colonialism. However, much like his stance on other European cultural and epistemological phenomena, Said does not advocate doing away with philology at all. In fact, he finds it to be the most important discipline for the humanities and passionately advocates a 'return to philology' in his *Humanism and Democratic Criticism.* The only thing is that it should not be Eurocentric but truly global in its outlook. Said also believes that for this to happen effectively, secularism and worldliness – two of his favourite tropes – must also inform new philological pursuits. It is pertinent to mention here that philology had become a dated concept and discipline replaced by linguistics, chiefly owing to the recommendation of the Swiss linguist Ferdinand de Saussure who believed that a language should be studied as it is at the present moment and not historically. This was agreed to by most structuralists and poststructuralists. However, Said always found this rejection problematic as it takes away the historical information that lies beneath the change of meaning of words over time. After Said's strong advocacy for a return to philology, there have been some changes in this direction and a new sub-discipline called postcolonial philology has also emerged.

PLO: is an abbreviation that stands for the Palestine Liberation Organisation. Founded in 1964, it is widely accepted as the sole legitimate representative of the Palestinian people. It was granted 'observer' status by the United Nations in 1974.

Postcolonial theory and criticism: This school of theory and criticism explores various implications of the literary and cultural texts that deal with the European colonisation of the non-European world and its aftermath. Said himself is often seen as the founding father of the field because of the impact of *Orientalism*. However, Said neither coined the term nor was he keen on being affiliated with the school, remaining loyal to his own concept of 'secular criticism' (see below). The allied term 'postcolonialism' is used in two senses: first, in the chronological sense of 'after colonialism'; and second, as an ideological position committed to the continuous critical examination of the process of colonisation and its aftermath. It may be noted here that the period designated by the unhyphenated term 'postcolonial' increasingly tends to include the 'colonial' period too. In other words, the term 'postcolonial' means after the beginning of colonisation and not just the period after the end of colonialism for which the hyphenated term post-colonial is more commonly used.

Professor of Terror: the epithet given to Said by an opponent named Edward Alexander in an article bearing the same title in the August 1989 issue of the American right wing magazine *Commentary*. Alexander alleged that Said was the mouthpiece of the Palestinian terrorist groups and was gathering support for them in the Western world via his access to the American academia and media. Actually, Alexander had wilfully obliterated the difference between opposition and terrorism. While all terrorisms are oppositions to some ideology, all oppositions to authorities or oppressive powers do not use terrorism. As we have seen the course of this book, while Said was always against authoritarianisms of all kinds and Euro-American interventionist politics, he never promoted or supported violent means to further his goals. He believed in dialogue, negotiation and humanist solutions. None the less, the term was reinforced by his detractors out of a spirit of vengeance and hatred towards Said's status as well as their disapproval of the Palestinian struggle for self-determination.

Secular criticism: by the term 'secular criticism', Said stresses the fact that criticism should be a non-dogmatic and constant interrogation of human ideas, ideals and institution. It should not be compartmentalised into subgroups by qualifiers and adjectives such as 'structuralist', 'feminist' and so on. It should aim at being relevant or applicable to a wide audience by shunning the use of jargon and obscure expressions. See *antidynastic* above, and Chapter 4 as well.

Worldliness: arguably the single most important notion at work behind all of Said's oeuvre, 'wordliness' refers to and emphasises the fact that literary and cultural texts (and their writers and critics) are produced in particular contexts: political, social, cultural, economic, and so on. Consequently, it is fallacious to portray them as occupying an aesthetic or non-political space that is beyond time and place. In other words, every text and its author, and by implication every human being, is a product of both their history and geography. Said's concept of worldliness, therefore, acts against a whole range of critical schools that include aestheticism, New Criticism, structuralism and poststructuralism. See Chapter 4 for further details.

Zionism: is the political and ideological movement which led to the establishment of the Jewish state of Israel in 1948. Theodor Herzl, a nineteenth century Jewish journalist from Austria, is generally regarded as the founder of the movement. Zionism strongly argued for an exclusive homeland for Jewish people, a claim which received wide support from several countries across the globe given the history of persecution of the Jewish people in Europe. However, the establishment of the Jewish state dispossessed countless Palestinians. This sense of dispossession is the key political and historical fact that informs almost all of Said's writings. In fact, the major and recurrent motifs in Said's writings, like the intellectual's prerogative to speak truth to power or the worldliness of texts and authors, stem from the dispossession of Palestinians brought about by Zionism. See Chapter 6 for further details.

Suggested Reading

Aram Veeser, H. *Edward Said: The Charisma of Criticism*. Routledge, 2010.

Ashcroft, Bill, Gareth Griffiths and Helen Tiffin. *The Post-colonial Studies Reader.* 2nd Ed. Routledge, 2006.

Ashcroft, Bill and Hussein Khadim, editors. *Edward Said and the Post-Colonial*. Nova, 2001.

Bayoumi, Moustafa and Andrew Rubin, editors. *The Selected Works of Edward Said.* Bloomsbury, 2021.

Bhabha, Homi K, editor. *Nation and Narration*. Routledge, 1994.

Bhabha, Homi K. and W.J.T. Mitchell, editors. *Edward Said: Continuing the Conversation*. U of Chicago P, 2005.

Brennan, Timothy. *Places of Mind: A Life of Edward Said*. Farrar, 2021.

Callaghan, Clare. "Selected Bibliography of Work about and of Edward Said's Texts". *CLC Web: Comparative Literature and Culture*, vol. 5, no. 4, 2003, https://doi.org/10.7771/1481-4374.1203. Accessed 25 January 2023.

Dabashi, Hamid. *On Edward Said: Remembrance of Things Past*. Haymarket, 2020.

Editors. "Legacies of the Future: *boundary 2* Editors on Edward Said". *b2o, the online community of the boundary 2 editorial collective,* http://www.boundary2.org/wp-content/uploads/2016/06/b2-Editors-on-Edward-Said.pdf. Accessed 25 January 2023.

Foucault, Michel. *The Archaeology of Knowledge.* Translated by A.M. Sheridan Smith. Routledge, 1989.

Ghazoul, Ferial J., editor. *Edward Said Critical Decolonization.* American U in Cairo P, 2007.

Guha, Ranajit. "The Tartar's Cry". *The Small Voices of History*, Permanent Black, 2010, pp. 635-44.

Innes, C. L. *The Cambridge Introduction to Postcolonial Literatures in English.* Cambridge UP, 2007.

McCarthy, Conor. *The Cambridge Introduction to Edward Said.* Cambridge UP, 2010.

Mignolo, Walter D. *The Politics of Decolonial Investigations.* Duke UP, 2021.

Poplawski, Paul, editor. *English Literature in Context.* Cambridge UP, 2008.

Radhakrishnan, R. *History, the Human, and the World Between.* Duke UP, 2008.

Said, Edward. *Beginnings: Intention and Method.* Columbia UP, 1985.

---. *Culture and Imperialism.* Alfred A. Knopf, 1993.

---. *Freud and the Non-European*. Verso Books, 2003.

---. *Humanism and Democratic Criticism*. Columbia UP, 2004.

---. *Joseph Conrad and the Fiction of Autobiography*. Harvard UP, 1966.

---. *On Late Style: Music and Literature Against the Grain.* Pantheon, 2006.

---. *Orientalism*. 1978. Penguin, 2001.

---. *Out of Place: A Memoir*. Granta, 1999.

---. *The Politics of Dispossession: The Struggle for Palestinian Self-Determination, 1969-1994.* Pantheon Books, 1994.

---. *Power, Politics and Culture: Interviews with Edward W. Said*, edited by Gauri Viswanthan, Pantheon Books, 2001.

---. *The Question of Palestine.* Routledge & Kegan Paul, 1979.

---. *Reflections on Exile and Other Essays.* Penguin, 2001.

---. *Representations of the Intellectual: The 1993 Reith Lectures*. Pantheon Books, 1994.

---. *The World, the Text, and the Critic.* 1983. Vintage, 1991.

Sokmen, Muge Gursoy and Basak Ertur, editors. *Waiting for the Barbarians: A Tribute to Edward Said*. Verso Books, 2008.

Spanos, William V. *The Legacy of Edward W. Said*. U of Illinois P, 2009.

Tally, Robert T. *The Geocritical Legacies of Edward W. Said: Spatiality, Critical Humanism, and Comparative Literature*. Palgrave, 2015.

Viswanathan, Gauri. *Masks of Conquest: Literary Studies and British Rule in India*. 1989. Columbia UP, 2015.

Other books in the series

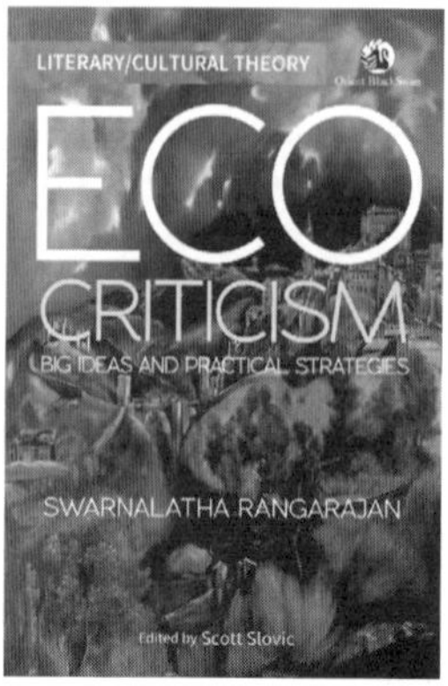

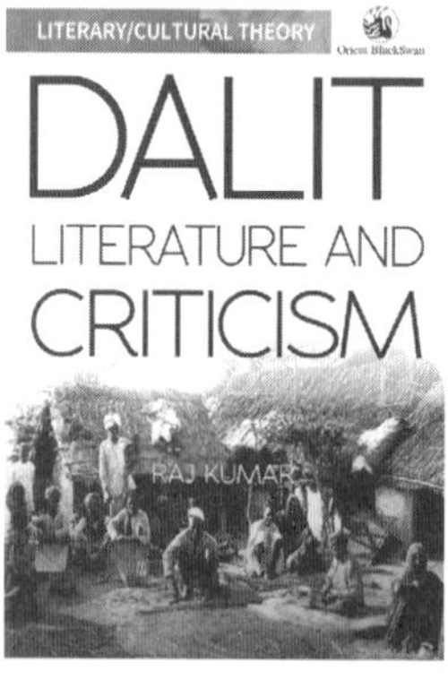

For more information, visit www.orientblackswan.com

Other books in the series

For more information, visit www.orientblackswan.com

Other books in the series

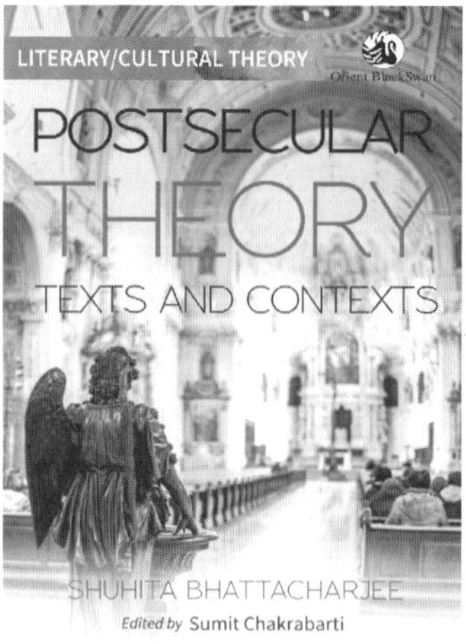

For more information, visit www.orientblackswan.com